'An excellent product of a lot of hard work and insights.'

— **Joe Studwell**, author of *How Asia Works*

'This book explains how Africa can emulate the best bits of Asia's journey from poverty to prosperity, and avoid the worst.'

— **Ernest Bai Koroma**, former president of Sierra Leone

'An enlightening window for Asia on Africa; for Africans, the step-by-step story of Asian development.'

— **Shu Zhan**, director and senior researcher, Centre for African Studies, China Foundation for International Studies

'Africa should use aid better – and avoid the pain of poor policy choices. These lessons – and much more – are front and centre of *The Asian Aspiration*.'

— **Jordan Ryan**, former head: United Nations Development Programme, Vietnam, and UN deputy special representative, Liberia

'Yet another outstanding volume from the Brenthurst team of distinguished statesmen cum analysts drawing pivotal insights and lessons for Africa from Asia's acclaimed economic and social development successes. It presents Africa with clear choices on how to become the next Asia while avoiding its mistakes.'

— **Emmanuel Gyimah-Boadi**, executive director, Afrobarometer

'The big difference between Asia and Africa, as this seminal book highlights, is leadership and governance. How Africa will respond to its crisis depends on its leaders.'

— **Hakainde Hichilema**, president, United Party for National Development, Zambia

'This compelling book puts things in perspective for African countries: you can transform your past into a positive experience.'

— **Souleymane Coulibaly**, World Bank, Malaysia

'*The Asian Aspiration* is the most profound policy book on how Africa can learn from the lessons of Asia. It's practical, it's deep and wide.'

— **Kingsley Moghalu**, 2019 presidential candidate, Young Progressive Party, Nigeria

'Very instructive and helpful for African leaders …'

— **Moeketsi Majoro**, minister of finance, Lesotho

'*The Asian Aspiration* is a captivating book with practical insights, full to the brim with useful lessons. A highly recommended read.'

— **David Monyae**, co-director, Confucius Institute, University of Johannesburg

'A fascinating account of Asia's modern economic miracle. A must-read for policy-makers, donors and anyone interested in Africa's future.'

— **Zitto Kabwe**, opposition leader, Alliance for Change and Transparency, Tanzania

'A toolkit and manual for development, useful to practitioners, leaders current or future, who believe in a New Africa and possibilities of thought leadership and ideas. This superb account should shock and shake readers into a sense of urgency.'

— **Nelson Chamisa**, president, Movement for Democratic Change, Zimbabwe

'There is a lack of a common vision for long-term development in Africa. This enlightening book, with insightful analysis and vivid examples, will greatly help forge a consensus for the continent's future growth.'

— **Tang Xiaoyang**, Tsinghua University, China

THE ASIAN ASPIRATION

THE ASIAN ASPIRATION

**Why and How Africa Should Emulate Asia –
and What It Should Avoid**

Greg Mills

Olusegun Obasanjo

Hailemariam Desalegn

Emily van der Merwe

HURST & COMPANY, LONDON

First published in the United Kingdom in 2020 by
C. Hurst & Co. (Publishers) Ltd.,
41 Great Russell Street, London, WC1B 3PL
© Greg Mills, Olusegun Obasanjo, Hailemariam Desalegn and
Emily van der Merwe, 2020

Printed in Great Britain by Bell and Bain Ltd, Glasgow

Distributed in the United States, Canada and Latin America by
Oxford University Press, 198 Madison Avenue, New York, NY
10016, United States of America.

The right of Greg Mills, Olusegun Obasanjo, Hailemariam Desalegn
and Emily van der Merwe to be identified as the authors of
this publication is asserted by them in accordance with the
Copyright, Designs and Patents Act, 1988.

A Cataloguing-in-Publication data record for this book
is available from the British Library.

ISBN: 9781787384453

This book is printed using paper from registered sustainable
and managed sources.

www.hurstpublishers.com

Editing by Sally Hines
Proofreading by Russell Martin
Indexing by Sanet le Roux
Design and typesetting by Triple M Design, Johannesburg

Cover design by publicide

Contents

Foreword

It seems extraordinary today that in the 1960s Singapore looked to Africa for insight on growing its economy.

In 1968, a team of Singaporeans came to Kenya to learn our lessons, since we were then a more developed country than they were. Four decades later I led a study trip to Singapore with six ministers. That was the latest in many trips taken by the Kenyan government to the island, about which no report was ever written, and where the participants kept everything to themselves.

I said that this trip had to be different, that we had to translate our findings into actions. On our return, I asked for a plan of action from each minister in learning from Singapore, since there was no point in reinventing the wheel. Each minister was tasked to prepare their action plan against our Vision 2030. But after I left government in 2013, nothing further happened.

This, I am sure, is the depressing experience of many an African government official and politician. Lots of studies, followed by much less in the way of action.

Of course, there were differences between Africa and Asia, which reflect in the different development paths they have subsequently taken.

Take Singapore. Once Britain had made the decision to withdraw its military forces east of Suez and close its bases on the island, Prime Minister Lee Kuan Yew and his colleagues were forced to think quickly and out of the box. They realised that their population was too small to rely only on their internal market, and instead had to attract international investors to grow their export industries. South Korea, too, found itself in a very difficult position. They needed to show how their system was better than the communist alternative promoted by the North. Whereas Africa suffered a Cold War, Asia experienced a 'Hot War', which focused the minds of leadership on growth, job creation and development. And where East Asia prospered, Africa largely wasted three decades in complacency and conflict.

But this begs the question: why did Asia possess such a sense of urgency? And why did its leadership, in spite of not always being democratic, make better decisions on behalf of the majority of their citizens than their African post-independence counterparts?

In answering these and other key questions, *The Asian Aspiration* shows exactly what Africa should emulate in catching up, and what it should best avoid from the East Asian development experience. It is a rich and powerful analytical collaboration, drawing on years of policy experience and the insights of top-notch academic minds.

If you want to avoid reinventing the wheel of development, and believe Africa can and must catch up, read this book, and learn.

Raila Odinga
Prime Minister of Kenya, 2008–13
Nairobi, October 2019

Preface

Why Asia, Why Africa, Why Now?

Hue is the embodiment of Vietnam's destruction. It was the site of the Battle of Hue in 1968, the epitome of the logic that 'it became necessary to destroy the town to save it', as expressed by an American military officer from the same Tet Offensive.

The Battle for Hue raged for the month of February 1968, destroying 80% of the city and resulting in the deaths of more than 10 000 soldiers and civilians, with many of the latter executed in acts of retribution by North and South Vietnamese forces. An estimated 116 000 of the city's pre-battle population of 140 000 were made homeless. From one perspective, Hue is seen in the same vein, today, as military operations in Beirut and Fallujah: a case of the cost of fighting in an urban terrain, where tactical success fails to translate into strategic victory.

Yet, now, Hue is a metaphor for Vietnam's recovery. Once the capital of the Nguyen dynasty, it has as its centrepiece a vast nineteenth-century citadel, encompassing the Imperial City with its palaces and shrines. A city of half a million, it receives more than two million foreign visitors annually, flocking to experience its rebuilt historic monuments up and down the Perfume River, which have earned it a place in UNESCO's World Heritage Sites.

Just 30 years ago it was virtually impossible to imagine such a transformation. Vietnam was emerging from the cost of years of colonialism, conflict and a command economy. At the end of the 1980s, per capita income levels were under US$100. Now they are 25 times larger. Following the regional patterns of stability, rapid growth and unimaginable prosperity within a single generation, Vietnam offers an example to African leaders and populations imagining how they might make similar progress.

In Vietnam, the war represents another country. More than 70% of the population was born after 1975.

This is particularly relevant as Africa stands on the cusp of a major demographic shift, with a projected doubling of its population within the next 30 years. The old economic drivers of raw commodity exports cannot provide the formula for sustainable growth and jobs, which are now urgently required. Already, two-thirds of Africa's population is under 30, and the majority are jobless.

In our role at The Brenthurst Foundation in providing advice to African policy-makers we are often asked: can Africa be the next Asia? *The Asian Aspiration* speaks to this ambition, and the almost blind admiration with which many Africans, particularly leaders, regard Asia. In answering that question, we detail not only the growth stories of Asia's economies, small and large, Singapore to China, but the key choices and priorities that these varied experiences present. It follows in this vein from two related and recent studies produced by the Foundation: *Making Africa Work* (2017) and *Democracy Works* (2019). This book does not aim to present a uniform or singularly positive picture of what Asia has achieved. There is much to be admired, even emulated; but there is also much to be avoided. All of this means, simply, that there is a lot to learn.

A relevant synthesis demands wide collaboration. The research presented here is a collective effort between two policy-makers and two researchers. With the generous financial support of Jonathan and Nicky Oppenheimer, this volume is based on extensive fieldwork across Asia. This is underpinned by long-term institutional relationships, notably including the S. Rajaratnam School of International Studies in Singapore, the Centre for Global Studies at Shanghai University and the Institute for African and Middle East Studies (IAMES) at the Vietnamese Academy for Social Sciences. The volume was reviewed at a round table hosted by the

Konrad-Adenauer-Stiftung in Como, Italy. Thanks go to Henning Suhr and Stefan Friedrich for their role in this regard, and to those who participated and also took the trouble to offer written comments on the draft, including Jordan Ryan, Saul Musker, Souleymane Coulibaly and Shu Zhan.

A number of individuals were invaluable in assisting with complex research itineraries, including Ambassadors Matthew Neuhaus, Martin Slabber and Barry Desker in The Hague, Manila and Singapore respectively; Professor Changgang Guo and Shimei Dong at Shanghai University; Ambassadors Norio Maruyama and Takashi Okada, as well as Sumie Arima of Japan's Ministry of Foreign Affairs; Audrey Wang in Johannesburg and Chen-Chi Wu in Taipei; in Malaysia Ambassador Nizan Mohamad, Tan Sri Rastam Mohd Isa and Dato Abdullah Mohamed; South Korea's Ambassador Jong-dae Park; and in Vietnam the director of IAMES, Le Phuoc Minh, along with Do Duc Dinh, Pham Thi Kim Hue and Do Duc Hiep. African field trips were facilitated by a large group of colleagues and friends, notably Karim Anjarwalla, David and Vicky Horsey, Ato Fitsum, Ahmed Mohamed Shide, Bart Nnaji, Mohcine Jazouli, Hicham Chaoudri, Rod Hagger and Mohamed Abdelkader Naji.

At The Brenthurst Foundation, Marie-Noelle Nwokolo supplied many of the graphs and tables used here, and like Ghairoon Hajad, Ray Hartley, Jaco du Plessis, Nicola Doyle, Henry Sands, Katy Roxburgh, Mariam Cassojee and Leila Jack, was always on hand to support the research behind this volume. Atom Lim, Maurice Babale and Taiwo Ojo facilitated former President Obasanjo's schedule, as did Dinayas Gemada and Bezawit Tefera that of former Prime Minister Hailemariam.

All mistakes and misrepresentations remain, as ever, the authors' alone, however.

As with other, recent Foundation projects, there is a song to accompany this book, written with the Cape Town-based singer-songwriter Robin Auld, 'Jambo Express', which is available to download at www.thebrenthurstfoundation.org.

Finally, this volume is dedicated to the memory of Brenthurst's research associate Johnny Clegg, an African musical icon, who passed away in the final stages of its production, and who was always a source of wise counsel, unique insight, inspiring intellectual curiosity and, in the process, extraordinary encouragement. In his own words:

> The world is full of strange behaviour
> Every man has to be his own saviour
> I know I can make it on my own if I try
> But I'm searching for a great heart to stand me by
> Underneath the African sky
> A great heart to stand me by.

About the Authors

Greg Mills heads the Johannesburg-based Brenthurst Foundation, which was established in 2005 by the Oppenheimer family to strengthen African economic performance. He has been a visiting fellow at the S. Rajaratnam School of International Studies in Singapore, the Strategic and Defence Studies Centre at Australia National University, Cambridge University's Centre for African Studies, the Vietnamese Academy for Social Sciences and Shanghai University's Centre for Global Studies. An Advisory Board member of the London-based Royal United Services Institute, he is the author of the best-selling books *Why Africa Is Poor: And What Africans Can Do about It* (2010), *Africa's Third Liberation* (2012), and, together inter alia with Brenthurst's chairperson Olusegun Obasanjo, *Making Africa Work: A Handbook for Economic Success* (published in four languages in 2017) and *Democracy Works: Rewiring Politics for Africa's Advantage* (2019). The national director of the South African Institute of International Affairs from 1996–2005, he has worked with the United States National Intelligence Council and the British Army's Development, Concepts and Doctrine Centre on their respective global trends projects, and the commander of the International Security Assistance Force in Afghanistan during four deployments between 2006 and 2012. He has directed reform projects in more than a dozen African countries, including Rwanda, Ghana, Kenya, Malawi, Ethiopia, Somalia and Mozambique. He served as a Danish Africa Commissioner and as a member of the African Development Bank's High-Level Panel on Fragile States. He was born and schooled in Cape Town, and he holds degrees from the University of Cape Town and Lancaster University.

Olusegun Obasanjo is the former president of Nigeria. He had a distinguished military career, including serving in the 1960 UN Peacekeeping Mission to Congo and receiving the instrument of surrender on behalf the Nigerian government from the opposing forces in the Nigerian Civil War in 1970. Having attended various educational institutions, including Abeokuta Baptist High School, the Indian Army School of Engineering and the Royal College of Defence Studies in London, he rose to the rank of general and became the Nigerian head of state after the assassination of the then military head of state in February 1976. He handed over power to a democratically elected government in October 1979. Jailed for his pro-democracy views for three-and-a-half years until the death of General Sani Abacha in June 1998, on his release he was democratically elected president in 1999 and served two terms. With over 30 books in print covering a variety of topics, he pursues a passion for conflict resolution, mediation and development through a number of institutions, including the Olusegun Obasanjo Presidential Library in Abeokuta, Tana Forum and The Brenthurst Foundation.

Hailemariam Desalegn was the second executive prime minister of Ethiopia, who served from August 2012 following the death of Prime Minister Meles Zenawi until his resignation and handover to his successor Prime Minister Abyi Ahmed in April 2018. Previously, he served as deputy prime minister and minister of foreign affairs, social affairs and government chief-whip minister under Prime Minister Meles Zenawi. He also served as governor of the Southern Regional State for six years. Born in 1965, he holds a civil engineering degree from Addis Ababa University. In 1990 he won a scholarship to Tampere University of Technology in Finland, earning a Master's degree in water and environmental engineering. He also earned a second Master's degree from Azusa Pacific University in California in 2006. Upon his return to Ethiopia, he served in various academic and administrative capacities, including as the dean of the Water Technology Institute. He is the first leader in modern Ethiopian history to step down voluntarily, setting the stage for sweeping reform. With annual economic growth rates averaging over 10% during his tenure as prime minister, he viewed his resignation as vital in the bid to conduct reforms that would lead to sustainable peace and democracy. He sits on the board of The Brenthurst Foundation.

Emily van der Merwe is an environmental and development economist at The Brenthurst Foundation. She graduated with a Master's degree from the London School of Economics in 2018, having previously studied economics and law at Stellenbosch University as a Mandela Rhodes scholar. Before joining The Brenthurst Foundation, she worked in London at Chatham House (The Royal Institute of International Affairs) and the Grantham Research Institute on Climate Change.

Abbreviations

ADB	Asian Development Bank
ANC	African National Congress
ASEAN	Association of Southeast Asian Nations
BPE	Bureau of Public Enterprises
BSA	Birmingham Small Arms Company
CDC	Council for the Development of Cambodia
CIER	Chung-Hua Institute for Economic Research
CSP	Concentrated Solar Power
DPP	Democratic Progressive Party
EAP	East Asia and the Pacific
EDB	Economic Development Board
ET	Ethiopian Airlines
FDI	foreign direct investment
GDP	gross domestic product
HDB	Housing Development Board
HIP	Hawassa Industrial Park
IAMES	Institute for African and Middle East Studies
IDZ	Industrial Development Zone
IMA	Institut des Métiers de l'Aéronautique
IPO	initial public offering
IT	information technology
ITRI	Industrial Technology Research Institute
KCM	Konkola Copper Mines

KMT	Kuomintang
METI	Ministry of Economy, Trade and Industry
MICE	meetings, incentives, conferences and exhibitions
MITI	Ministry of International Trade and Industry
MRT	Mass Rapid Transit
NEP	New Economic Policy
ODA	official development assistance
OECD	Organisation for Economic Co-operation and Development
1MDB	1Malaysia Development Berhad
PDC	Penang Development Corporation
Pemandu	Performance Management and Delivery Unit
PRC	People's Republic of China
R&D	research and development
RVR	Rift Valley Railway
SEZ	special economic zone
SGR	Standard Gauge Railway
SME	small and medium enterprise
SOE	state-owned enterprise
SSA	sub-Saharan Africa
TAT	Thailand Tourism Authority
TDRI	Thailand Development Research Institute
TFP	total factor productivity
THSR	Taiwan High Speed Rail
TIMSS	Trends in International Mathematics and Science Study
TSMC	Taiwan Semi-Conductor Manufacturing Company
TWA	Trans World Airlines
UMNO	United Malays National Organisation
UNCTAD	United Nation Conference on Trade and Development
UNDP	United Nations Development Programme
URA	Urban Redevelopment Authority
VSIP	Vietnamese Singapore Industrial Park

INTRODUCTION

The Asian Aspiration

More than half the people in the world are living in conditions approaching misery. For the first time in history, humanity possesses the knowledge and skill to relieve the suffering of those people.

— President Harry Truman, Inaugural Address, 1949

Asia has lifted one billion people out of poverty in a single generation, thereby defining the term 'inclusive growth'. Can Africa be the next Asia?

Yes, but only if the continent's leaders commit to making very difficult policy and governance choices. It demands that Africa's citizens also play their part, holding their leadership accountable to a higher standard. And, in some respects, it requires taking a different path from Asia, one more sensitive to issues of human rights, democracy and the environment.

There is an imperative to this because, without sustainable and inclusive growth, Africa is likely to be engulfed by the unrealised aspirations of a rapidly growing and urbanising population.

Not so long ago, many Asian countries found themselves in circumstances very similar to much of contemporary Africa: poverty-stricken, commodity-dependent, facing problems of political and social instability and with few prospects of employment for burgeoning urban populations. By the late 1970s, swathes of East Asia had been devastated economically by a combination of conflict and isolation from global markets. But, following from the early example set by Japan and, later, the so-called tiger

3

economies of Singapore, South Korea, Hong Kong and Taiwan, the region has quickly and dramatically reduced the number of people living in poverty. In so doing, it has enabled huge gains in human development, from child mortality to education.[1]

But such broad strokes, like statistical hyperboles, risk underplaying the human aspect and impact.

The Reunification Express Train, which links northern and southern Vietnam along a railway originally conceived in the late nineteenth century as the 'backbone of Indochina', was completed in 1936 under French colonial rule. Not long after, the line and its 191 stations became a target of incessant attacks by the Viet Minh and North Vietnamese units during the 40 years of war to liberate the country, forcing the abandonment of large sections, while in North Vietnam, American bombing targeted the railway infrastructure. After Saigon fell in 1975, the Hanoi government repaired 1 334 bridges, 27 tunnels and 158 stations, returning the line to use as soon as December 1976.

The train, officially the North-South Railway, was an immediate, tangible symbol of a reunited Vietnam. Still, without the right overall policies, in spite of the huge effort in its rehabilitation, it could not alone take Vietnam from stability to prosperity. Enabling this move would require a different set of policies from the command economics offered by the Hanoi government after 1975, no matter the strength of leadership and political will. Good policy that gave oxygen to the entrepreneurial energies of the Vietnamese would make the difference.

As a result, by the early 1990s, Vietnam was still remembered for its wars, and their costs and consequences. Hanoi was little more than a run-down provincial capital, devoid of the shops and buzzing activity of millions of motorcycles that characterise it a quarter-century later. Ho Chi Minh City had the potential to reclaim its spot as one of Asia's great cities, but, in reality, this seemed a long way off given the lack of investment and international isolation. The country was still under international sanctions nearly two decades after the war with America had ended.

Given a glimpse of opportunity, however, with the installation of its Doi Moi (or renovation) reform policies in the mid-1980s, Vietnam had already set off down the road of reform travelled by so many others in Asia before it. This has enabled the country to replicate a pattern of social transformation and wealth creation, which they could only have dreamt of in the 1980s, when survival, not prosperity, was foremost on their minds.

The North-South train now carries 6.5 million passengers annually through the contrast of luminous-green paddy fields dotted with the coni-cal hats of workers and serial nondescript towns on its 'hard seats', 'soft seats' and 'VIP suites'. It has been turned from a symbol of unity and a conduit for agricultural trade in the 1970s and 1980s into a more modern service to access Vietnam's export markets. Its stations are clogged with containers moving goods, while the state railway also encourages its use by foreign tourists. Over 15 million such tourists visited Vietnam in 2018, an unimaginable figure 25 years before, bringing in more than US$25 bil-lion in income, no less than four times the whole gross domestic product (GDP) of Vietnam in 1989.

By putting the war and failed economic policies behind it, Vietnam has proven again the necessity for policy-makers and people not to be prison-ers of their past or of ideology.

As a miniature, Vietnam captures all the lessons identified in this book as worth learning from Asia about inclusive growth: looking forward and being willing to change policy tack; the need to start with the basics, in Vietnam's case agriculture and education reforms; the central importance of opening up to business and foreign markets; the premium of good lead-ership; the need to make tough and pragmatic structural reforms even if counter to ideological beliefs; and the centrality of growth per se.

Africa's failure to develop like Asia over the last 60 years, it is argued, has not been due to a lack of good ideas or even 'well-meaning' authori-tarians, but a chronic poverty of leadership across all sectors, failure of delivery against plans, and the inability to identify a crisis and act on it.[2]

This failure shows up in some key numbers from the World Bank's World Development Indicators:

	Share of world GDP (%)		Share of world population (%)	
	2000	2017	2000	2017
Sub-Saharan Africa	1.1	1.9	10.9	14.1
China	3.6	15.2	20.6	18.4

Table 1: Africa and Asia: share of global GDP and population

Sources: World Bank national accounts data; OECD national accounts data; United Nations Population Division, World Population Prospects: 2019 Revision; Census reports and other statistical publications from national statistical offices; Eurostat, Demographic Statistics; United Nations Statistical Division, Population and Vital Statistics Report (various years); US Census Bureau, International Database; Secretariat of the Pacific Community, Statistics and Demography Programme.

These figures show that sub-Saharan Africa has a small (and declining) share of global income and rising share of global population, while China (as a proxy for East Asia) has enjoyed both a rising income and falling population share, becoming in World Bank parlance more 'economically dense' while Africa is not.

Since even the best lessons have little worth without learning and transfer, the aim of this volume is to identify the key tenets of leadership, policy choices, trade-offs and execution required.[3]

The rapid changes in Africa's demography demand an urgent change to business as usual. Time, however, is not on the side of the continent's leaders if they are to ensure the twenty-first century is the African century for development.

'Use, don't lose, a crisis': The urgency for change

Africa's leaders have to adopt a similar sense of urgency to Asia's if they are to ensure that their countries not only survive but prosper in the face of the huge demographic changes they face. It is projected that the African continent north and south of the Sahara together will double its population to 2.5 billion by 2050, with the bulk of this increase being in its cities, where more than half of African citizens will be living by 2030. In 1960 this figure was just 10%.

Africa's contemporary cohort of some 420 million young people, aged 15–35, already faces a daunting future. Only one in six is in stable wage employment,[4] and just 75% are literate – the lowest of any region globally.[5] With the number of young people on the continent set to double within the next generation, they will no doubt disrupt the economic, political and social status quo. How this turns out is dependent on the decisions that are made today.

Absent the necessary reforms, the more pressured urban setting, too, can only become one of heightened contestation. With the right preparation and better management, Africa's cities can, however, become poles of rapidly improving prosperity. After all, Asia has been able to reap a demographic dividend – where birth rates have fallen in tandem with skilled, healthy adults coming into a booming job market – through education, family planning, and fit-for-purpose infrastructure and institutions. Asia should offer Africa hope given its remarkable development path.

Why Asia is important

Global poverty reduction since 1990 has been hailed as the greatest human achievement of our time, as a result of which, a generation later, less than 10% of the world's population lived in extreme poverty.[6]

Much of this improvement is due to developments in East Asia, and in China in particular. As will be seen, the transformation started with Japan after the Second World War, when it redirected its undoubted industrial prowess towards consumer manufacturing rather than imperialist ambition. The tigers followed. South Korea transformed itself from the debris of conflict. Between 1962 and 1989, the Taiwanese economy grew at nearly 10% each year. The same happened in Singapore between 1967 and 1993. Proximity helped as trade and investment flowed across regional borders.

But all these populations were relatively small compared to that of Western Europe and the United States.

Then along came China. The sheer scale of its population, coupled with an average of nearly 10% annual growth, has been responsible for three-quarters of this poverty-alleviation effect by lifting 680 million people out of misery. It reduced its extreme poverty rate from 84% to just 10% in 33 years from 1980 – a by-product of which means over half of the world's poorest now live in sub-Saharan Africa.[7]

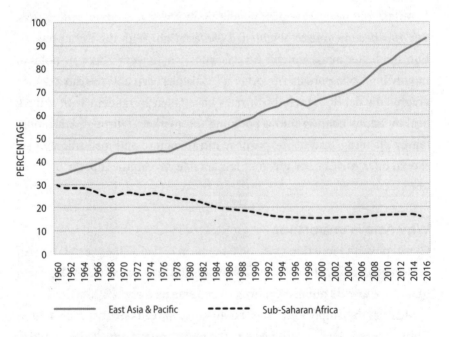

Figure 1: Asia and Africa: share of world GDP per capita (constant)

Source: World Bank Databank, 2019; own calculations.

This geographical shift in poverty signals a change in the underlying global balance of power. In 2014 the International Monetary Fund calculated that three of the world's four largest economies (by purchasing power parity) are in Asia: China in first spot, overtaking the US, with Japan at number three, and India at number four.[8] China had already become the world's largest merchandise exporter by 2009.

Hans Rosling, the renowned Swedish academic, spoke of the world's contemporary 'pin code' as being 1114: roughly one billion each live in Europe, the Americas and Africa, and four in Asia to make a population of seven billion. By 2050, it will be 1125: with Africa and Asia each adding a billion people.[9] The US government's own National Intelligence Council predicted that 'by 2030 Asia will have surpassed North America and Europe combined in terms of global power, based upon GDP, population size, military spending and technological investment'.[10]

Lessons but little learning

Thousands of Africans visit East Asia annually to study the lessons from its economic success. This naturally leads to the question: if these lessons are plentiful and useful, and information not hard to come by, why are they so hard learnt?

One reason why Africa has not followed the Asian development story may be its preoccupation until now with the Western model, whether with admiration or dismay. In a survey of African individuals conducted in July 2019 by The Brenthurst Foundation, 44% noted that this is so. Another reason is simply that the Asian story is not well understood, at least in Africa – a shortcoming this book aims to address – or that cultural, linguistic and geographical differences have hampered learning. Some 28% of respondents believed that this was the case.[11]

Nearly 80% of those asked responded positively to the question: should Africa be willing to learn lessons from the experience of other regions when it comes to development models? There was, however, widespread agreement – by no less than 67% of respondents – that Asia is the world region that Africa has most to learn from. Unsurprisingly, growth and poverty reduction, urbanisation and infrastructure were identified as areas in which Africa can learn the most from Asia. China was prominently noted in all these.

This concurs broadly with a 2014/15 Afrobarometer study of African perceptions towards China, which found that China ranks second as a preferred development model behind the US.[12] No other Asian countries were noted, revealing an opportunity missed to learn from even more relatable examples such as Vietnam, the Philippines and the island-state of Singapore.

And while no country or region is a complete analogue of any other, the East Asian experience illustrates the astonishing results a determined government can deliver. China, for example, for many years was seen as hopeless, a view confirmed, seemingly, by the catastrophes of the Great Leap Forward (1958 to 1962) and the Cultural Revolution (1966 to Mao's death in 1976).

Then, with 40 years of growth touching 13%, the interesting story is about the process of change that brought China to this point: how it acknowledged the failure of Mao's policy, and seemingly turned on its own axis to embrace free markets (see Chapter 9). As a result of this admission, the rise of China has changed the world, challenging the centuries-long domination by the West of global political and commercial affairs, and signalling a shift of power and wealth to Asia – a process so profound that the author Gideon Rachman describes it as no less than 'Easternisation'.[13] This path of growth and development on such a scale also poses, as we note later, questions about sustainability, especially concerning the environment, which have to be factored into any growth formula for the twenty-first century.

Obvious parallels

Despite the obvious differences, Africa and Asia share many similarities: in fact, East Asia seemed to have very few advantages over Africa at the point of decolonisation.

In some respects, African countries were better off than their Asian counterparts at independence. Few African countries, after all, can claim the bitter cost and damage wrought by the wars in Vietnam, Laos and Cambodia. The US dropped an estimated seven million tonnes of bombs on these three countries – unleashing more than twice the destructive force of those bombs dropped on Europe and Asia during the Second World War, including on Hiroshima and Nagasaki. More than three million died in these 'Indochina' wars; another three million, many of them skilled, and most of them indubitably highly motivated, fled the region, and a further five million were internally displaced.[14]

Like Africa, East Asia suffered a colonial inheritance of complex ethnicity and undeveloped human and institutional capacity. Yet, it has prospered despite this colonial legacy, because it pragmatically built on the past and refused to be a victim.

The unity of purpose pursued relentlessly by the leadership of many Asian counties has helped to dilute tensions around identity. By contrast, the political economy – essentially the manner in which history and politics shape economic policy choices and vice versa – of African development has been defined by clientelism, by the management of elite access and preferences in exchange for support, leading to 'rent-seeking' – the creation of wealth not by investment but by the connections of organised interest groups. Finding the institutional and constitutional means to curb such elite predations and open up opportunities beyond a small group has characterised the East Asian development story. Where unsuccessful, as in Myanmar for example, growth and development have suffered.

East Asia's development has pivoted on changing the relationship between government and the private sector. By ensuring conditions favourable to investors, East Asia was able to transform the extractive colonial economic model, thereby ensuring the benefits of growth have been spread beyond a thin elite. Real investment growth and long-term capital that diversify economies and create jobs, notably in industry, have remained very low in Africa compared to Asia, as Figure 2 illustrates. This reflects hostility to foreign capital and private sector-led growth, something that Asia's leaders realised long ago were intrinsic to inclusive growth.

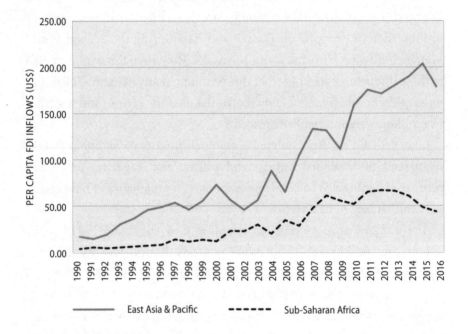

Figure 2: Africa and East Asia: inward investment per capita

Sources: UNCTAD, FDI/MNE database (www.unctad.org/fdistatistics); population data from World Development Indicators; World Bank classification of East Asia and the Pacific; own calculations.

The importance of differentiation

Of course, Asia is not one country. We do not presume it to be so since Africa, too, is not a single country.

It is uncertain even what exactly the term 'Asia' represents. Parag Khanna, for one, sees it as representing five billion people stretching from the Mediterranean to the Pacific, encompassing 53 countries, nearly five billion of the world's eight billion people, the top two most populous countries of China and India, two-thirds of the world's megacities and the same proportion of the world's economic growth, almost one-third of the Fortune 100, six of the world's ten largest banks, eight of the ten largest armies, five nuclear powers, and some of the richest countries in the world but also some of the poorest.[15] But the Asia region can be divided into three distinct entities: East, South and Central Asia.

Even East Asia, the focus of this study, is disparate, containing great differences within and between states. The region is home to hundreds of languages, all the major religions, and various systems of government from open democracies to monarchies and military dictatorships. There are massive wealth divides between urban and rural areas, too, and between countries: per capita income in Singapore is more than 20 times greater than that of Myanmar and Cambodia, for example.

The use of the term Asia as a geographic descriptor is not, however, one that this study seeks to employ. Rather, we are interested in the term as a label of reform, of the high-growth economies in which billions of people have experienced both the rapid rise in incomes described earlier, and rapid and positive change in stability and personal security. Hence the selection of case studies in this book, which describe the changes and, in particular, the policies that lie behind what is less an 'Asian miracle' than a calculated revolution.

There are parallels of transformation, both historical and contemporary.

Singapore's example is much admired across Africa. In the abovementioned Brenthurst poll, for instance, some 42.5% expressed their support for this model for Africa, nearly three times more than the next country, Malaysia, at 15%.

Singapore, which obtained its independence in 1965, a year after Zambia, illustrates a tale of two countries and continents. Whereas Zambia's per capita income in 2019 was, at US$1 672, scarcely US$150 greater than at independence in 1964 (in constant 2010 US$ terms), Singapore's GDP per capita at US$58 248 was 15 times more than it was in 1965. Much like Zambia at the time, Singapore was born in crisis out of the separation of the Malaysian Federation, amid Konfrontasi with Indonesia, and riven with multiracial, ethnic and religious sensitivities and differences. But these countries, and indeed the regions they represent, had divergent responses to these crises.

Admittedly, Singapore's example – and its contemporary levels of wealth and development – makes it at best aspirational for Africans. Its contemporary challenges and their answers bear little relevance to those of most African countries.

There are instead more recent examples of fundamental transition from seeming hopelessness and trauma to upward mobility.

Take the case of Cambodia: Siem Reap International Airport is a model of efficiency, despite its small size and meagre resources. Several stations are alert to process visas on arrival, their aim to get the visitor in so that they can spend their money in their country as quickly as possible. 'No photo? No problem, we'll do it anyway.' Within five minutes you are through, visa in hand.[16]

And this was not because of small volumes of visitors. Far from it. The plane was packed. The airport saw over three million passengers in 2018. No wonder Cambodia's tourism business is booming, up more than tenfold from 437 000 visitors in 2004. Many spend time at Angkor Wat near Siem Reap. It helps having the world's largest religious temples, but you still have to make it easy and enjoyable for people to visit. While temple gazing is the hook, many stay longer, spending time in the city's markets, restaurants, cooking classes, museums and, for some, massage parlours.

It is light years from the reality of the euphonic Pol Pot, 'brother number one', and the Khmer Rouge's 'Year Zero' in 1975: the start of a genocide that wiped out perhaps as many as two million Cambodians, including those exhibiting any sign of education, cutting off the country from the rest of the world, and abolishing money and religion. Such autarkism served to deny Cambodians for a generation, though the inheritance even prior to Pol Pot, the chosen name of schoolteacher Saloth Sar, was hardly impressive. King Norodom Sihanouk's eccentric rule was curtailed by a 1970 coup led by his prime minister, Lon Nol, his feckless government best summed up by the name of his military spokesperson, Am Rong.

There are few countries that suffered as much, as violently and as traumatically.

It has taken a long time to recover. A few of the temples opened to visitors again ten years after the Vietnamese invasion, which turfed out Pol Pot's government in 1978. Now tourism accounts directly for around 10% of GDP and an estimated 800 000 jobs.

But it is not the only driver of Cambodia's annual GDP growth of over 7% since 2011. Increased rice cultivation, both by area and by yield, has helped, but it is the garment and footwear sector that provides 90% of the country's exports. The number of apparel factories has increased from fewer than ten to more than 600 in the last 20 years, with industry growth touching 20% annually.

Cambodia is one of Asia's poorest countries, where half the population of 16 million is under the age of 25, and the per capita income a shade over US$1 200 in 2019. Yet, it has increased nearly threefold this century, from just US$440 in 2000.[17] The garment sector is a major source of this growth, employing 400 000 people, accounting for a third of GDP, with investment principally sourced from China, Taiwan, Korea and Vietnam.

Cambodia, as cited above, offers but one illustration of East Asian industrialisation: low wages, minimum government interference, and openness to capital and trade. But the Cambodian example is not the only development model prevalent in East Asia. Joe Studwell's engrossing *How Asia Works* describes how the Japanese copied the US, British and German industrialisation model of protectionism, built behind tariffs and using monopolies, and founded on close co-operation between business and government through, in the Japanese case, a technocracy centred on the Ministry of International Trade and Industry (MITI). This government-business prototype was emulated, in turn, by the Taiwanese and (South) Koreans.[18]

The effectiveness of this blueprint depended on government discipline: a willingness to efficiently administer the relationship with business, demanding a top-class interlocutor. It is questionable whether African countries possess the capacity of an MITI or Taiwan's Industrial Development Board and South Korea's Economic Planning Board. But it is more interesting to ask if and how this capacity might be acquired and institutionalised.

Indeed, the extent of openness of East Asian countries as measured by the Index of Economic Freedom is considerably higher than the African average. Stronger freedoms correlate with higher GDP per capita, as is depicted in Figure 3.

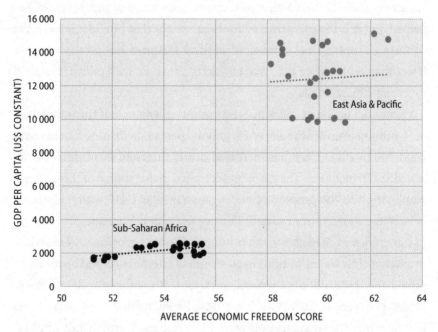

Figure 3: Correlating regional economic freedom and wealth

Source: World Bank Databank, 2019; Heritage Foundation, Index of Economic Freedom, 2019; own calculations.

Whether it be manufacturing or services, factories or tourism, Asia has offered opportunities to break out of cycles of poverty: low-yield agriculture, poor health care and education, vulnerable communities, weak government, and high population growth.

In Cambodia, waiters can earn ten times what their parents would make in the fields, ensuring a fresh cycle of growth, savings, entrepreneurship, investment and affluence.

Admittedly, theirs is an industry built on cheap labour, with some of the lowest wages in the region. This attempt to pick up the low-wage manufacturing jobs discarded by higher-cost markets, including China, is not without stories of injustice and misery. Working conditions are often not pretty, and tales of the plight of workers pitiful. Children frequently work on short-term contracts, up to 14-hour days six days a week, with daily shirt sewing quotas of 950, and just US$0.25 paid for every additional 100 shirts.

Still, without the garment sector, in the opinion of local specialists, the country's economy would collapse. There are more recruits than available jobs. While there is a tough side to this business, it is not as if global consumers of Nike, Puma and Adidas, among others, are volunteering to pay more.[19]

As wages have risen, some jobs have been lost and some have moved to cheaper locales. This is commonly characterised as a 'race to the bottom'; in East Asia, however, there has been a continuous rise in wages and reinvention of economies, with a narrowing in wealth divides, contrary to the supposedly close relationship between growth and inequality.[20] In fact, remarkably, East Asia's rapid growth has been characterised by improving equality in a cycle of growth and reinvestment.[21] One measure of this reinforcing quality is the rate of savings, which averages 35% of GDP in East Asia compared to half of this figure in sub-Saharan Africa.[22] In Asia growth has not been only about the increase in GDP, but fundamentally about wealth creation across the population, as measured in Figure 4 by income inequality (where 0 represents perfect equality and 1 perfect inequality).

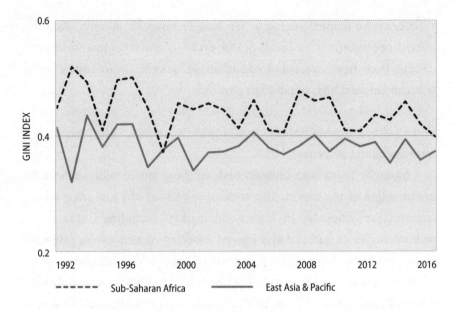

Figure 4: Africa and Asia: measuring inequality

Source: World Bank, Development Research Group. Data is based on primary household survey data obtained from government statistical agencies and World Bank country departments. For Asia and the Pacific, data is available for 25 countries, including the region's developed countries (Australia, Japan and New Zealand). For sub-Saharan Africa, data is available for 48 countries.

Regional integration has helped facilitate this growth process, in keeping the peace and ensuring a steady flow of trade and opportunities, reducing, too, the premium of risk. As noted above, proximity helped in that the presence of regional exemplars – starting with Japan – has provided a model for change and the imperative of incessant innovation.

This is not without its challenges. Decent work and living wages are but one of the humanitarian conundrums implicit in Asia's development. Few would be able to justify today replicating the sweatshop model in Africa, and, as access to information improves, consumers are finding it harder to turn a blind eye to the inhumanity of product supply chains. Yet, in Ethiopia, industrial parks employing workers at less than a dollar a day are heralded as a way out of poverty. These questions don't have easy answers.

Neither does the matter of environmental sustainability. Asia's development is rife with degradation and harm to the planet, for which, in the case of climate change and ocean pillage, the whole world, including Africa, is paying. We cannot be uncritical of Asia's chosen path.

The reasons why Africa shouldn't

For those Africans tending towards autocracy, the Chinese model is an enticing one of economic growth without serious political competition. The same can be said for those businesses that might prefer not to have to negotiate the vagaries and inertia of African bureaucracies and have to obey the written rule of the law.

The Chinese development experience does not offer a perfect model for African governance. The Chinese don't claim that it does. For starters, the vast majority of Africans prefer democracy to autocracy, not least since the experience under the latter system has been so adverse.[23] In Africa, as in Asia, strong men (or women) cannot make up for weak institutions.

We do not assume either that East Asia's progress has been perfect or without cost. On the contrary, there are many downsides, not least the environmental effects of rapid industrialisation, including local air and water quality challenges and global climate change. While China and India have to deal with deadly air pollution, which kills millions prematurely every year,[24] states elsewhere, such as Cambodia, have some of the highest incidences of death from water pollution, mostly due to industrial effluent.[25] The cement model of China, as we term it, also runs the risk of high levels of debt to keep fuelling growth, and the infrastructure providers who profit from this mode of development. Yet, it has to be asked: to what extent does infrastructure alone drive growth and development, and when is there 'sufficient' and 'sustainable' growth?

Such concerns have given rise to a different prism for evaluating the quality of economic advancement. The global economy is worth, in 2019, some US$80 trillion, or US$1 500 for each man, woman and child. It has grown by some 5 000% since the 1960s.

Traditionally, there are three measures of GDP growth: the total value of goods and services produced; the total amount spent in the economy; and the total amount of income from profits and wages. But this calculation misses out on several aspects, including work in the household, volunteerism and much of the informal sector, along with the downside costs of environmental degradation and wastage inherent in over-production (such as food). It also, crucially, does not take into account the distribution of wealth and income. And it makes few allowances for the quality of life: how long one has to toil to produce the output, and how unhappy or fulfilled one is at work. Hence, the debate in the developed world about the need for 'degrowth', emphasising sustainability, that enough is enough, and the need to decouple growth from carbon emissions.[26]

Yet, degrowth is not an option for the 3.4 billion people worldwide, almost half the global population, who live on less than US$5.50 per day. Growth that is both sustained and more sustainable is thus a key consideration for Africa in forging a steeper developmental path. Difficult choices have to be made on the policies that feed growth; for example, on the type of power that will be sustainably and cheaply generated to allow diversification, or the policies that encourage inward investment while incentivising local business to scale up, that enable governments to permit growth without losing control, and that improve productivity while recognising the rights of workers, and women, in particular.

Such difficult decisions (although made in a different era, for a set of different realities, which preceded contemporary social and environmental concerns) were the cornerstone of Asia's transformation – much more so than chance or luck or history.

Structure of this book

This study is divided into two main parts: the first, which focuses on ten 'growth stories', starts with Japan and the power of its example, deals with the tigers, cubs and what has now become the regional (and global) locomotive of China, and ends with a more recent example of transformation in Vietnam.

The second part draws what we see as the five key lessons for Africa, illustrating these with comparative African and Asian examples. It also explains some of the pitfalls that Africa should avoid (see Table 2) in following Asia's fast-track development path.

What Africa should do	What Africa shouldn't do
Listen to business	Favour elites
Ensure openness	Mistake trading for a means to develop
Instil the basics: political and macro stability	Seek silver-bullet solutions
Boost agriculture yields	Focus on land alone as the solution
Prioritise necessary infrastructure	Adopt high-debt infrastructure-led growth
Invest in education and skills	Close avenues to outside talent
Pursue growth as an inclusive agent	Ignore the environment for the next generation
Improve productivity	Fail to improve the quality of life
Attach laser-like focus to job creation	Look to the state as the solution
Act fast and decisively	Attempt authoritarianism as a political solution

Table 2: Summary of suggestions for Africa

Finally, while recognising the differences within Asia and Africa, and the importance of differentiation, the conclusion asks what Lee Kuan Yew, the iconic turnaround politician from Singapore, would do if he had found himself leading in Africa.

The continent's ambition cannot be to duplicate the Asia path, but rather to learn from Asia and other fast-growing regions through a process of 'translative adaptation' – a concept that defined the transfer of Japan's lessons to the rest of Asia. In this sense, the lessons presented in the second part of this book are meant as guidelines for self-exploration, rather than hard rules for development.

While identifying and using a sense of crisis, African leaders will have to strive to escape the 'tyranny of the emergency' and instead create a shared vision of how their countries will progress. We were reminded by one colleague that 'a disciplined nationalism is the secret sauce of development'. This can be interpreted as the deep commitment to popular welfare that defines inclusive growth and that has been routinely exhibited by East Asian leaders, whatever the formal system of government.

In May 2000, *The Economist* led with the headline 'The Hopeless Continent'. Eleven years later, in 2011, it had the heading 'Africa Rising'. There is truth to both these statements and to the grey area that lies between them. Africa is, we realise from personal experience, neither a continent of chronic despair nor one of unchecked optimism. For us, the key lesson from Asia is to deal with the facts on the ground as they are. In this, we would hope that sound advice could bear fruit in order to be able to take the next generation from poverty to prosperity.

Africa would do well to heed Asia's experiences and lessons, avoiding its faults and replicating its successes.

PART ONE

CASE STUDIES FROM ASIA

Chapter 1

Japan
The Power of Example and Innovation

The contrast between that which preceded the funeral car and that which followed it was striking indeed. Before it went old Japan; after it came new Japan.

— *New York Times* on the funeral of the Emperor Meiji, 13 October 1912

By 1945, an estimated 800 000 Japanese civilians had been killed in Allied bombing attacks, more than 100 000 alone on one evening in Tokyo in March 1945. Traumatised and beset with famine and poverty after the war's end, Tokyo's citizens would clamber aboard trains to the countryside in the hope of finding something to eat. These trains were so crowded, writes David Pilling in *Bending Adversity*, that people hung onto the outsides of carriages, and windows were barricaded with planks from the inside to stop them from cracking.[1]

Yet, within a generation, Japan had rebuilt itself from the ground up, reaching high-income status in 1977. Between 1950 and 1987, for example, Japan's GDP growth rose annually by 7.9%, while labour productivity increased by 8%. The corresponding figures were 4.6% and 4.3% in Germany, 2.5% and 2.8% in the United Kingdom and 3.2% and 2.6% in the United States.[2]

After its subsequent slow-down and the 'lost decades' of stagflation and stagnation in the 1990s and 2000s, many have taken Japan's rapid post-war rise for granted, viewing it as a fluke rather than acknowledging the leadership and grit it demanded.

One region this was not lost on, however, was East Asia. Japan quickly became the prototype for the regional development 'miracle'. 'Translative adaptation', to use the phrase popularised by the economic anthropologist Keiji Maegawa, was possible within the unique cultural and other characteristics of each country, as it had been from the West to Japan during the late nineteenth century. Product designs were absorbed, modified and re-exported back to the West as early as 1929 with Toyoda's and Suzuki's automated cotton weaving machines.

The message implicit in Japan's rise, which was noted by the leaders of the tigers in Singapore, Hong Kong, South Korea and Taiwan that also followed an export-led growth model, was that it was possible. This prospect had, ironically, been strengthened by Japan's smashing military victories over the Allies in 1942, which shattered the twin illusion of Asian mediocrity and Western supremacy. It was certainly no fluke. In fact, on the day after Japan surrendered, on 16 August 1945, a small group of bureaucrats and economic experts met in a burnt-out building in Tokyo to discuss how Japan would be restored, not through military might, but with technology and economic power.[3] This signalled the end of *Fukoku Kyohei*, or 'rich country, strong military', the maxim that led Japan's militarist leaders to enter the war. It showed that the politics – and the leadership – had to be right, in giving direction.

But Japan's extraordinary story of growth and peace is not one of simply rebuilding the country after 1945. It is a longer story of development, the recent phase going back 150 years to the start of the Meiji Restoration, which put in place the foundation of education and encouraged openness to foreign expertise. The transformation after 1945 was less a case of a turnaround than redirection to democracy and selling to the global consumer.

The Meiji Restoration, which started in 1868, unified Japan's feudal states into a centrally organised empire. 'Meiji' translates as 'enlightened rule', with the objective to combine modernisation with traditional values. Learning became a top priority. There was little option for a country so poor in natural resources. Emperor Meiji announced in his Charter Oath that 'knowledge shall be sought all over the world, and thereby the foundations of imperial rule shall be strengthened'.[4] And government sought to strengthen the modernisation by helping business to modernise, including encouraging foreign technology and skills, traits which have stood Japan in good stead since. In this way, the Second World War, and the terrible events at Hiroshima, were an aberration in a 150-year period of continuous reform and innovation-led industrialisation.

Two industries around Hiroshima are testimony to these foundations and the need for grit.

The Kure shipyard is an example of the importance of continuity in building skills and of positive policy direction. Opened in 1889, the Kure Naval Base was developed alongside the local steelworks, which accounted for half of Japan's production and the naval arsenal. In 1937 it laid down the heaviest and most powerfully armed battleship ever, the 72 800-tonne *Yamato*.[5] The technology developed in the construction of the *Yamato* was evidence of the standard of Japanese engineering and the means whereby it would enable the country's reconstruction.

Then, as now, Mazda had its headquarters in Hiroshima's Aki District. Started in 1920 as the Toyo Cork Kogyo Company, which manufactured machine tools, it branched out into three-wheel auto rickshaws in 1931, before diverting into rifle production during the Second World War. Its founder, Jujiro Matsuda, celebrated his 70th birthday on 6 August 1945, the day the atomic bomb was dropped on the city. Despite losing many workers in the devastation, Mazda was able to restart production just four months later, living up to what Matsuda saw as Mazda's oath: 'contributing to the world through manufacturing'. Mazda is now the 15th-largest carmaker globally, producing 1.6 million vehicles in 2019. Like other Japanese car manufacturers, it has leant heavily on foreign innovations, famously attracted to the German Wankel rotary engine, first using it in 1967 in its Cosmo sports car. Again, like others, Mazda has used motorsport to advertise and improve such technology, becoming the first Japanese manufacturer in 1991 to win the gruelling Le Mans 24-hour endurance race. Unusually, however, Mazda has accommodated foreign partners not only in technology sharing but also management based on its long-term tie-up with Ford. Today it is pushing, once more, the technological envelope with its production techniques and its Skyactiv engine systems. Its Hiroshima plant can assemble a car every 30 seconds. With such a contrasting combination of innovation and pragmatism, it is no wonder that Japan became the world's largest car producer (until 2008 when overtaken by China) and that Toyota is the world's second-largest carmaker, or Honda the world's largest motorcycle manufacturer.

Like Mazda, Toyota, Honda and many other industries, Japan rose from the embers of war, and in so doing showed the way for others.

Educate and import ideas

The Toyota Commemorative Museum of Industry and Technology in Nagoya has a large circular loom in the entrance, invented by Sakichi Toyoda, whose family fortune from his designs seeded the Toyota empire. His Type G loom was sold to Platt Bros & Co. Ltd in 1929 for £100 000. Not only did the Type G permit non-stop shuttle changing,[6] but its system automatically shut down the loom if a warped thread snapped. An illustration of Japanese focus on incremental but continuous improvement, or *kaizen*, Toyoda's design increased productivity, as workers were freed from monitoring looms, being able to operate up to 30 machines per worker. Once the world's largest textile manufacturer, with more than 15 000 workers in 1913, Platts went out of business in 1982 when it was faced with the closure of Lancashire cotton mills and tough competition in foreign markets.

Not forgetting their roots, however, half the Toyota museum is dedicated to the evolution of Japan's cotton industry, and Toyoda's role in it. Still, today, Toyota industries produce hi-tech looms. The difference is that it is less than 1% of its business for a company that produced 8.8 million vehicles in 2018.

Sakichi Toyoda's maxim was to work with 'the spirit of being studious and creative'. It is a metaphor for all of post-war Japan.

Japan's industrialisation was based on three key elements: a strong private sector, a supportive state and an ability to adapt and absorb outside influences, including technology, ideas, machines and capital. The Perry naval expedition, which landed near Edo (present-day Tokyo) in July 1853, resulted in the signing of the US-Japan Treaty of Peace and Amity the following March. While the mission threatened violence, the Americans found in the Japanese willing modernisers and collaborators. Nariakira Shimazu, a leading political figure at the time, concluded that 'if we take the initiative, we can dominate; if we do not, we will be dominated'.[7]

But simply being receptive to outside ideas was not enough. The government deliberately went out to learn lessons, and to import technical and commercial partners. This was achieved by sending government officials abroad to study, for example through the Iwakura Mission to the US in 1871. In pre-war Japan, as much as 2% of government's budget was expended on the advice of European and American corporate and industrial specialists.[8] The Department of Science and Technology spent nearly half their annual budget on foreign expertise.

Japan actively diffused and internalised the technologies and practices foreigners had left behind, often alongside external capital and technology. This pattern of engagement has been a constant. Despite the archetype of a closed society to outsiders, the spinning mills owed their origins to British technology, electrical machinery to a relationship with GE, AEG and Siemens, the telegraph to French involvement, ship-building to British and US firms, while the steel industry was based around collaboration between the state-owned Yamata Iron Works and Germany's Gutehoffnungshütte and, later, between the Mitsui *zaibatsu* and Britain's Armstrong and Vickers. In 1872 the first Japanese railway was built with British help, the start of a massive network of railways. If American or French railways had been chosen instead, Japan might well be driving on the right side of the road.

Japan borrowed car and motorcycle expertise from Britain and others in its early years: Isuzu from Wolseley Motors and Nissan from Austin, Toyota from US carmakers and Mitsubishi from Fiat. After the war, Honda and Suzuki, as will be seen, among others, were willing to study European models and reverse-engineer and improve on their products.

Openness to ideas proved simultaneously necessary and advantageous.

'Bending adversity'

A further, important aspect of Japan's success has been an ability to turn crises into opportunities.

After Japan's declaration of surrender in August 1945, nine days after the Hiroshima bombing, the country was placed under American authority, with the goal of demilitarising Japan and preventing future war. There was even a Nuremberg-style trial, the Tokyo War Tribunal, sentencing former militarist leaders to death or imprisonment, including the Japanese wartime prime minister, Hideki Tojo.

Japan's recovery benefited from a measure of post-war pragmatism in the face of fast-cooling relations between the US and the Soviet Union, and a dollop of idealism. 'We were lucky after the Second World War when the New Deal guys came,' says Masa Sugano, the deputy for the Africa region of the Japan External Trade Organisation. Many of the officials who accompanied General Douglas MacArthur to Japan after the war, writes Pilling, were 'idealists who wanted to fashion a peaceful and democratic society from the broken shards of Japan's failed modernisation.'[9] Along with delivering US$15.2 billion of foreign aid between 1945 and the end of their occupation in 1952,[10] the Americans also effected important reforms, encouraging labour unions, land reform and women's suffrage in the late 1940s.

Military spending by the US government also enabled Japanese fiscal resources to be more productively diverted to infrastructure development. As the Americans dismantled Japan's industrial complex, prohibiting the manufacturing of warships and military aircraft, many companies adjusted by producing products for domestic household markets instead. These reforms, aimed at liberalisation, also led to the break-up of the monopolistic *zaibatsu* conglomerates, making way for *keiretsu* or loose federations. But support for communist and socialist ideas were soon gaining momentum, leading the US to clamp down again on the newly established labour unions, along with the media and left-wing politicians. US-sanctioned growth and liberalisation, it would emerge, had conditions.

During the Korean War, Japan became the main supplier of US matériel, with manufacturing growing by 50% between 1950 and 1951. Some US$3.5 billion (or US$33 billion in 2019 terms) was spent by the US for the duration of the war, from 1950 to 1953, on Japanese companies, including Mitsubishi and Sumitomo. Within ten years of Japanese shipyards being allowed to produce again in 1954, Japan overtook Britain as the world's biggest shipbuilders, the Kure yard foremost among them. The vanquished quickly became the victors.

Similar stories were repeated in the automotive and motorcycle industries.

Continuous improvement and investment

The coastal city of Hamamatsu, 260 kilometres west of Tokyo, is the motorcycling equivalent of Silicon Valley, and is the birthplace of Yamaha, Suzuki and Honda.

Michio Suzuki founded the Suzuki Loom Works in Hamamatsu in 1909. His business took off with the invention and export of a new automated weaver 20 years later. Intent on diversifying, Suzuki started a small car project in 1937, the same time as Honda set up his piston ring manufacturing operation in a small Hamamatsu garage. Suzuki's motoring plans were halted by the war, after which the company returned to producing looms. Faced with the collapse of the cotton market in the early 1950s, Suzuki restarted his transport project, building, as Honda did at its start, a 'clip-on' small engine to power bicycles in 1954 to meet a dearth of post-war motorised transport.

It grew quickly. In 1955, Suzuki produced 9 000 motorcycles, changing its name to the Suzuki Motor Co. Ltd. By 1960, however, it was churning out 155 000, nearly the annual output of the entire British motorcycle industry.

For the first half of the twentieth century, Britannia ruled the motorcycle world.[11] Birmingham Smalls Arms Company (BSA), the biggest industry name of all, had been founded in 1891 as a consortium of Birmingham-based arms manufacturers. In its heyday, it claimed one in four motorcycles worldwide was a BSA. When British motorcycle production peaked in 1954 at 187 000 units, the industry was the country's third-largest source of foreign exchange after cars and whisky.

But it lost its way because it failed to move with the times.

By 1974, British motorcycle brands held only 1% of the US market and just 3% of their domestic market. BSA was no more. The consortium of Norton Villiers Triumph was officially dissolved in 1978.

While Japan ascended, led by the likes of Honda, Yamaha (today the world's second-largest motorcycle producer), Kawasaki and Suzuki, the British motorcycle industry went into terminal decline. A 1975 UK parliamentary study found that Japanese workers were not paid less than their British counterparts, but rather that the manufacturing techniques simply were more capital-intensive, resulting in increased productivity and better quality.

While the likes of Suzuki killed off the British industry, increasingly the Hamamatsu company is exiting the motorbike business, which by 2019 was responsible for only 6% of its US$37 billion in annual revenue.

Suzuki's success in car manufacturing (it was in 2019 the world's 10th-largest car[12] and sixth-largest motorcycle manufacturer[13]) has, in part, been due to taking a different direction from its competitors, in focusing on the small car market from the start. Secondly, it has followed the trend in offshoring the bulk of its production in the search for cheaper labour and markets, concluding several ultimately lucrative joint venture deals with Vietnam, Myanmar, Hungary, Indonesia and Pakistan. Of 3.3 million cars sold in 2018, 1.7 million were made in India, and fewer than a million in Japan. One in every two cars sold in India in 2018 was a Suzuki.

And the third reason is the company's continued willingness to introduce new technology, just as Michio Suzuki did with his looms. Its first car, the 1955 Suzuki Suzulight, possessed a transverse engine driving the front wheels, four-wheel independent suspension and rack-and-pinion steering, all of which were revolutionary for the time. Like Honda and Yamaha, Suzuki has not been shy to learn from outsiders in improving the stock, from the early 1960s using foreign riders and engineering talents. Today Suzuki spends US$1.3 billion annually – or 4% of turnover – on research and development (R&D), a large share of which is earmarked for electric vehicle technology.

The power of reinvention

Chalmers Johnson's seminal account of Japanese development, in which he coined the term 'developmental state', highlights the importance of nationalism (where economic means are seen as the principal way of ensuring national survival), state control of finance, labour relations, the role of the economic bureaucracy especially through the Ministry of International Trade and Industry (MITI), the use of incentives, and the existence of conglomerates.[14]

One contributing factor of Japan's early success was the presence of a corporatist state, although sometimes inefficiently so. In the 1950s the role of MITI (which transformed to the Ministry of Economy, Trade and Industry – METI – in 2001) was to target key sectors, particularly textiles, through foreign exchange allocation. The following decade their focus shifted to promoting domestic technology through R&D subsidies, and in the 1970s it promoted alternative energy sources (notably nuclear) in the wake of the oil shock, along with deregulation. Now its role is mainly as a 'troubleshooter' within government ministries – or 'troublemaker', as one former official put it.

It is questionable, however, whether companies such as Honda and Sony prospered because or in spite of government, given the focus of the latter particularly on heavy industrial giants such as Mitsubishi and Mitsui. Picking winners did not always serve those who were selected, but the process did build some resilient challengers.

The MITI/METI role is sometimes taken as evidence of the Japanese conformist, rigid, corporatist trait. Yet, this may be overstated. For one, the bureaucracy was better geared to business than most. 'Our role was', reflects Dr Yuko Yasunaga of the UN's Industrial Development Organization, who earlier headed up METI's semi-conductor wing, 'to understand what was going on outside. I had 15 minutes a day with my boss, but four to five hours a day with industry.'

History suggests there is also a constant appetite for change. The flexibility of Fujifilm to switch its focus from film (on which 90% of its business depended in the mid-1990s) to medical imagery, unlike its principal competitor Kodak, which is highlighted in Chapter 12, confirms this astonishing adaptability. Mazda similarly changed tack when it became clear that the rotary engine was not going to produce the desired emissions and fuel economy, no matter its advantageous power-to-weight ratio. Or Honda, among others, was willing early on to test itself on the racetracks of the world, in both motorcycling and Formula One, bucking the trend in terms of the engine technology chosen.

Honda is the world's largest motorcycle manufacturer as well as the world's largest producer of internal combustion engines, more than 31 million units annually. It is also the seventh-largest car manufacturer in the world, with more than 220 000 employees.

Given his background, Soichiro Honda personally did not operate in the manner of the oligarchic *zaibatsu*, preferring a garage overall to a suit. The company has remained consistent, however, in being led by sound engineering production practices. It has invested heavily in R&D, with a minimum commitment of 3% set aside annually for design and prototypes. The firm encourages flexible hours for its R&D team to spur innovative thinking, quite contrary to the conformist stereotype of Japanese workers.

In 2014, Honda's worldwide motorcycle production went through the 300-million mark. There are three significant gear changes in this otherwise seamless ascent from adding on a war-surplus engine to a bicycle in 1948 to dominant global force.

The first was in the development of the Super Cub motorcycle in 1958. Until then, Honda's production was under 50 000 units annually; by 1965 it was nearly at 1.5 million. Super Cub production went through 100 million units in 2017.

Aimed initially at a local market, the Super Cub had to have mass appeal: to be affordable, cheap on fuel, and easy to ride by both sexes. Honda scoped out European models in the design, while the mass production system required a heavy investment in machine tools. While MITI assisted with cheap capital, the risk of over-investment in such new machinery was largely Honda's. Honda was open to learning from others, including top European racers, bringing them to test machines in Japan, and to campaign for it on the world's racetracks. The world took notice when it won its first victory on the testing Isle of Man track in 1959, going on to subsequently dominate GP racing.

Second, reflecting the early partnership between Soichiro Honda (the engineer) and Takeo Fujisawa (the marketeer), Honda aggressively accessed the critical American market, where in the 1950s half a million new motorbikes were registered, learning and adapting its approach continuously. To do so it had to change the image of motorcycling from a 'black-jacketed man on a Harley' to one of wider appeal, hence the 'You'll meet the nicest people on a Honda' campaign, now widely studied in business schools as an example of success. Honda sold 40 000 motorcycles in America in 1962, then 10% of its production. There was no looking back. The development of the world's first mass superbike in the four-cylinder CB740 and, later, the Gold Wing tourer increased the Honda slice of the US premium market, entrenching the brand. By 1984, Honda had a 50.4% market share of the 1.3-million American motorcycle import market, when Honda's total production was just under 2.6 million bikes.

Honda produced 20 million motorbikes in 2018/19, alongside 5.3 million cars and 6.3 million power products, such as agricultural equipment, marine engines and generators. Virtually no Honda motorbikes are produced in Japan, however, signalling the third big shift of production, especially towards Southeast and South Asia, centring on Vietnam, Thailand, Malaysia and the Philippines, the largest consumer markets.[15] It has two small sub-Saharan African facilities, in Nigeria and Kenya, producing little more than 60 000 bikes in 2018, despite the growth in the African market to total sales of more than four million units.[16] Naofumi Sakamoto, who joined the company in 1982 and headed up the American marketing operations, sums up Honda's philosophy: 'Our decision-making is always driven by what is best for the customer.'

Is there a Japanese model?

Asia has, as is suggested above, long looked to Japan as an example of success. 'Learning from other countries is a common success factor for Asian countries,' observes Keijiro Otsuka, a professor of development economics at the National Graduate Institute for Policy Studies in Tokyo.[17] India's and Malaysia's Look East policies, for example, reflect Japan's efforts, nearly 150 years before, to learn from other nations on its path to development.

Japan's historical example shows how a focus on education can carry a country through different stages of industrialisation and make it resilient. Yet, closer study reveals a belief that Japan is inherently 'different' – exemplified by the once-popular genre of *Nihonjinron*, which studies the factors that make Japan 'separate'. Japan has an economy so unique that outsiders have had to invent a whole jargon to describe it – from Abenomics to lean production. This is not to mention expressive Japanese words like *karoshi* – death by overwork – and *otsukaresama desu* (a popular greeting, also meaning 'your week must have been tough, and you must be tired'), which embody Japan's unique corporate culture.

But this uniqueness ought not to be overstated. Nor should it be taken to mean that Japan's success cannot and should not be repeated.

Japan, itself, managed at least three great restorations over the last 150 years, each one faster than and different from the last. The latest one, their recovery from the devastating 2011 earthquake, which turned into a triple disaster with the tsunami and nuclear accident, reminded the world just how resilient the Japanese are, and how well they respond to a crisis.

If there are aspects in which the Japanese have not succeeded during their industrialisation, it is geographical parity and openness. Rapid growth was achieved by concentrating on large cities, particularly Tokyo and Osaka. There was comparatively little regional distribution of wealth.

For all of its problems of ageing and stagnation, 'Japan', notes Pilling, 'remains an adaptive and resilient society. Its history suggests it has the ability to confront and eventually overcome many of the difficulties it faces.'[18] It is blessed with virtually full employment (unemployment is just 2.8%). There are valuable lessons for other countries with ageing populations, and in dealing with the challenge of reinvention – just as Fujifilm has managed so well by comparison with others.

Yet, Japan's earlier economic transition is still pertinent to developing economies. In so doing, it smashed Western prejudice. It led the consumer digital revolution. It changed our timescale expectations about development. It illustrates still the power of innovation and example.

Conclusion: Translative adaptation and Africa

One priority for Japan's development spending in Africa is on *kaizen* – the 'continuous improvement' of the workforce. To this end, a Kaizen Institute was established in Ethiopia in 2013, while the Japan International Co-operation Agency continues to fund seminars, experts, training and other skills improvement initiatives in Africa as part of its US$1 billion in annual African aid. This engagement has accelerated and deepened as Japan has apparently felt marginalised by China's ambitious Africa plans, and Tokyo has learnt lessons from the effectiveness (or not) of its aid, in terms of the necessity of using soft power to encourage the private sector, as well as the imperative of feasibility studies and local ownership of development plans.[19]

But such a focus on skills and education is not going to be enough to replicate, or even adapt, the Japanese model. One indication of the conditions necessary is in the answers provided to the question asked of auto executives in Tokyo, Hamamatsu, Nagoya and Hiroshima in 2019: 'what would it take to open a new factory in Africa?' This is not an unreasonable expectation given the growth in Africa's population and the offshoring production trend.

Almost universally, the key determinant was that there had to be a large market, preferably growing in population size and wealth: in a word, demand. It assumed that there are 'reasonable logistics', 'quality fuel' allowing for the use of the latest engine technologies, 'favourable taxation and other incentives', and 'macro-economic stability'. The 'motorisation point' at which the population was wealthy enough to contemplate purchasing a car was US$3 000 per capita. There was a need, too, to 'avoid focusing on trying to protect industry, as this will worsen production standards and competitiveness. If you protect the market, you will slow down growth.'[20]

Japan's own history speaks to these challenges.

During the nineteenth century, China, like Japan, imported foreign ideas and technology. But these did not 'stick' then in the same way as they did in Japan. One reason may be that China was still a dynasty and that it was difficult to absorb Western technology into what was a feudal system. Today, these lessons should be asked of African countries interested in borrowing from the success of Asia. 'You need to have fierce policy competition, which is focused principally on the benefit to business as the key customer of government,' notes Kenichi Ohno, who has advised the Ethiopian government, among others, over many years. 'This is why and how Asia works,' he states.

At its core, this ranges from understanding the nature of business and its needs to seeing the customer – whether a business or an individual – as being at the centre of government's actions. And all this demands a depth in human resources and an appetite to learn, translate and adapt, the most salient lesson of Japan's 150 years of transition.

Chapter 2

Taiwan*
The Subcontractor

> A country's ability to compete is not bred in the bone. In the past, a country could become rich by simply depending on natural resources. Today, rich countries must create wealth through the long-term accumulation of high-quality technologies, management, and system integration ... In the past, a country's rise and fall is calculated on a hundred-year cycle. Now every one or two decades will produce a replacement. Therefore, the effective development of 'brain power' within a nation will decide the prosperity of a country in the future.
>
> — Stan Shih, founder of Acer Computers, 1996

The Apple iPhone is, as is well documented, made up of components that are sourced mostly from China, South Korea and Japan.[1] This is captured by the words 'Designed in California, Assembled in China' printed in very tiny letters at the back of each iPhone. This also means that any US trade war with China is in part also a trade war with its very own companies, notable among them the iconic Apple.

But what is less known is that Taiwanese firms supply 70% of iPhone parts.[2] Local companies Taiwan Semi-Conductor Manufacturing Corporation,

---

* As of September 2019, 16 countries officially recognised Taiwan's government as independent from mainland China, while the Chinese government, along with the United Nations and 180 countries, regard Taiwan as a region of the People's Republic of China under the 'one country, two systems' principle, thus eschewing any description of Taiwan as a 'nation' or 'country'.

Foxconn, Foxlink, Advanced Wireless Semiconductor, Winbond and Delta collectively supply (and therefore 'own') an overwhelming share of the supply chain for the world's most aspirational phone, one that has become synonymous with cutting-edge innovation and quality. Even if these components are manufactured elsewhere, they originate in Taiwan, which is driven by a hi-tech, R&D-friendly environment.

It may come as a surprise, as a few decades ago 'Made in Taiwan' was still associated with low quality, plastic and disposable.

Taiwan has gone through several distinct stages of development: from agriculture and textiles and apparel in the 1950s and 1960s respectively, to petrochemicals in the 1970s, and finally to economic liberalisation and the advent of the Information Technology (IT) sector in the 1980s. Personal computers (PCs) and opto-electronics followed in the 1990s and early 2000s, and today so-called integrated circuits and green technology (photovoltaics and LED) are responsible for the bulk of Taiwan's exports.

Meanwhile, most key exports don't even carry the Taiwanese label, being components in a larger network of international brands, which subcontract to Taiwanese businesses. This is the story of Apple and Foxconn. And it is analogous to the way Taiwan has, largely to its own benefit, become a cog in China's machine.

Taiwan's development progression sounds logical and simple, almost inevitable. But it was the outcome of deliberate policy choices. In part, it reflected Taiwan's 'performance through paranoia', a result of its strained relationship with the People's Republic of China (PRC) next door, which has laid claim to the island since the Kuomintang (KMT) fled there in 1949 to set up a Republic of China government to rival Beijing. Beijing, meanwhile, has not ceased to claim the island as part of its territory under the 'one country, two systems' policy.

Undoubtedly, the need for economic development in the face of such an existential political risk has been a key motive for Taipei's leadership.

Even so, Taiwan's example shows that success is systematic: you start with

land reform and stabilising the macro-environment, dealing with inflation and exchange rate volatility. Next, you incentivise exports and enable
small and medium enterprises (SMEs) by all means possible, ensuring
government is a friend of business: create an integrated system of support,
including fiscal incentives at the start, technological incubators, science
and industrial parks, and trade promotion agencies. Infrastructure must
be used to stimulate down periods in growth, but also to make growth as
inclusive as possible. And finally, you keep evolving, creating a continuous policy feedback loop, not least through deepening democratic reforms
(once Taiwan's strength and perhaps now its weakness).

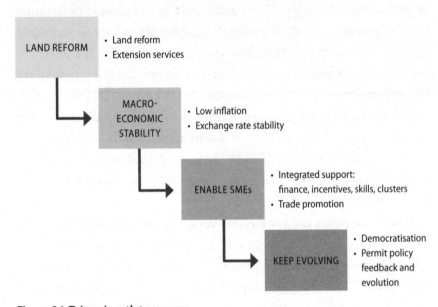

Figure 2.1: Taiwan's path to success

Hardware and software transitions

As one of the original Asian tigers, Taiwan presided over an economic
miracle that transformed the former Japanese colony to one of the leaders
in global exports in just two generations. Its extraordinary growth record

enabled it to achieve per capita incomes firmly in the developed economy league. In 1951, Taiwan had a per capita GDP of just US$154.[3] Twenty years later, this had risen to US$451; by 1982 to US$2 700. At US$8 216 in 1990, it had doubled further within two decades.[4]

This has been achieved alongside political and price stability, with inflation averaging under 5% since the 1960s, following a phase when it topped 100% in the 1950s. There has also been a consistent spreading of economic benefits between the wealthy and poor, despite a gradual widening of income inequality. The Gini coefficient for Taiwan measured 0.281 in 1981 and 0.337 in 2018,[5] which puts it in the company of Switzerland and France. By comparison, Zambia has a Gini coefficient of 0.571, with similar population size, while South Africa, which ranks among the most unequal countries worldwide, is at 0.631.[6]

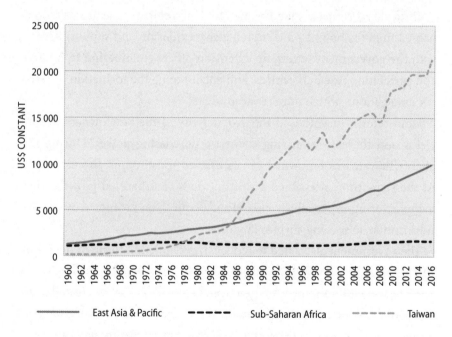

Figure 2.2: GDP growth: Taiwan versus Africa and East Asia

Source: World Bank Databank, 2019

Stages in economic development

There are a number of clearly identifiable stages in Taiwan's economic development, in which internal and external factors both played a role.[7]

The first was the 'pre-plastic' chapter.

During the 1950s, the government embarked on a three-phase land reform process, which secured the rights of tenant farmers, reduced their rent payable, and transferred public and private land by setting the maximum farm size at six hectares and the upper limit of rent paid to landlords at 37.5% of harvest. In the land-to-the-tiller phase from 1953, landlords were compensated partly through shares in state-owned companies. As a result, some 140 000 hectares of farmland were transferred to nearly 200 000 households.[8] This is covered in more detail in Chapter 13.

Critically, this was not land reform for land reform's sake. It was accompanied then (as now) by a comprehensive extension and support service, with the government setting up extension offices (numbering 16 in 2019) and agriculture research centres, and encouraging the formation of farmers' associations, which number around 300.

Land reform incentivised the productivity of the new owners, raising yields and thereby improving domestic purchasing power. During this phase, Taiwan was renowned for its canned mushrooms and asparagus. At the same time, it enabled a shift in focus to urban-led growth. Light manufacturing, especially in apparel and textiles, was promoted by import-substitution, absorbing surplus labour.

The government also acted to reduce hyper-inflation through the imposition of high interest rates, while the workforce received a boost with the arrival of two million (mostly) men from Chiang Kai-shek's defeated army, one-fourth of the number already on the island. Government also spent heavily on education and training, realising that no macro-economic policy can work without skills.

Also, from 1951, Washington provided US$100 million annually in aid, then some 6% of Taiwan's GDP, which was useful in ways more than just the financing and stabilisation effect: it facilitated the creation of a technocratic class and technology transfer, while the prospect of its culmination in 1965 also helped to focus the minds of Taiwanese policy-makers – they had to make a plan, and quickly.

			GDP per capita (US$) (% of 1950 levels)
1950s	Import substitution	High interest rate policy Unify exchange rate Land reform US aid starts	$154–$163 (100%–105%)
1960s	Export growth	Export processing zones Implement nine-year mandatory education National Science and Technology Development Plan Family Planning Plan US aid ends	$161–$397 (105%–258%)
1970s	Infrastructure and heavy industry	Ten construction projects ITRI Hsinchu Science Park Loosen import restrictions	$451–$2 389 (292%–1 551%)
1980s	Economic liberalisation	Environment Protection Bureau Exchange rate liberation Incentives for strategic industries Privatisation of SOEs	$2 721–$8 216 (1 766%–5 335%)
1990s	Industrial upgrading	Six-year National Development Plan Set up private banks Expand Science Park	$10 778–$14 941 (6 998%–9 701%)
2000s	Global deployment	Knowledge Economy Development Plan Admitted to World Trade Organization Devalue New Taiwan dollar Service industry promotion	$13 448–$19 278 (8 732%–12 518%)
2010s	Diversify investment	5+2 Industrial Innovation Plan Southbound (ASEAN) investment drive	$20 939–$25 026 (2018) (13 596%–16 250%)

Table 2.1: Phases of Taiwan's growth

Similarly, close ties with the Japanese economy (despite their tumultuous colonial past) acted both as an example of reform and conduit for technology and policy. But while establishing extensive trading links, Taiwan was able to build its own internal industrial production system. There is no doubt, too, that its relationship with the mainland PRC also helped to concentrate efforts aimed at survival. Increasingly diplomatically isolated, Taipei knew (and still knows) that if it got into trouble it could not hope for an international bailout, especially after Taiwan's loss of its seat at the United Nations in 1971 and the subsequent recognition of the mainland by Washington in 1979. Ironically, this fear also keeps Taiwan engaged with the rest of the region – especially the PRC.

During the 1950s, economic growth averaged 8.4% per annum.

Plastics best describes the second chapter, during which export development followed a path, in turn, from agricultural goods, processed food, light machinery and textiles, and heavy industry (steel, ships) to, finally, the shift away from labour-intensive industry towards hi-tech goods.[9] Centrally designed and implemented development plans also included the establishment of the first export processing zone in 1966; by 2019 these zones numbered no less than 62.[10]

During the 1960s, the average annual economic growth rate reached 9%.

A third phase, during the 1970s, focused on petrochemicals and infrastructure. The economic dip during the 1970s oil crisis (Taiwan is a net importer of energy) was countered by government investment in infrastructure, such as the construction of harbours, a new international airport and network of freeways, as well as the electrification of the railways. The establishment of the petrochemical industry provided an impetus for the manufacture and export of plastic products.

The economic growth rate averaged 10.1% during this period.

During the 1980s, the focus of growth shifted from plastics to the PC. With the economy apparently reaching something of a manufacturing peak, the government relaxed state controls and protection, liberalising finance and trade and privatising SOEs. There was a deliberate, accelerating trend towards science and technology, as exemplified by the creation of the science park at Hsinchu.

During this period, Taiwan's economy grew 7.7% annually.[11]

Since that time, as labour costs have risen and competition increased, particularly from elsewhere in the region, and coupled with the floating (and appreciation in relative US$ value) of the New Taiwan dollar, the focus has continued to shift to higher-tech, higher-value products in the IT sector. This growth took advantage of and underpinned the emergence of hi-tech globalisation in the 1990s. During this decade, per capita income went through the US$10 000 level (in 1992), while there was considerably greater investment by the state in infrastructure, including mass transport, roads and environmental protection.

Despite the impact of the Asian financial storm, Taiwan's economy still grew 6.3% annually during the 1990s.

The opening up to mainland China represented a big shift, too, in the 1990s. In spite of the absence of political ties, and despite a ban on direct contacts, Taiwan is now the fourth-largest investor in the mainland, with an official stake of an estimated US$60 billion (some put it as high as US$100 billion) – more than Taiwan has sunk into all of Southeast Asia combined. Mainland China is also Taiwan's single-largest export and import market, constituting around one-third of the island's trade. Opening up to the mainland – paradoxically its greatest source of insecurity – has latterly been a crucial component of Taiwan's enduring success.

At the same time, Taiwan democratised in the 1990s. The island was ruled for many years by the KMT after they lost the mainland to the Chinese communists, even though the mainlander migrants were outnumbered nearly three to one by the indigenous Taiwanese population in their new home. Chiang Ching-kuo succeeded his father Generalissimo Chiang Kai-shek as leader on his death in 1975. A decade later, Chiang pledged political reform, including a free press and lifting bans on new political parties and street protests. Emboldened, dissidents formed Taiwan's first opposition party, the Democratic Progressive Party (DPP). Martial law was lifted, having been in place for 38 years. When Chiang died in 1988 and Taiwan-born Lee Teng-hui took power, he lifted restrictions on the press, eliminated parliamentary positions that had been frozen since the 1940s and prompted constitutional changes that eventually led him to become Taiwan's first directly elected leader in 1996. In 2000, the DPP candidate, Chen Shui-bian, won the leadership race, ending the KMT's monopoly on political power.

Democracy has gone hand in hand with better governance and accountability. Chen Shui-bian and his wife Wu Shu-chen were convicted in 2009 on two bribery charges; Chen being sentenced to 19 years, reduced from a life sentence on appeal. This is a punishment of a former leader that few countries could imagine. In 2013, a trial cleared Lee Teng-hui of involvement in a corruption scandal. Chen's successor, Ma Ying-jeou, has faced his own charges of embezzlement while he was mayor of Taipei, being cleared just before his inauguration in May 2008.

Taiwan ranks high on various international governance indicators. The World Economic Forum, for example, places it 13th of 140 on its Global Competitiveness rankings in 2018, and first for macro-economic stability.[12] Meanwhile, the World Bank has it at 13/190 on its Ease of Doing Business indicators in 2019.[13] As another measure, by 2019, Taiwan had instituted visa-free access (including visa waivers for 111 countries) for 171 countries for up to 90 days.

For Taiwan, the 2000s was the era of integration of global markets and suppliers, as well as technology. Some things, however, remained similar. Agriculture is still a significant sector, employing 560 000 people and contributing 11% of GDP if agro-tourism and processing are added. And Taiwan is still a manufacturing-based economy, even though the character of industry has changed markedly to offshoring and higher-tech. Today, manufacturing accounts for 36% of GDP.

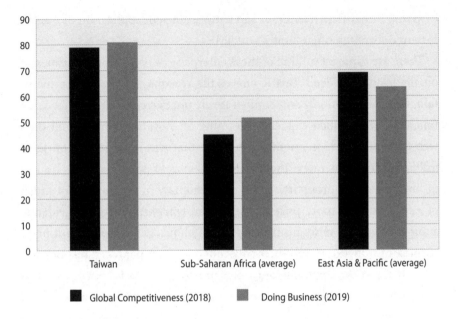

Figure 2.3: Measures of competitiveness

Source: World Bank Doing Business Index 2019; WEF Global Competitiveness Index, 2018.

Since then, Taiwan's economy has continued its reorientation towards a knowledge-based system, with per capita incomes (in 2019 at US$25 000) ranking in the top 35 worldwide, in the league of Slovenia, Bahrain, Portugal and Saudi Arabia.

Small and anonymous is beautiful – or is it?

Taiwan, a small island of just 23 million people – about the same size as Côte d'Ivoire, Cameroon or Niger – has enjoyed a large global impact. Its global profile is down to its economic and development success. This success is largely a story of people realising their talent.

Taiwanese prefer not to talk of their economic transition in terms of a 'miracle'. Many put their economic success down to a combination of simple factors: hard work, investing in education, improving skills, a trait of saving rather than spending, and a more efficient application of limited resources through often family-run SMEs.

There are some 1.4 million of these enterprises – or 98% of all businesses on the island.[14] Indeed, this is one of the reasons, the Taiwanese maintain, that their economy was comparatively unaffected by the 1997/8 Asian financial crisis, which exposed the frailty of those economies built on a web of political and economic patronage that was often reliant on large industrial conglomerates. Then, as now, its vibrant democracy was backed up by Taiwan's rigorous free press – an anomaly in the context of much of Asia, and even more puzzling in Taiwan where the media is evidently a target of China's news insurgency[15] – which has helped to prevent nasty surprises for investors and their consequently often-panicked responses.

Such rapid development did not happen by osmosis, but rather was the result of a deliberate series of premeditated government actions and institutions.

An example is the establishment of the Industrial Technology Research Institute (ITRI) in 1973 by the Ministry of Economic Affairs. ITRI is Taiwan's largest R&D organisation, part think tank and part incubator, which had by July 2019 developed nearly 26 000 patents and continues to do so at the staggering pace of about five patents per day (of which three are approved).[16] This ensures a regular income outside of government grants, ITRI turning over nearly US$700 million in 2018.

Among ITRI's major successes was the design and subsequent licensing to Giant of carbon fibre bicycle frames in 1985, which was a major part of the company's success. Today, Giant is the leading global bicycle manufacturer, Taiwanese brands being responsible for no less than 33% of all bicycles produced worldwide. Meanwhile, ITRI operates as a non-profit, managing to cover its expenses only by commercialising its designs as fast as possible.

This has included designs for sophisticated carbon capture and storage for cement factories, now used by most Taiwanese concerns, and a formaldehyde-free adhesive for the building industry. They have also developed patents for novel cancer medication, brain surgery aids, utility drones and waterless clothing dye. ITRI's success, it admits, is down to having (and finding) the right people.

They do this through extensive international relations (with liaison offices in Silicon Valley, Moscow, Tokyo and Berlin), and by hiring the smartest engineers and problem-solvers. ITRI has 6 150 permanent employees, with over 1 200 PhDs among them. This approach is reiterated by the management of the nearby Hsinchu Science Park, which counts as its single most attractive feature its pool of talented people, both locals and expats, who do the work.

Hsinchu Science Park was established in 1980. In 1986 just 59 companies were located in the park, employing 8 275 workers, turning over US$151 million. Twenty-five years and various expansion plans later, it has grown to house over 500 companies and 153 000 employees, turning over US$35 billion in 2018, and contributing around 6% of Taiwan's GDP. It is called a 'science park', says May Hsiu, a research associate at the park, because it links academia and industry, taking companies 'from IP to IPO'.[17]

Taipei encouraged hi-tech through supply-side measures, 'showering' the sector with tax concessions, including holidays and rebates.[18] Yet, even a combination of technology, access to foreign markets, a critical mass of expertise through clustering, low manufacturing costs and margins, and government support is not, if the Taiwan example is anything to go by, enough. A further key component of the Taiwan tech transition is the establishment of a venture capital market, which both spawned and fuelled local firms. One key tax incentive was to allow venture capital funds to offset 20% of their investment against income tax.

The creation of the park followed extensive studies of the US experience, including Silicon Valley, Research Triangle in North Carolina and Massachusetts' Route 128, which were led by K.T. Li, a senior adviser to Lee Teng-hui. Hsinchu has been able to leverage a global reputation to attract talent and industries, but at the beginning it had to create a positive one. It did so, in part, by recognising that it could attract Taiwanese talents home, who realised that they were unlikely to rise to the very top in their adopted homes. In 1998, Forbes praised Hsinchu for 'helping to reverse the brain drain' from Taiwan, attracting scores of talented expats back to Taiwan.[19]

Morris Chang is perhaps the best-known illustration of this 'brain regain'. Born into the family of an official in the Yin county government on mainland China, Chang graduated from the Massachusetts Institute of Technology in 1955, moving immediately into the semi-conductor field. He joined Texas Instruments three years later where he spent the next quarter-century. In 1985 he was recruited by Sun Yun-suan, a former Taiwanese minister of economic affairs and prime minister, who was also behind the land-to-the-tiller programme and who is viewed as the architect of Taiwan's economic transformation, to head up ITRI. Once there, Chang launched a semi-conductor fabrication plant, having sent 50 specialists to RCA in the US to study semi-conducting. In 1987 he founded Taiwan Semi-Conductor Manufacturing Corporation (TSMC) as a joint venture between the local government (21%), Dutch electronics giant Philips (28%) and other private investors. Chang pioneered the idea of attracting new customers through aggressive pricing to gain market share, which would turn TSMC into one of the world's largest producers, responsible for nearly a 50% slice of the global US$30-billion semi-conductor industry. The story goes that Chang made the first TSMC sales calls in 1987 with a single brochure.

Chang and TSMC are not the only example of starting small. Having made a name for himself in developing Taiwan's first electronic calculator at Unitron, Stan Shih, along with his wife Carolyn Yeh and a group of five others, in 1976 founded Acer, formerly known as Multitech and head-quartered also in Hsinchu City with just US$25 000 in capital. As will be seen in more detail in Chapter 15, after the bubble burst in its PC market in the mid-2000s when it was the world's second-largest producer, it has reinvented itself as a gaming and slim notebook market leader, turning over US$8 billion in 2018 and employing more than 7 000 people with

95 000 retail stores in 160 countries. Figures such as Morris Chan and Stan Shih have become role models for a generation of Taiwanese techies – local versions of Steve Jobs and Bill Gates.

Agribusiness has successful examples, too, of global brand-building.

Located on the borders of the Yilan Mountain and the Pacific Ocean, a 45-minute drive from Taipei through the 13-kilometre Hsuehshan tunnel, Kavalan distillery first produced whisky in 2008. Within ten years it was an established international brand, exporting 80% of its 10-million-litre annual production. The owner, the Lee family, started with a pesticide business in the southern Taiwanese city of Kaohsiung before branching out into household cleaning products, coffee with the Mr Brown brand, and soft drinks. By 2019 they had factories in Vietnam, Guangzhou in China, and Taiwan.

Though the Lees initially favoured brewing beer, the barriers to entry were difficult, not least the state monopoly held by Taiwan Beer, causing an initial application to be rebuffed in 1995. But they persevered and with increased liberalisation were granted a licence to produce whisky in 2005. The whisky is produced in a state-of-the-art facility in the springwater-rich area of Taiwan, using Scottish and German stills and employing a Scottish distiller.[20] The Kavalan holding company, King Car, turns over at least US$500 million in annual revenue.

Hub and spoke of the bicycle world

Another little-known fact is that Taiwan, and specifically the city of Taichung, just one hour south of Taipei on the Taiwan High Speed Rail, is the global leader in bicycle manufacturing. This is thanks to two companies, Giant and Merida, who have proved that it does not always pay, in the words of Merida's head of marketing William Jeng, 'to be an instant noodle' – referring to the mass-volume, small-margin but quick-return original manufacturing model of most Taiwanese firms.

Both Merida and Giant were started as family-run SMEs in 1972, just as Japan shifted bicycle production to a cheaper labour market in Taiwan. This was possible since bicycles were not a government-protected sector, another key lesson in those seeking to create commercial opportunities.

Early on, both companies were principally suppliers to overseas-based brands: Merida to GT and Raleigh, and Giant to Schwinn. After Schwinn decided to set up its own factory in China, faced with the disappearance of 80% of its market Giant was forced to establish its own brand of mid-sector bikes in 1987. The same happened to Merida with GT in the UK, 'teaching us a key lesson', says Jeng, who has been with Merida since 1988, 'that we were taking all the risk but not getting all the profits'.

Merida took two strategic decisions: to build its own brand, and to diversify by entering a partnership with Specialized in the US – a relationship that is still going strong. Along the way, it maintained its family values. Its CEO, Michael Tseng, son of the founder Ike Tseng, is still in the office each day from his home just ten minutes away, while his son Vansen (an MBA graduate) is learning the business from the bottom up. The family and employees are bike fans, as happy to gossip about their team's performance in the Tour de France as they are about the latest and lightest carbon technology and production techniques, and the routes they plan to cycle on the weekend.

The volume of bicycles produced in Taiwan was 2.5 million in 2018, less than one-quarter of its 1986 peak. China is now the largest producer in the world, with somewhere 'between 20 to 30 million bikes annually', says Jeng, with India adding a further ten million. Merida has three factories in China, and one in Germany. It produced nearly 945 000 bikes at the Taichung factory in 2018, or 38% of the overall Taiwanese total, earning US$750 million in exports. The big change for Merida is thus less in volume than price. Whereas its average bike price (free on board) was US$200 some 20 years ago, today it is over US$1 000.

Presently, 1 300 workers at the Yuan Lin factory south of Taichung, most bedecked in the company colours of green and white, produce all the company's e-bikes, which hit the stores for US$5 000 compared to half this amount for their average mountain bike. Thirty per cent of Merida's turnover is e-bikes, and one-third of its production is made from carbon, fed by a global supply chain, with many of the major factories (including Rock Shox and Fox) clustered around Taichung.

Many of the manufacturing techniques – from cutting, milling and welding tubes to assembly – are labour-intensive. Yet, contrary to the assertion that labour-intensive industries are always a race to the bottom, the company has continued to move up the price ladder, finding a more profitable niche in high-quality bikes. Around 5% of its US$900-million annual turnover is spent on R&D.

Acer, Giant and Merida are unusual as Taiwanese companies in that they rely on their own global name. If one great Taiwanese development strength has been the flexibility of Taiwanese entrepreneurs in finding a way around the political challenges with China and subcontracting to multiple manufacturers, this has been at the expense largely of creating household brands such as Samsung and Hyundai in South Korea, or Sony and Sanyo in Japan. This makes the Taiwan story more difficult to sell and to emulate, and threatens to undermine its economy in the long term in a brand-conscious world.

Yet, Giant and Merida, like Kavalan and Acer, show that building brands is possible for Taiwan. It does not always pay more to be a subcontractor.

Conclusion: Treating business like a friend

Irrespective of whether Taiwan's success has been deliberate or accidental, the lessons are clear.

Jiann-Chyuan Wang of the Chung-Hua Institute for Economic Research (CIER)[21] highlights four key Taiwanese takeaways: raise the productivity of the agricultural sector, extend obligatory schooling years, diversify into light industry through export incentivisation, and welcome foreign investment as it brings people, technology and money. In all of this, notes

Chen Chung-Chiang of the Industrial Development Board within the Ministry of Economic Affairs, 'We treat business like a friend.'

It is not as if this central lesson is not widely shared. This century, no fewer than 72 African delegations, comprising more than 3 500 African officials, have undertaken official study tours of Taiwan. But evidently little has been learnt or implemented. Why?

Perhaps one reason is the lack of capacity to do so elsewhere. It is not only the private sector that relies on the quality of its workers in Taiwan. In a system that traces its roots back 1 300 years and specifically, in a modern age, to 1931, the Ministry of Examination, or Examination Yuan (one of five arms of the Taiwanese government), tests more than 250 000 candidates per year. Just 10% pass these rigorous exams, ensuring those civil servants who join the 350 000 already in the service are of the highest quality. It turns out that to have a government, you need to staff one with people, systems, structure and a plan, and have goals and a strategy to achieve them.

The quality of personnel and systems is illustrated by the establishment of the Taiwan External Trade Development Council in 1970, Taiwan's version of Singapore's Economic Development Board or Japan's External Trade Organisation. Through its 63 international offices, it hosts regular trade shows and helps local businesses to improve their international competitiveness. Under their watch, exports grew from US$6 billion in 1971, when it recorded its first trade surplus, to US$317 billion in 2017.[22]

Perhaps the failure to learn these lessons is also down to Taiwan's economic slowdown this century. Growth has fallen off since the heady days of the 1970s and 1980s, averaging 3.3% since 2000.

Or perhaps it is because of the fraught relationship with mainland China. This does not, however, necessarily mean that democracy has caused growth to slow down, or that China has been bad for business. Taiwan's entrepreneurs ironically led the charge to move factories and jobs to the mainland in search of lower costs and better export terms, to the detriment of the Taiwanese worker, leading to a 20-year stagnation in wages. Average real wages declined in real terms from 2000 to 2016.[23] An estimated two million Taiwanese are working in mainland China, and more are expected to jump ship after Beijing announced measures in 2018 to make it more attractive for Taiwanese to work and live on the mainland.[24] 'It's a war of talent with China,' says Hsinchu's May Hsiu. 'We fear a loss of talent, not rising costs.'

Or perhaps the failure of the transmission of lessons from Taiwan relates to the increasingly difficult domestic decision-making process, where Taiwanese policy-makers are reportedly less receptive to advisers outside of government. Dr Wang of the CIER observes that the influence of outside actors, including his own institute, has diminished since 2000 as political parties have retreated into their own advisory inner circles. Hence, the renewed imperative for policy evolution and flexibility.

In a world where power is economic rather than political, and where people are worried more about money and consumer brands than values, Taiwan is increasingly a forgotten international actor. The impact of this trend has seemingly been compounded by the realisation of middle-class status by many Taiwanese, and with it a changing set of concerns about their quality of life, less the quantity of income. These include democratic freedoms and growing fears about environmental sustainability. Then again, Taiwanese firms are already positioning themselves to do business in the latter area. Taiwan has seldom, if ever, squandered even the tiniest scrap of an opportunity.

Taiwan remains a model for both Asia and Africa of how to modernise your economy through macro-economic stability, careful planning and institutionalisation, and the right people.

Chapter 3

Singapore
Have a Good Crisis

> A nation is great not by its size alone. It is the will, the cohesion, the stamina, the discipline of its people and the quality of their leaders which ensure it an honourable place in history.
>
> — Lee Kuan Yew, *The Wit and Wisdom of Lee Kuan Yew*

It is difficult to think of Singapore as a fragile, poor backwater. Yet, it was born in crisis out of the separation of the Malaysian Federation, amid Konfrontasi with Indonesia, and riven by multiracial, ethnic and religious sensitivities and differences. Thus, economic and social delivery – from jobs to housing – was politics by other means. While the state under Lee Kuan Yew was at the helm of this transformation, its actions were guided by commercial principles.

The pace and scale of Singapore's transition from urban slum to global city are unparalleled. Despite the common narrative of critics and wannabe despots that this action was down to authoritarianism, the ability to get things done has relied principally on the government's performance record and commitment to popular welfare. Success has depended, too, not on a few big or iconic infrastructure projects or even the provision of necessary funding, housing and land, even though all these were necessary aspects, but fundamentally on ensuring a complete cycle of economic growth, governance and job creation within an overarching 'can do' political framework.

Singapore's infrastructure and housing development is a symbol of much that has been achieved since its unwilling divorce in 1965. It is testimony to the importance of having a good crisis in creating a laser-like focus on development needs, from housing to jobs, and of a willingness to take tough decisions to ensure progress and public support – what has been termed 'performance legitimacy'.

The immutable value of location

Contemporary Singapore is a metaphor for world class.

The city-state's skyline reflects a continuous, driving reinvention and fast-paced expansion; one year an idea, the next a Singapore Flyer, Marina Bay Sands, ArtScience Museum, 42 million tonnes of underground oil bunkering, a US$1-billion Gardens by the Bay, and so on. 'It is because we don't want to fail,' one official has reflected. 'We also have no natural resources to fall back on,' she added. The city is the epitome of globalisation, possessing the world's second-busiest container port, handling more than 34 million containers annually, a ship arriving or leaving every two to three minutes, while Changi Airport is consistently ranked as the world's best airport,[1] handling 150 000 passengers daily and 6 700 flights weekly. This is more than logistics. Singapore is now home to 121 foreign banks and 7 000 multinational companies, two-thirds of which have their Asian headquarters on the island.

Fifty years after separation from Malaysia, in 2015 Singapore's GDP per capita was, at US$54 000, nearly five times greater than Malaysia's.[2]

Employing the benefits of its geography has always been at the heart of modern Singapore, and so has its people's industriousness. The founder of modern Singapore, Sir Stamford Raffles, commented that 'it is impossible to conceive of a place combining more advantages', referring to its proximity to China and its positioning in the Malay Archipelago. Or, as Lee Kuan Yew noted in 2012, 'We became a hub because of the convenience.

For shipping, you have to pass Singapore, it's the southernmost point [of continental Asia] ... we were poor and we were underdeveloped, so we had to work hard.'[3]

Following its birthing in 1819 by Raffles and Major William Farquhar as a free port, which Raffles declared would be 'open to ships and vessels of every nation free of duty', the *towkays* (Chinese merchants) quickly came to dominate regional commerce.

As the British Empire flourished, so did Singapore; its growth powered by trade and its role, not unlike today, as an international financial centre. The front page of the first issue of *The Straits Times* on 15 July 1845, for example, is filled with notices on shipping activity, lists of foreign goods for sale, market reports from around the world and warehouses to let.[4]

Declared a crown colony in 1867 along with Malacca and Penang, by the time of its centenary in 1919, Singapore boasted modern conveniences, including telegraph and telephone connections, electricity and cars, along with the world's second-largest dry dock. Jules Verne described Singapore in *Celebrated Travels and Travellers* in 1881 as 'simply one large warehouse, to which Madras sent cotton cloth; Calcutta, opium; Sumatra, pepper; Java, arrack and spices; Manila, sugar and arrack; all forthwith dispatched to Europe, China, Siam, etc.'[5]

With the opening of the Suez Canal in 1869, more vessels called at Singapore's deep-water harbour at Telok Blangah, the site of the contemporary container operations known as Keppel Harbour. The completion of the causeway in 1923 connecting the Malay Peninsula enabled Singapore to profit from the booming Malaysian mining and rubber industries, the latter driven by the advent of the motor car.

With prosperity, Singapore's population grew quickly. From just 5 000 inhabitants in 1819, it had doubled in size by 1825, by which time trade had reached US$22 million, more than the established port of Penang. By the turn of the nineteenth century, Singapore housed an estimated 225 000, more than 550 000 by 1930, and touching a million by 1950. This reflected the growth in commerce. The US Treasury estimated the trade of Singapore at US$210 million in 1898, more than that of Japan and the Dutch East Indies. Between 1873 and 1913, Singapore's volume of trade increased eight-fold, making it the second-busiest port in the world after Liverpool.[6]

Jewel of the British Empire it may have been, it was a site of great hardship, of callous division, a world of European *tuans* and coolies, bumboats and *memsahibs*, two cities and societies: one driven by international finance, steam and the telegraph, whose members enjoyed lifestyles of leisure; the other a rickshaw society, marginalised, violent, poor, disease- and drug-ridden, for whom laws and justice did not equally apply.

Those rickshaw pullers, often Chinese migrants, would work up to 12-hour shifts for as little as 60 cents a day, much of which would be invariably consumed on *chandu* (opium), given the levels of addiction among pullers. As the National Museum of Singapore notes, 'Because of the physical toll on their bodies, coolies usually worked for five to seven years before returning to China.' This occasionally flared into violence, such as the Post Office Riots of 1876 or the so-called Verandah Riots of 1888. In 1896 Dr Lim Boon Keng led an enquiry into the 'four social evils': gambling, alcoholism, prostitution and 'chasing the dragon' (opium smoking). After the Second World War, these frustrations found voice in the expressions of *merdeka* ('freedom' in Malay) and the pan-Malayan independence movement.

Still, after its departure from the short-lived Malaysian Federation in August 1965, independent Singapore was faced with fewer resources in meeting the aspirations of its people. Lee's team of 'founding fathers'[7] and subsequent governments relied on gathering and deploying efficiently scarce resources. Their success exactly illustrates the value of decisive domestic leadership concerned less with grand visions, governance frameworks and mobilising aid, than with the things they were themselves in control of – policy tools, tax revenue and execution.

To reiterate, the challenges at independence seemed formidable: high levels of poverty and inequality, limited infrastructure geared for the

British naval presence, limited literacy (just 60%), widespread squalor with half a million in slums and high unemployment. Goh Keng Swee, deputy prime minister under Lee Kuan Yew, who is regarded as the father of Singapore's modern economy, learnt from the 1952 Social Survey that of the 1 814 people who lived in Upper Nanking Street close to his own home just three households had their own toilet, bath and kitchen. The others shared open-bucket toilets and open coal fires to cook. As a result, 'he decided that his priority should be to provide jobs. And the best way to do this was to encourage capitalism and private enterprise.'[8]

The government's response was to align the economic, social, international and legal context to the nation's needs: land, housing, jobs and investment were the priorities.

Land, housing, jobs and investment

Liu Thai Ker returned from his studies in Sydney and at Yale and a stint working under the renowned architect I.M. Pei[9] to serve, first, as the deputy CEO, then CEO, of Singapore's Housing Development Board (HDB) for 20 years from 1969 and, then, the chief planner and CEO of the Urban Redevelopment Authority (URA). In 2008 he was appointed as the chairperson of the Centre for Liveable Cities within the Ministry of National Development.

His career provides a unique window on Singapore's transformation-from a city where, at independence in 1965, two-thirds of its 1.6 million people lived in overcrowded slums, most without waterborne sewerage, and many without employment, on a tiny island-state of just 580 square kilometres. Fast forward 50 years, 83% of the 5.5-million population lived in publicly supplied HDB apartments, 90% owned their own homes, the rivers were clean, the island was 15% larger as a result of land reclamation and, despite the population increase, green cover had increased to nearly half of the territory.

Thai Ker observes that this extraordinary transition has hinged on the government's credibility among its population. And that, in turn, has depended on delivery and, 'behind that', he says, 'is its record of transparency, frugality and the absence of corruption'.

To support the priority of urban renewal, Lee's government enacted the Land Acquisition Act in 1966, which granted the power to acquire land quickly and at reasonable rates of compensation. This was followed, later, by an amendment of the Foreshores Act of 1964, which enabled the government to embark both on reclamation and to build the East Coast Parkway linking Changi Airport with the city centre. By 1979, 80% of land belonged to the government to be sold on long-term (usually 99-year) leases to developers. 'Without land', says Cheng Tong Fatt, permanent secretary in the Ministry of National Development in the 1970s, and later ambassador to China, 'you can't talk about planning'.

Today 12% of Singapore's land is allocated to roads, and just 17% to residential areas.

Land acquisition was sometimes only grudgingly accepted. 'Government had a vision', reminds the URA's Peter Ho, 'and knew what had to be done, even if unpopular, for the greater good of the people.' But it was more palatable with the payment of compensation and promise of resettlement.

The resulting resettlement of those living in the CBD required alternative housing through the HDB. At the end of the HDB's first decade in 1970, one-third of the population lived in public housing, and it had built 120 669 units, compared to the 23 019 constructed by its predecessor, the Singapore Improvement Trust, in 32 years. Now apartments are funded through a combination of homeowner grants and loans, the latter both commercial and from the Central Provident Fund, a mandatory savings scheme in which employers and employees contribute (a maximum of) 16% and 20% of salary respectively. Central Provident Fund loans, in 2016, were at 2.6%, repayable over 30 years; the aim, says the HDB's chairperson, remaining now, as in the 1960s, 'to provide affordable housing'.

63

Home ownership, emphasises the HDB's Sng Cheng Keh, gave the population a 'stake in their society, building a strong work ethic, a store of value to be monetised, and a sense of belonging.'[10] Effectively, it turned a radical discontented society into one with conservative values and suspicious of populist solutions as they saw themselves as owners.

The son of a 'mother who survived as a hawker and taught me the value of multi-tasking and hard work', Alan Choe was the first architect-planner of the HDB and the founder of the URA. Having returned with a town planning degree from Melbourne University in 1959, he was quickly recruited into the nascent HDB. After the failure of the Singapore Improvement Trust to deliver more than 1 000 units a year, due to, he says, a lack of empathy with local culture and needs, the HDB was tasked with delivering 50 000 units in five years.

One of his early projects was at Toa Payoh, situated on 600 hectares in the central part of the island. 'The land was full of squatters with their thatch and tin-roofed shacks, and infested with gangsters, who unofficially provided different services to the community. It was dangerous to go in and try to remove them, and there was a lot of resistance. To achieve this,' Choe recalls, 'we needed to resettle the residents to other, nearby flats. Changing the culture, too, of the people used to living in such *kampongs*, with animals out the back and fruit trees, into a high-rise was also challenging.' Aside from the compensation paid under the Land Acquisition Act, 'our most formidable weapon was that this was for the good of the nation, and that no one could challenge the order'.

By 1963, having completed 'around 20 000 units, Lee Kuan Yew realised that just rehousing squatters was not enough, and shifted focus to the city centre. I was asked to shadow a UNDP [United Nations Development Programme] expert to learn about how we should go about this. Additionally, I took study tours organised by the Ford Foundation to the US, the British Council to the UK, and to Germany and to Japan to understand urban renewal. In all cases, with the exception of only the US, it was urban reconstruction that they were involved with. And in the US, urban renewal was a dirty word, seen as corrupt.'

A report to Choe's minister, Eddie Barker, followed, and the UNDP sent a further three experts – legal authority Charles Abrams, traffic engineer Susumu Kobe and urban planner Otto Koenigsberger – to Singapore for three months, again shadowed by Choe and his team of two. Their job was to demarcate an area for central development. The resulting four-year Urban Development and Renewal Project, started in 1967, cost around US$15 million, of which a third was contributed by the UN. The concept envisioned a circle of high-density development around three sides of the central water catchment area, as well as a southern development belt that spanned from the industrial area of Jurong to the airport at Changi.

Redevelopment of the city centre required amalgamation of the 18- to 22-foot riverfront properties. Again, the Land Acquisition Act served this purpose, though 'tension between the URA and the HDB over whether this land should be used for housing (the HDB's preference) or commercial property (the URA's) led to the latter's establishment as an autonomous body in October 1974'.

Cheng Tong Fatt joined government in 1957 fresh from his veterinarian studies at Glasgow University. 'Then the city was just 15 square kilometres under the City Council, the rest of the territory being under the control of the Rural Board. Nothing much', he recalled of nearly 60 years ago, 'was going on. There were no big buildings and very limited authority. Things changed when the PAP [People's Action Party] came in', he says, 'in 1959, merging the two boards into a single administration.' In the run-up to the Federation in 1963, he spent a lot of time in the company of Lee Kuan Yew, canvassing support in the rural areas. 'I bought a new car with a government loan on my return', he smiles. 'Within three years it was gone already, destroyed by the poor rural roads and the demands of getting things done.'

After the merger with Malaysia, 'things were still very poor, very haphazard, with very few resources, with most development still within a

30-square-kilometre area around the city centre'. His record in turn-ing Singapore into a self-sufficient food producer, however, saw Cheng appointed in 1971 as the permanent secretary in the Ministry of National Development. 'There were eight new permanent secretaries appointed at the same time. I inherited a more or less complete five-year master plan, which the UNDP had assisted in drafting, and which provided for differ-ent types of land usage – residential, defence, commercial, recreational, industrial, transport – across the island. With continuous reviews and adjustments, this remains the basis of development in Singapore today', he notes.

The plan was intended to ensure the optimal use of limited land resources to meet the residential, economic and recreational needs of a population projected to reach four million by 1992. It provided for the location of the airport at Changi, the construction of the Mass Rapid Transit (MRT) system and the network of expressways.[11]

In all of this, Cheng recalls, Lee Kuan Yew was 'in absolute control. He was always sending me notes. Although he learnt from other cities, he formed in his own mind a vision of what Singapore should be, and he implemented this step by step, throughout his life, learning all the time as he went along.'

This was not without its tense moments. 'In the mid-1970s we were work-ing on what has become the Marina Sands area. Lee Kuan Yew wanted to know why we had narrowed the entrance to the river with the reclama-tion, when he believed that a wider mouth was necessary to remove the pollution. When I explained to him why, he went very quiet for a while. He was thinking. He then came up with a solution, which was to clean the river up at the source of the problem, rather than try to deal with the consequences of pollution. That is where his clean-up programme for the rivers came from.' As Lee put it publicly at the time, 'It should be a way of life to keep the water clean, to keep every stream, every culvert, every rivu-let, free from unnecessary pollution. In ten years let us have fishing in the

Singapore River and in the Kallang River. It can be done.'

Frugality required taking a long view. Although Marina Sands reclamation was completed by 1980, the building development only took off 20 years later.

Under Lim Kim San, known as 'Mr HDB', a Public Utilities Board was set up in 1965 to oversee the provision of water, electricity and gas, ensuring better sanitation and amenities. This included the 'Clean and Green' Singapore programme, and the clean-up of the Kallang River Basin and Singapore River, which took ten years from Lee's statement in 1977 that he wanted fishing on both waterways.[12] It was a signal, also, of Singapore's economic transition, from the lightermen who plied their trade on the creek to a new stage of development, from a heavily polluted port to a fashionable commercial and residential neighbourhood.

This was not the only action on water. In addition to securing its potable water provision from Malaysia through a treaty, Singapore focused on developing its own resources, including converting more than one-third of the island into a water catchment area, desalination and reclamation.

Outsiders and politics

As the UN's role in planning suggests, Singapore has been open to external advice and ideas, not just on urban development, but also on wider issues of growth and development, notably with the involvement of the (unpaid) Dutch consultant Dr Albert Winsemius, who advised the government for nearly 25 years until the mid-1980s.

Winsemius was central in the early plans to expand the embryonic country's economic base.[13] The strategy to do so focused, first, on heavy industry and electronics, which would provide, Goh Keng Swee envisaged, 50 000 jobs in the first five years. Land was set aside for export industries, notably the Jurong Town Corporation complex created in 1968. Manufacturing's share of GDP increased from 20.5% in 1967 to 29.5% by 1980, driving the country's annual economic growth at over 12% from 1966 to 1973.

While it built on Singapore's trading legacy, the openness underpinning the socio-economic transition was not preordained. Indeed, the opposition Barisan Sosialis (Socialist Front), formed in 1961 by left-wingers expelled from the ruling People's Action Party, offered a more state-directed and state-centred alternative, 'more akin to the Communist Chinese model at the time'.[14] Despite initial suspicions of Lee's leftist political leanings, which led to some industrialists relocating to Kuala Lumpur, his administration soon gained a name as honest and pragmatic administrators. As *Time* noted in its report of 7 November 1960, 'Lee … soon grasped that Singapore by itself is an island emporium ill-suited to revolutionary socialism since, among other things, it lacks any major industries to nationalise. His revised economic policy: "Teaching the capitalists how to run their system."'[15] Lee could move to the centre once the left had hived off into the Barisan.

With full employment in 1972 came a shift from labour-intensive manufacturing to skill- and capital-intensive operations. 'We needed labour-intensive industry to suit our needs in the 1960s,' remembers Ngiam Tong Dow, who served as Goh's permanent secretary, 'but you cannot compete on low labour costs alone. We asked the employers to provide the training if we provided the facilities, since you cannot train in a vacuum but rather with a job in mind.'

This required ongoing investment in training through technical schools, vocational institutions and joint government-business training centres for workers. Early emphasis was placed on mathematics, technical subjects and science, a bilingual policy insisted on the widespread use of English, and television was used early on (in 1967) as a medium for learning. With few exceptions, all secondary school students had to undergo, from 1968, a two-year course, including technical studies. By 1972 Singapore's nine vocational institutes produced more than 4 000 graduates, compared to just 324 in 1968.

This was not the only 'soft' aspect. Singaporeans were actively encouraged to reduce family sizes, which put a strain on health care, education and housing. In 1966 the government established the Family Planning and Population Board and launched a national programme to encourage smaller families. The 'Stop at Two' policy was backed up by financial incentives, resulting in a decline in Singapore's fertility rate from 4.7 in 1965 to 2.1 in ten years, and 1.7 in 1980. This has created a different challenge of renewal, however.

Rather than numbers being decisive, the opposite has held true. Singapore's population growth rate is linked to the likely pace of economic expansion. Thought is now given to the viability of further expansion and the future city model required – Vertical City, Sci-Fi Utopia, Compact Nation among others – with the holding capacity potentially as high as 10 million people.

Politics is more than power

While Singapore, like others in the region – including South Korea, China, Indonesia and Taiwan – has developed and modernised under a system of rigid political control, the image of Lee Kuan Yew as the 'big man' lacks sufficient nuance. Singapore's economic development involved much more than one person and fundamentally relied on the establishment of robust institutions with strong and honest leadership and commitment. Although Lee presented the articulate public face and adroitly managed the politics and personalities, his was a formidable team. Lee's memoirs are testimony to how highly he regarded the opinion of his colleagues and how often there were differences of outlook within government on key issues.[16]

Goh Chok Tong, 78 in 2019, became Singapore's second prime minister on 28 November 1990. After stepping down, he served as senior minister until May 2011 and as chairperson of the Monetary Authority of Singapore. He continues to serve as a member of parliament, holding the honorary title of emeritus senior minister. His administration introduced several political reforms, including non-constituency and nominated MPs and group representation constituencies, parliamentary committees, and an elected presidency. He led the ruling People's Action Party to three general election victories, in 1991, 1997 and 2001, in which the party won 61%, 65% and 75% of the votes respectively.

Yet, in his view, 'authoritarianism is not essential for success'. Lee Kuan Yew sometimes said 'that if he did not have to win elections he could have done much more for Singapore. I am not sure,' smiles Goh, 'he might have become arrogant and over-confident. He would not have allowed his successors to do so.'

While democracy was, as mentioned above, 'essential for our success, we had to modify the political system to suit our local situation'. Goh recalls that since Singapore 'inherited the British Westminster system, [democracy] was a given for us. But the framework of democracy alone was insufficient for economic development as a newly independent country, [though] democracy focused the minds of leaders on what it took to win the next election.' As a primary objective, Singapore 'had to reduce unemployment. Then we had to address what would win the hearts of the people. In our case it was housing.

'Rather than a sign of authoritarianism, or a lack of democracy', Goh says, 'having one party in power [since independence] is a consequence of being able to deliver. Singapore avoided [entrenching power] by a team led by Lee Kuan Yew. He taught us always to allow us to be challenged by others. To do this we needed to create an opposition within our own party. [When] we could sense that people wanted to have genuine opposition voices, we experimented by having non-constituency MPs.'

Goh cites a large number of fierce debates within government. Amid the debate around how to improve the system of public transport, 'one clan led by the transport minister and Lee Kuan Yew favoured the subway system', known as the MRT. Another, led by the deputy prime minister, Goh Keng Swee, favoured a bus-based system. A tremendous debate followed. Both sides engaged consultants paid for by the government, with the ministers and the consultants arguing against one another with no resolution. The subway system was going to cost US$5 billion at a time when we could hardly afford it.' In the end, Lee resolved the matter by funding the MRT system through the sale of public land, so 'pulling the carpet from under [Deputy Prime Minister] Goh'.

Goh Chok Tong cites a further example when 'Mr Lee suggested changing the voting rules to ensure that minority candidates would always be represented in parliament through the twinning of candidates. This resulted in another intense debate, especially in the Malay and Indian communities who were against this, and in the parliamentary select committee.' Other controversial matters include government's changing of the rate of contribution to the Central Provident Fund, and that around the controversial Graduate Mothers' Scheme, which 'caused a loss of votes'. The scheme, formulated around Lee's eugenic beliefs, aimed to give children of graduate mothers priority in school admission. It was reversed in 1985.

Once decisions were taken in cabinet, Goh notes, they would then go through parliament where 'in certain issues the whip was lifted'. Performance legitimacy played a part. As the eminent Singaporean academic Barry Desker has noted about the region, 'The reality is that East Asian leaders need to perform, even in an authoritarian setting, as their legitimacy and tenure is due to their successful growth performance, even in the absence of free and fair elections.'[17] While performance was, in Goh's view, 'one factor, the other is the trust that the leaders built up with the people, including the personal character of the leader in government. They had to be seen to be fair.'

This, too, was driven by a fear of failure and loss of control. 'For us, the thing was always how can we win the next election,' Goh reflects, 'and to do that, we needed to work out what would cause people to vote for you.' Or, as the former deputy prime minister, Tharman Shanmugaratnam, notes, this was based on a performance ethos, where 'incumbents are only at an advantage if they deliver to their constituency. The [ruling] People's Action Party is not entitled to rule Singapore; it depends on how we deliver.'[18]

Goh thus refutes the depiction of Singapore as a benevolent dictatorship – 'benevolent, yes, but a dictatorship, no. I would describe our system as strict, disciplined, no-nonsense and paternalistic. Our prime minister [Lee Kuan Yew] took the view that this was a family, and we had to do what was best for Singapore. But he also took the view that he did not have to consult in the process with everyone as he had been elected.

'The key was not authoritarianism, but that we were able to win election after election as we delivered economically. The focus was always on the well-being of people, not the self-interest of the party. I notice', he cautions, 'that in other countries once they win elections, they look after themselves.'

But, for Goh, the ultimate determination of success is Singapore's foundation of 'values of governance. Now', he notes, as a result, 'we have a thriving Singapore without Mr Lee. He planned for his retirement. But when I look at Africa today, most leaders hang onto power.'

Conclusion: Leadership, application and context

In the foyer of the URA is a display outlining 'ten qualities of a good city: Good transport, good amenities, clean and green, good governance, ease of business, liveable, people-centric, 24-hour activity, vibrant and unique'. This display forms part of an attempt to engage the public, reflecting the long road travelled since the more draconian days of the 1960s. Achieving these qualities is more complex. Throughout interviews with the politicians, planners and doers (an unusually inseparable bunch in Singapore's case) of the 1960s, a number of issues came up time and time again. These can be summarised as leadership, execution and compromise.

LEADERSHIP	EXECUTION	COMPROMISE
Political will and integrity of government.	Policy is implementation and implementation is policy.	Establish priorities.
Employ a sense of desperation and crisis in driving Singaporeans to action.	Action-oriented institutions and agencies.	Adopt a whole-government approach where compromise and co-operation are standard.
Establish an overall plan and design.	Not only incremental improvement, but more radical step-change when the situation demands it.	Do not reach for 'first-world' solutions, but pick appropriate solutions for each circumstance.
Aim to be as good as your competitors, or the money will go elsewhere.	Spend frugally.	

Figure 3.1: Leadership, execution and compromise form part of Singapore's success

Overall, Singapore's continuous transformation and development speak of the importance of matching deeds with words and of careful planning. Its success illustrates the necessity of rooting actions in the population's principal needs: jobs and housing were the priorities in the 1960s, and better infrastructure and urban renewal those of the 1970s. It has required security, achieved through local capacity and international diplomacy.

More than anything, Singapore's transformation illustrates the necessity of getting the overall environment right. You can't do big infrastructure without building an economy, and you cannot build an economy without security, savings, both local and foreign, and skills.

This is the bedrock of a functioning democracy: that those in power are motivated to deliver what the people need because they know that they won't otherwise be re-elected. If this is not the case, democratic freedoms are hollow.

The transformation in Singaporean living standards over the last 60 years is what motivated the population to repeatedly support the People's Action Party government in every election. At Lee Kuan Yew's death in

2015, even the government did not expect the spontaneous outpouring of grief by ordinary Singaporeans, according to Desker.[19] This is what legitimacy through performance implies.

Chapter 4

South Korea
Incentivising Competitiveness

> There was a constant pressure on the government to outperform North Korea in terms of economic development. This was all the more reason for Park to vigorously launch the national modernisation campaign in order to consolidate the legitimacy of his rule.
>
> — Jong-dae Park, 2018

In August 2012, a short, plump pop star from Seoul burst onto the global music scene virtually overnight. 'Gangnam Style' became the most-watched video on the internet *ever*, exceeding YouTube's previous limit at more than two billion views. While Park Jae-sang, or PSY, was already well known in Korea, he had suddenly also 'made it big' in the US, becoming the first-ever artist from Korea to do so, and propelling K-pop along with him.

The rise of his sensational hit, which parodies his native 'Gangnam' neighbourhood in Seoul for its opulence and exclusivity, was made possible by social media more than anything else. Shares on the platform Reddit and tweets from high-profile artists led to PSY's unexpected global stardom. To the north of the Korean border, meanwhile, where just 10% of the population had mobile phones at the time of PSY's spectacular rise,[1] the video was barely noticed.

A comparison of North and South Korea is a particular favourite of development economists. Because it so closely resembles a laboratory trial, it is hard to imagine designing a better social experiment. A view of the Korean Peninsula from space at night shows an invisible border between a territory in the South with large concentrations of night lights, and one in the North that is all but shrouded in darkness.

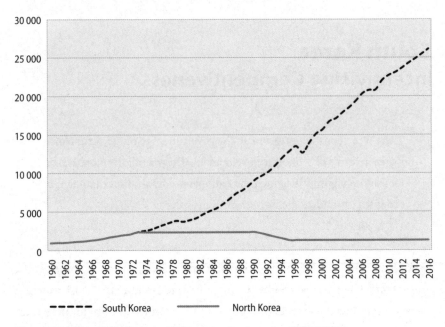

Figure 4.1: Tale of two Koreas: GDP per capita (constant 2010 US$)
Source: World Bank Databank, 2019.

What makes this comparison so enticing is that these countries had been one until 1945. With most productive industries in both countries reduced to rubble after the war of 1950–3, the stage was set for reconstruction and development along two entirely separate paths. The divergence did not happen at once, with the two countries' GDP per capita remaining more or less on par until as late as 1973.

Then, from 1965 to 1990, South Korea achieved an average growth of 9.9%, the highest in the world. As a result, its per capita income is now US$30 000, and a number of its companies are global market leaders. The benefits of growth can be measured in other ways too. Infant mortality declined from 9.6% in 1960 to 0.4% in 2010, life expectancy over the same period from 54 to 80, and teacher to children ratios from 1:47.4 in 1980 to 1:18.7 in 2010. North Koreans, meanwhile, measure on average 8 centimetres shorter than South Koreans, due to the prevalence of growth stunting, and lag 12 years behind in life expectancy.

'Get on with it' best summarises the thinking of President Park Chung-hee, the 'boss' and president of South Korea for 18 years.[2] Or as he put it more politely, 'We need wordless deeds and ambitious construction programmes.'[3] While he was democratically elected five times, Park was no democrat. His instinct and focus were elsewhere. He oversaw a rapid economic take-off, driven by an export-led industrialisation strategy. From 1965 to 1990, the country increased its annual exports more than five thousand times. In the process, along with the other Asian tigers (Hong Kong, Taiwan and Singapore), it altered perceptions and expectations of development worldwide.

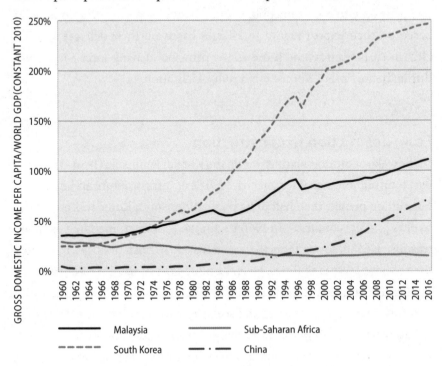

Figure 4.2: GDP per capita as a share of global income

Source: World Bank Databank, 2019; own calculations.

South Korea's economy grew as much in a single generation as America's did over a century.[4] This growth model has been taken over by China, leading to a massive decline in global poverty over the last three decades. Both China and Korea are used to promoting a 'growth through authoritarianism' or 'development through a benevolent dictator' thesis. Yet, the evidence shows that the key components of Korea's path were far more complex than just having a strongman; indeed, Park's style of rule threatened and ultimately undercut his success.

There was much more to it than perspiration and militarism. With a belief in *Shin-Sang-Pil-bul* (Never fail to reward a merit), Park's ideology centred on what Sung-hee Jwa, the head of the Park Chung-hee Foundation, describes as 'economic discrimination', as opposed to 'egalitarianism'.[5] Economic discrimination was the process of inserting the element of competition into economic policy, from favouring performing companies based on their export record to villages based on their delivery to their citizens. It is regarded by some as the principal driving force for growth during the period of Korea's rapid industrialisation.[6]

From destruction to construction

In the wake of the devastating war on the Korean Peninsula (1950–3), which cost four million casualties, destroyed 70% of infrastructure and displaced ten million people, then half of its population, South Korea was one of the world's poorest countries. In 1960 its annual (nominal) income per capita was just US$80, lower than the sub-Saharan African average. It seemed then to have few possibilities, given its poor store of natural resources, low savings and tiny domestic market.

It was poor, broke, insecure and seemingly with few options.

Park had come to power after Syngman Rhee, the country's inaugural president and hero of the war, was forced out by a student-led uprising over his increasingly authoritarian rule and widespread corruption. Already in

1950, the British chargé d'affaires in Korea, Sir Henry Sawbridge, wrote to the Foreign Office from Pusan (Busan): 'It appears from here that this war is being fought *inter alia* to make Korea safe for Syngman Rhee and his entourage. I had hoped that I might find it otherwise. I may be wrong, but I fancy that the experience, incompetence, and possibly corruption of the present regime are in some measure responsible for this crisis.'[7]

Whatever his excesses, Rhee laid a foundation for Korea's subsequent success through a land reform programme, a strong relationship with key ally (and aid provider) in the US, and an education drive. Illiteracy fell from 70% to 15% in a decade. Peasants were encouraged to gain land ownership and increase production through a scheme whereby they paid half the crop over to the government for five years, their improved financial situation creating a positive cycle that enabled them to send their children to school.

South Korea's ambassador to South Africa, Jong-dae Park, argues that this land reform programme is one of four 'cornerstones' of his country's successful development, alongside empowerment of people, a revolution in education and governmental reform.[8]

Although a democratic government initially took over from Rhee, Park (Chung-hee) led a coup in May 1961 upon learning he was to be retired from the military. Park's regime was no less authoritarian, but as an admirer of Napoleon and Bismarck and student of German and Japanese industrialisation, he had a far more ambitious economic plan than the 84-year-old Rhee. At the time, South Korea was three times poorer than its northern neighbour in per capita GDP terms, with Seoul's politicians being wedded to the idea of agrarian-led growth and import substitution.

Park's strategy, by contrast, was dependent on shifting from import substitution to export-led industrial growth, given the tiny domestic market. Labour-intensive manufactured exports offered a competitive advantage, but the challenge was to build businesses of scale.

Government incentives were to play a part, but first he had to get the business people on side. As in most of East Asia at the time, much of business was focused on rent-seeking from American aid, which provided about half of the government budget in the 1950s.

Here authoritarianism might have helped at the outset to speed things along. Park swiftly gained the attention of business by locking up 12 captains of industry, under a 'Special Measure for the Control of Illegal Profiteering', at Seoul's Seodaemun Prison, which had gained notoriety under Japanese colonial rule. This was a blunt signal that the era of crony capitalists, those whom Park termed 'liberation aristocrats', who took a slice while doing little for their country, was over. Those suspected of having made illicit gains were 'invited' to form a Committee for Economic Reconstruction, a forerunner of the Federation of Korean Industries. In addition, the Economic Planning Board was set up to facilitate the development process.

Later, entrepreneurs were regularly called to the presidential palace to report on their progress. Park proved a willing listener in formulating successive five-year national development plans from 1962, early on sending out teams to gather information from Hong Kong and Japan.

Despite some early recalibration of initial targets, which necessitated liberalising the exchange rate, by 1964 Korea reached a benchmark US$100 million in exports. Thereafter, 30 November became National Export Day, on which companies were publicly ranked by the scale of their achievement.

The start was modest in developing textile, footwear, toy, wig and light electronics industries. But the result was the development of large-scale conglomerates, the *chaebols*, modelled on the Japanese *zaibatsu*, of the likes of Samsung and Hyundai. Seoul's National Museum of Korean Contemporary History details the transformation from an agrarian to hi-tech society, displaying the first attempts at a Korean radio in Lucky Goldstar's white plastic A501 of 1959, the agricultural Kia three-wheeler truck and Hyundai's early, clunky 1982 Pony sedan through to the Baekgom missile produced under the Yulgok military modernisation programme. Plastic was, at least then, the future. In 1969, just 6% of South Korean families owned a television. Within ten years, this had increased to 80%.

Lucky Goldstar became LG, and Kia and Hyundai are now global brands. Hyundai's factory in Ulsan is the largest car production facility in the world, where 34 000 workers can produce 5 600 vehicles daily, this from assembling Ford Cortinas under licence in 1968. Such *chaebols*, family-managed conglomerates, started small but were responsible for two-thirds of the growth in the South Korean economy during the 1960s.

Park did not just strongarm businesses, but provided the conditions they needed, especially tax breaks and export finance. And crucially, his administration invested heavily in infrastructure, including the nationwide expressway system and the Seoul subway. The construction of the 428-kilometre Seoul-Busan highway (known also as the Gyeongbu Expressway) started in February 1968 and was completed in July 1970, slashing travelling time across the country. Kim Jung-ryum, who was chief presidential secretary at the time, recalled later, 'The rapid economic growth we saw during the 1970s and '80s would not have been possible without the expressway.'[9] One of Park's early accomplishments was to ensure the 24-hour provision of electricity by 1964, which previously had been available just a few hours each day.

Innovation and evolution

Park was also willing to innovate and evolve his plan. Once light manufacturing was up and running, he turned his attention to building heavy industry in the late 1960s, focusing on automotives, chemicals, shipbuilding, steel and electronics. Aid was used creatively. For example, the steel plant at Pohang was funded by Japanese war reparations.

These five sectors today total 70% of Korea's exports, a third of economic output and a quarter of all jobs. Domestic savings grew tenfold to over 35% by 1989.

Having been born into a poor peasant family, in 1970 Park also turned his attention to modernising rural life through the Saemaul Undong, or

New Village Movement, focusing on improving basic conditions, then income and infrastructure. His rural upbringing apparently made an indelible impression on Park; as a youth his ambition was reportedly to 'escape' the Korean countryside.[10]

All of this happened while under extreme military threat from the North, whose forces were lined up on the border just 40 kilometres from Seoul. This inspired economic performance as a pillar of national strength and security, but also drew off considerable financial resources into a domestic arms industry capable of developing and manufacturing hi-tech equipment from aircraft to electronics, naval vessels to rockets. 'This drive to increasing self-sufficiency was sparked by [US President Richard] Nixon's 1972 visit to China, and the fear that US troops would be pulled out from the Korean Peninsula,' says Park Jin, the head of the National Assembly Futures Institute. But the strong anti-communist motive also excused excesses, including the absence of a free press, imposition of a nationwide curfew, forced movement of homeless people, and the detention of activists.

And while Park's authoritarianism may have got the economy moving quickly, it also nearly undid the whole thing.

'Essentially there were two phases to Park's rule,' says Park Jin. 'Between 1961 and 1972 he was a remarkable president, pressurising the country for development. After 1971, when he nearly lost his re-election to Kim Dae-jung, he changed the constitution to allow himself a third term and to be elected indirectly via an electoral college system, rather than directly so. He remained economically sound but became politically terrible.' Park introduced, amid growing public opposition and student-led protests, the Yushin (Renovation) Constitution in November 1972.

After that time, his rule hardened as he was less willing to take external advice. 'He changed, especially after his wife was killed [in a failed assassination attempt on Park's life in August 1974], and he turned to his brothers and nephews in the military for input,' says Chung Hee-lee of Hankuk University of Foreign Studies. The Hanahoe, comprising mostly graduates from the 11th class of the Korean Military Academy, and formed by the future president, Chun Doo-hwan, especially grew in influence.

Despite the political ructions, by 1979 South Korea's per capita GDP had grown to US$1 800, or US$6 600 in 2019 money.

Park was killed by his former classmate at the military academy, Kim Jae-gyu, the director of the Korean Central Intelligence Agency, ostensibly due to an argument as to how to confront domestic demonstrations. What became known as the '10.26 incident' inside the Blue House presidential compound in October 1979 set in train events resulting in the country's democratisation in 1987. Park had apparently rebuked Kim for not being tough enough on protesters in Busan, so Kim shot him and his head of security, among others.

A coup two months later brought General Chun Doo-hwan to power until 1987. Willing to take advice from the experts in the Korean Development Institute, Chun cooled what had become an overheated economy, including freezing the national budget for two years in 1983–4, setting the stage for a subsequent export boom as Korea's competitiveness increased. This period signalled a radical departure from the state-led growth and development of the 1960s and 1970s, to a more market-led model, with the government prioritising economic stability and liberalisation, and encouraging private initiatives outside of just the *chaebols*.

Chun's party, the Democratic Justice Party, and its leader, another general and Hanahoe member, Roh Tae-woo, won the first election in 1987 against veteran activists Kim Dae-jung and Kim Young-sam, who effectively split the opposition vote. Kim Young-sam thereafter served a term in alliance with Roh during 1993–8. The transition from autocracy to democracy was marked by key events, including the hosting of the Olympics in 1988, signalling Seoul's emergence into the global community of nations, and the election of liberal political icon Kim Dae-jung ten years later.

By this time, however, bubbles had formed in the economy, which partly had their origins in politically connected practices and loans. A combination of over-borrowing with government backing, investment in unproductive assets, including real estate, and the opening of the capital markets led to the 1997 crash. 'In a way this was a real blessing,' reflects Park Jin, who was called to serve in Kim Dae-jung's reform office for three years. 'We needed to restructure a lot of sectors: private, labour, public and finance. Kim Dae-jung did this, acting like a president from the outset.' Korea also accepted a US$58 billion international bailout, which it paid off by 2001.

Kim Dae-jung reduced the nepotistic connection between the government and the private sector, so much so that subsequent heads of government have been indicted for corruption. Most infamously, Park's eldest daughter, Park Geun-hye, who had become the first female president of South Korea in 2013 in an election that was seen by some as reinforcing her father's legacy, was impeached four years later in an influence-peddling scandal and sentenced in April 2018 to 24 years' imprisonment. Her predecessor Lee Myung-bak, president from 2008 to 2013, and a former CEO of Hyundai, was arrested in 2018 on bribery and tax evasion charges, and in October was sentenced to 15 years.[11] In 2016 former Prime Minister Lee Wan-koo was convicted of taking illegal funds, and in 2018 his successor, Choi Kyung-hwan, was jailed for five years for bribery. The message: business as usual was unhealthy.

Despite the Asian financial crisis and the democratic transition, growth in Korea continued apace, GDP per capita reaching US$20 000 in 2006, rising again to US$30 000 by 2017, making it the world's 11th-largest economy, and the fifth-largest exporter.

Conclusion: Authoritarianism as a chimera?

Is authoritarianism thus necessary for economic triumph?

While it is an enticing 'silver-bullet' developmental answer, authoritarianism is no guarantee of success on the Korean Peninsula as elsewhere:

look at the record of Mao Zedong or myriad African authoritarian failures, along with the North Korean regime. It only works if you have a 'good' authoritarian, and the easiest way to get rid of a bad one is paradoxically through democracy.

'If you have a benevolent dictator,' says Park Jin, 'it would be a good thing, at least in the early stages. But there is no guarantee that it will be a good thing; that the person in charge will turn out to be good. Rather democracy is a safer bet.'

Korea also enjoyed three features largely overlooked in the pro-authoritarian argument: first, while Park's regime can hardly be described as liberal, there was an active civil society throughout, despite the absence of a free media and pervasive militarism. Indeed, Park came to power because of people's activism against Rhee, and was re-elected five times.[12] And whereas Park may have been no liberal, by the standards of the (Cold War) era and his region, the extremes of his rule were unexceptional, especially considering the overarching security imperative. Indeed, three major civil society demonstrations define Korea's recent history: the April 19 Revolution of 1960, the Gwangju Uprising of 1980 and the June Democratic Uprising of 1987. To this can be added the 2016 Candlelight Revolution, which helped to bring down Park's daughter, President Park Geun-hye.[13]

The overriding national mood ensured that liberal democracy was not only inevitable, but that when it happened, the transition stuck. Regardless, in evaluating Park's regime, there is a concerted contemporary effort made to whitewash his rule in the collective memory – despite polls finding that he remains the 'greatest leader of the country since South Korea's liberation from Japanese colonial rule in 1945', with a 44% approval rating overall, followed by Roh Moo-hyun and Kim Dae-jung with 24% and 14% respectively. There is a wide generation gap, however, regarding his popularity. Some 62% of those surveyed in their fifties and 71% in their sixties preferred Park while 60% in their twenties and thirties preferred Roh and Kim.[14]

The left and right are closer on one issue. Nam Kyu-sun, the head of the Korea Democracy Foundation, and a former student activist, says, 'Authoritarianism is not needed for development, both of the economy and of our politics; on the contrary if we didn't have 18 years of authoritarianism, the economy would have been more developed.' Sung-hee Jwa emphasises that there are 'no grounds' to argue that Park's success is a by-product of his authoritarian politics and similarly 'to claim that no lessons can be learnt for twenty-first-century democracy. Rather,' he adds, 'democratic leadership that embraces economic discrimination is a precondition for economic take-off.' The failure to embrace such a competitive ideology explains, he says, along with 'creeping socialism', why Korea's growth rate has slowed considerably: from 8.8% in 1987–97 to 5% in 1997–2007, and just 3.3% in 2007–17.[15]

The second factor explaining why authoritarianism was not critical, as Park Jin again notes, is that 'there was always a well-functioning civil service. Our national exam for civil servants started 1 000 years ago, and our bureaucracy was modernised by Japan during their period of colonial rule.'

And third, unlike other authoritarian socialist regimes, which feared the creation of alternative centres of wealth and power, Park realised that the success (or not) of business would define Korea. As a result, the transition has been staggering. Samsung was, for example, once a small exporter of agricultural and fishery products. Hyundai started as a small car repair business. The LG Group was once a factory making face cream and toothpaste. SK started out as a small textile manufacturer and has grown into SK Telecom. Embracing corporate growth has fundamentally facilitated Korean economic development.

'What Park was able to change', reflects Park Jin, 'was to incentivise hard work by increasing the rewards for performance.' Famously this was done in the programmes for cement distribution to villages in the early 1970s, when those who were adjudged to be in the top half of performers received double the allotment the next year, and those in the bottom half, zero. Park did not care whether he upset those groups, just as he did not care about the reaction of business.

The focus on authoritarianism as the reason for Korea's rapid growth and transformation obscures complex, myriad programmes and tough policy choices that had to be made in the process. This involved, at its heart, the strategic reorientation from protectionism to export-led growth and the rapid refocusing of society on competitiveness. Looking back over nearly 60 years, this seems logical and, following Southeast Asia's subsequent development path, passé even. At the time, it was revolutionary.

Korea's transformation from a poor, developing country to a developed one is known as the 'Miracle on the Han River'. But it was no miracle, requiring a lot of hard work, discipline, leadership, innovation and education, incentivisation, a focus on growth above all else, and, ultimately, democracy.

Chapter 5

The Philippines
Beware Elites

> The Philippines, it has a politics of patronage. Family and favours, in addition to the old cliché of guns, goons and gold, really do still hold a lot of sway.
>
> — Miguel Syjuco, *Ilustrado*

> The Marcos era was the golden time for the Philippines. We had the lowest crime rate in the world in Manila and real development then. At last, people are starting to understand this.
>
> — Imelda Marcos, 2010

General Douglas MacArthur, the retiring chief of staff of the US Army, was invited to the Philippines in 1937 by President Manuel Quezon to oversee the creation of a new armed force. Imbued with an inflated sense of self-importance, MacArthur asked to stay in Malacañang Palace, the official presidential residence. Instead, Quezon commissioned a penthouse suite for the MacArthur family at the luxurious marble and mahogany Manila Hotel.[1]

Promoted to field marshal, MacArthur was tasked with building a Filipino army as a regional American surrogate, Washington being concerned (correctly, as it turned out) by the rise of Japanese militarism. MacArthur's tenure was cut short by the Japanese invasion of the Philippines in December 1941 when he was recalled to active service as commander of US Army Forces in the Far East. Never a man lacking self-confidence, and a master of grandstanding, but whose inspirational leadership was viewed as being, as Dwight Eisenhower wrote, 'worth five army corps', MacArthur decamped from the Philippine capital to the fortified, if tiny, tadpole-shaped island of Corregidor at the mouth of Manila Bay, where he fought on until ordered to safety in Australia.

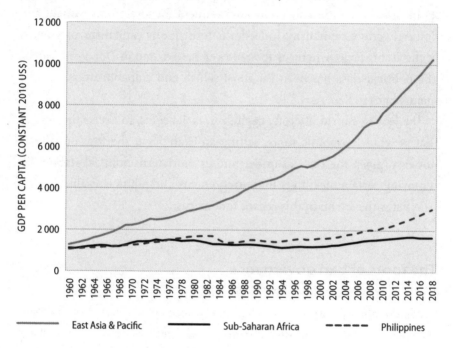

Figure 5.1: Rising tiger? The Philippines' growth in perspective

Source: World Bank Databank, 2019.

Washington oversaw independence in the Philippines in July 1946, the deal permitting long-term leases for American military bases and protection for US products.

Despite, and perhaps because of, this dependency, the Philippine economy performed well below the average of its East Asian tiger counterparts until the twenty-first century. Viewed as the 'sick man of Asia', despite considerable wealth in natural resources and population size, the second largest in Southeast Asia after Indonesia, the Philippines experienced slow growth because of consistent mismanagement and congenital corruption, reflecting weak leadership in a powerful presidential system. It was deeply extractive, thanks to a handful of business families and politicians in a tight network. In a vicious cycle, the Philippines was overly reliant on commodity income, given the unfriendly environment for foreign investment and domestic crony capitalism. Indeed, the term 'crony capitalism' originated in the archipelago, where, as Joe Studwell has written in *How Asia Works*, 'the political class has been the most selfish and culpable among all the major states in East Asia.'[2]

The way to get rid of crony capitalism is, it seems, to excise the system that provides economic rents, setting an example at the top. But this is not easy, given the risks of undermining short-term political stability in removing certain incentives for entrepreneurs and politicians alike.

What is the lesson in this regard for Africa?

The roots of bad governance

Bad governance is a function of leadership.

MacArthur was not the only big man whose ego darkened the Filipino archipelago. The 22-year dictatorship of Fernando Marcos and the shoe-aholic Imelda defined a combination of Latino influence and American-style executive presidency, but one where the 'grand spoils' are dispatched by the leader virtually unhindered by institutional checks and balances.

While the Philippines had the trappings of a constitutional democracy from the time of the achievement of independence in 1946 until the Marcos coup in 1972, 'in practice it was an intra-elite struggle based on powerful patron-client relations, at the apex of which were the landed families.'[3] After defeating Spain in 1898 in the distant war over Cuba, Washington ran the archipelago through local power-brokers. The central government was weak; the regional potentates dominated. Politics was based on the economy: a feudal structure of peasants and powerful landlords, where the state, including the military and the police, have been used to subdue the discontent of the *masa* – the masses. The oligarchs were fed by cheap credit and protected by a US export quota and tariff protection for sugar through which 'rent-seeking tycoons' were 'able to sell globally uncompetitive agricultural products into the US market while manipulating a political system that was ostensibly undemocratic.'[4] The spoils of the relationship continued into the post-independence era, with the abovementioned bilateral trade agreement and the staging of US military bases guaranteeing a steady supply of funds for politicians who were distinguished only in seeking out the best opportunities for themselves. Little wonder Filipinos have referred to their congressmen as *balimbing* – a star-shaped fruit that looks the same from either side.[5]

Following a pattern of regular elections and a turnover in leadership from 1946, a 'brilliant young lawyer', Fernando Marcos, was elected president in 1965. In September 1972 he suspended the constitution, curtailed press freedom and imposed martial law, citing communist subversion.

While some see the Marcos period as a 'golden age' for the economy, by its end in 1986 the country was deep in debt, with widening poverty and unemployment amid extensive corruption and human rights abuses. Notable business people and connected families swirled around the Marcos elite. Large-scale international borrowing was not used, as in Taiwan or Korea, to drive industrialisation, but for elite plunder – borrowing heavily on preferential terms and failing to repay these loans. The political system enabled the elite to take the money and run without suffering the consequences.

Over the past 50 years, economic growth in the Philippine economy has averaged 4.2% compared to the regional Association of Southeast Asian Nations average of 5.7%.

Marcos lifted martial law in 1981. But his main political opponent,

Benigno 'Ninoy' Aquino, was assassinated at Manila International Airport upon his return from exile in the US. Under pressure from Washington among others, Marcos held a snap election in February 1986. Although he was declared the winner, the process was marred by violence and reports of vote rigging, including a claim by 35 government election commission computer technicians about such malfeasance. When the head of the Philippine Constabulary, General Fidel Ramos, and Defence Minister Juan Ponce Enrile withdrew their support for 'Macoy', as Marcos was nicknamed, the die was cast, 'People Power' public protests under the EDSA Revolution (so named after the main highway in Manila) forcing the longtime president out and into self-imposed exile in Hawaii.

Marcos died there in 1989 but his widow and children returned to the Philippines, many having been elected to public offices in an impressive political comeback, including his wife Imelda, infamous for her shoe collection in the conjugal dictatorship.

Known as the 'Steel Butterfly' during her husband's reign, the 90-year-old Imelda is a more benign version, more forgetful grande dame than fierce consort. Yet, she brooks no criticism of her husband's regime. Still a congresswoman in 2018, she argued that 'for all the bad publicity we received', Marcos brought the country 'freedom, justice and democracy. We could not have had freedom while we had US bases with 99-year leases, which Marcos cut off. We could not have had justice if 60% of our lands and wealth belonged to foreigners. He changed this. And,' she says, 'we did not have a democracy since feudal lords were ruling the country. Marcos anchored democracy on the family, the *barangay* [settlement].' It was someone else's fault. In November 2018, a Philippine court found her guilty of corruption for funnelling US$200 million to Swiss foundations in the 1970s as Metropolitan Manila governor, sentencing her to 77 years in gaol and disqualifying her from public office.

Corazon 'Cory' Aquino, widow of Benigno, became the 11th president of the Philippines on 25 February 1986. Yet, her 'indecisiveness, inexperience, and ineptness as a political leader were no match for the challenges of democratic governance' and she failed to measure up to perhaps unrealistically high expectations.[6] 'There was chaos around her,' says one former senior member of her government, 'perhaps reflecting that she was more comfortable with NGO types than those with experience in government.'

Things started to improve with the election of retired General Ramos as president in 1992. Ramos opened up the economy to encourage private investment and reduce corruption under his vision of 'Philippines 2000'. This included the development of the special economic zone (SEZ) concept. As one measure, over the last 20 years, growth in the economy has averaged 5%.

Ramos was succeeded in 1998 by his deputy, Joseph 'Erap' Estrada, a veteran and popular film actor. In 2000 Estrada declared an 'all-out war' against the Moro Islamic Liberation Front. But he did not do the same with corruption. Instead, he was undone by a 2001 senate impeachment trial for taking US$80 million from the government coffers. His deputy, Gloria Macapagal Arroyo (widely known as GMA), a former professor of economics, stepped in, and was re-elected in 2004, serving as president until 2010. She had originally entered government in 1987 in the Department of Trade and Industry.

Under GMA's leadership, the economy picked up with some gusto. Two-thirds of growth was, according to the Asian Development Bank, driven by domestic demand among the 107 million-strong population. This has increased as per capita income reached the US$3 000 level in 2017. Growth has been fuelled, too, by continued remittances. More than 11 million overseas Filipino workers labour in the diaspora, sending home over US$28 billion in 2017, or just under 10% of GDP, doubling over the last decade.[7] Tourism has been a significant growth sector, arrivals more than trebling from 2000 to number 6.6 million in 2017. Meanwhile, there has been a near doubling in the volume of offshore revenues between 2013 and 2017, with US$22 billion repatriated in 2017.

The Asian Development Bank estimates that services are responsible for creating 60%–70% of all new jobs in the Philippines, with as many as three million in the IT sector alone. Increasing consumerism is also driven by a change of employment. The Philippine economy has been revolutionised in this regard by the drive to Business Process Outsourcing, with more than 1.3 million working in an industry worth US$22 billion to the economy, or as much as 15% of the global total, and which has enjoyed consistent double-digit growth.[8] Between 2007 and 2017, growth in the Philippine economy has averaged 5.6%, twice that of the 1970s, for example, and from 2013 to 2017 it was over 6.5%, the highest in Asia after China and India.

Country	FDI, in US$000		FDI, % of GDP	
	2010	2017	2010	2017
China	114 734	136 320	1.9	1.1
India	27 397	39 916	1.7	1.5
Singapore	55 076	62 006	23.3	19.1
Indonesia	13 771	23 063	1.8	2.3
Vietnam	8 000	14 100	6.9	6.3
Malaysia	9 060	9 543	3.6	3.0
Thailand	14 568	7 635	4.3	1.7
Philippines	1 298	9 524	0.7	3.0
Myanmar	6 669	4 341	14.6	6.3
Cambodia	1 342	2 784	11.9	12.6
Laos	279	813	3.9	4.8
Brunei	481	-46	3.5	-0.4

Table 5.1: Comparative Asian FDI inflows

Source: World Investment Report 2017; World Bank, World Development Indicators.

Much growth is linked to the establishment of SEZs (under the Philippines Economic Zone Authority), such as those in the former US air base at Clark Field and the naval port at Subic Bay. By 2017 there were 366 SEZs across the country, including 74 manufacturing zones.[9] This drove up annual foreign direct investment (FDI) inflows threefold to US$10 billion between 2013 and 2017, for example. More than 40% of FDI in 2016 went to the manufacturing sector in such zones, despite the country's restrictive FDI policies, which include constitutional provisions prohibiting more than 40% foreign ownership and national preference in key sectors.

Some of this is the reward from cleaning up government. As Benigno Simeon 'Noynoy' Cojuangco Aquino III, president between 2010 and 2016, put it in his last State of the Nation address, 'a significant portion' of growth was, during his predecessor's term, 'fuelled by remittances from Filipinos who had lost hope in our country'. As a result, 'We went after the corrupt and we cleaned the systems, which redounded to confidence in our markets. Businesses came into the country, opportunities expanded ... This is a cycle: justice, trust, economic growth, the creation of opportunities, progress. This is the very spirit of "where there is no corruption, there is no poverty".'[10] Or, as he noted on a different occasion, 'good governance is good economics'.[11]

Overall, the biggest accomplishment of the last generation, reflects Delia Albert, a former foreign secretary, is that 'we have been able to improve social mobility, as a result of which people feel more optimistic, that there is more of a future here'. This improvement, however, has a lot to do with the (literally) get up and go of Filipinos, especially the overseas Filipino workers, rather than politicians.

Getting rid of the rent-seekers?

Leaving with his family from the jetty at Corregidor's Lorcha Dock in March 1942, MacArthur reached Australia after a risky 600-kilometre journey through the Japanese blockade by torpedo boat to Mindanao and from there by a B-17 bomber. A bitter guerrilla and liberation struggle against Japanese militarism ensued, followed by clamours for independence. This was gained, controversially, on 4 July 1946, initially fraught with American conditions imposed on its sovereignty, as noted above.

MacArthur famously declared on arrival in Australia after leaving Corregidor that 'I shall return', which he did at the war's end three years later, wading purposefully ashore behind his ubiquitous aviator sunglasses. The ego had landed.

He was, again, not the last. Many Filipino politicians do, over and over again.

In 2007 Estrada was sentenced to a life sentence for corruption. Pardoned by his one-time deputy (and automatic successor), Gloria Arroyo, he ran for president in 2010. Defeated resoundingly by Benigno Aquino III, son of Cory, Estrada was elected mayor of Manila in 2013. In July 2018 Arroyo was elected speaker of the House of Representatives. Both she and Ramos have enjoyed something of a political renaissance, given their support for the current president, Rodrigo Duterte.

Yet, most Filipino presidential careers end badly, it seems. Estrada's dismal presidential conclusion was not unique. General Ramos is one of the few whose careers have not been embroiled in some form of post-presidential scandal. For example, in November 2011, Arroyo was arrested on charges of electoral fraud and later arrested again on charges of mis-use of state lottery funds, both of which she was later acquitted after four years under 'hospital arrest'. Her oldest son, Mikey, is a former congress-man (2004–10) and actor, who has run into scandal over a failure to declare earnings. His younger brother, Dato, who worked as one of his mother's speechwriters, won election as representative of the First District of Camarines Sur Province.

Arroyo was succeeded by Benigno Aquino. Keeping things among fami-lies, his vice president was Mar Roxas, son of a senator and grandson of Manuel Roxas, the first president of the Philippine Republic (1946–8).

The persistence of such dynasties and corruption controversies reflects the weakness of government institutions against personalities in the Philippines. Politics, put differently, is a family business where personalities and their networks are more important than ideas, ideology or parties.

Imelda, unsurprisingly, has not seen anything particularly problematic about this. Her oldest son, Ferdinand 'Bongbong' Marcos Jnr, is a senator and vice presidential candidate, having first been elected to the House of Representatives at the age of 23 and succeeding as governor of the province of Ilocos Norte, his father's power base, from 1983 to 1986. His sister, Maria Imelda 'Imee' Marcos, is the governor of Ilocos Norte. Before that, she served three terms as representative of the Second District of Ilocos Norte in the House of Representatives from 1998 until 2007. 'Bongbong was only six-and-a-half years old,' reminds Imelda without a hint of irony, 'when we got into the palace. He has all the ingredients [to run the country].'

There are other more extreme examples. Also in the province of Camarines Sur, the sitting governor, Miguel Luis Villafuerte, 29, defeated no less an opponent than his grandfather, Luis, in the last (2018) election, who had been a congressman from 2004 to 2013 and governor of the same province from 1995 to 2004. His father had earlier, too, served as governor, while his grandmother is a former member of the Philippine Monetary Board.

It is not only politicians who succumb to cronyism. The chief justice of the Supreme Court, Maria Lourdes Sereno, a key opponent of President Duterte, was under impeachment charges in 2018 for failing to declare assets.

Senator Gregorio 'Gringo' Honasan, who led several failed coups as a Special Forces officer against Ferdinand Marcos and, then, Cory Aquino, says that 'we are a product of our limited choices. Political parties do not exist in this country. It's all about personality choice.' 'When you cast your ballot, you think it's a tragedy that we have these slim choices before us,' says the retired colonel. Honasan, who stood unsuccessfully for vice president in 2016, says this is worsened by the funding regime for parties, which receive no money from the state. As a result, whoever funds the party is usually its leader; a patronage principle exacerbated by the 30 000 or so jobs the president can immediately, upon assuming office, dispense.

This, too, relates to the relative absence of ideology as an organising principle in elections.

While the political divide is ostensibly between the 'liberals' (represented by the Aquino and Roxas dynasties) and the 'nationalists' (Marcos, Arroyo, Duterte, Ramos), in practice this means little. Where, to cite one former senior government official, 'allegiances can be bought and where it is the politicians and not the state that provide social services, from paying for schools to funerals, political dynasties flourish'. And elitism plays into other areas, including the weak institutional basis of government, centralism over federalism, and a dismissive attitude towards poverty. Hence the term '*padrino* cycle', a sense that 'nothing really changes in the Philippine government except for the rotation of a handful of politically powerful families whose heads, i.e., *padrinos*, take turns either taking up residence at the Presidential Palace or falling from grace'.[12]

Another consequence is that economic policies and plans suffer from a lack of continuity, when it does not suit the personalities to honour previous commitments. The pliability of state institutions, which undercuts the effectiveness of Philippine democracy, suits these elites, with a resultant democratic fatigue, so that citizens have come to prefer an authoritarian, tough-talking alternative.

Managing divides

Skipping puddles of sewage is a main preoccupation in the muddy alleys of Manila's Helping Land slum. Sandwiched between two container depots at the capital's port, its inhabitants process rubbish for their living. *Sari-sari* 'hole-in-the-wall' convenience shops ply their penny-packet wares and women wash pots where children and mangy dogs and cats splash their way. The purpose is to separate rubbish from income, one corner devoted to plastic, another to paper, and the most overpowering to the production of *pagpag* from fast-food waste, which is then recooked and sold.

Manila Bay it may be, but the reality of the Tondo district is a long way from the Manila Hotel and the wealth of the capital's Makati business district. While the average Gini coefficient in Southeast Asia is 0.38, relatively low by global standards, in the Philippines this is 0.40, with higher scores indicating more inequality.[13] Inequality in the Philippines has hovered above 0.40 since the early 1990s, without noticeable improvement.

Manila is the most densely populated city in the world, with 42 857 people per square kilometre, while its wider National Capital Region, where 40% of GDP is generated, accommodates an estimated 13 million people. The slums of Tondo, including Helping Land and Happy Land, contain no fewer than 73 000 people per square kilometre.

Problems with logistics and infrastructure are linked to lifting the quarter of Filipinos who are currently in poverty. This has a clear rural dimension. Agriculture employs a third of the population, yet the sector makes up just 10% of GDP. Protectionist deals with the US kept the country focused on agriculture, which constituted 80% of exports in the 1930s, for example, and which remained inefficient. Poverty in the rural areas is also linked to a failure of land reform. A plethora of plans ran up against vested interests: most politicians were from or supported by landed gentry. As a result, by the time of Marcos' fall from power, he had achieved less than a quarter of his limited targets, while the subsequent Comprehensive Agrarian Land Reform Law of 1988 did little to accelerate change.[14]

But all poverty is not rural. Far from it. The divides are regional – and, as the plight of those in the slums of Tondo illustrates, within regions. North of Tondo but still within the confines of the Manila Metro lies 'Plastic City', or Valenzuela City, which has become a dump site for not only the Philippines' but also the world's plastic.[15] The Philippines is the world's third-largest contributor to ocean plastic and just the 13th-largest population. The big culprit is a single-use plastic sachet, itself a result of poverty, as people buy from their *sari-sari* stores in small quantities as the need arises and their income allows.[16]

Politics and economics in the Philippines are shaped by criss-crossing fault lines, whose extent partly relates to the distance from the national capital region (Manila), and in which religion, ethnicity, and the presence of economic opportunities and investment from the central government all play a part. While the average per capita income across the Philippines touches US$3 000, citizens in the National Capital Region enjoy three times this amount, and those in some outlying provinces just half.

Whereas the National Capital Region, for example, is the commercial and financial centre with minimal agriculture and predominantly a services and manufacturing economy, enjoying the majority of government spending (80% of which runs through central government currently, even though there are 18 regions, 81 provinces, 135 cities and 1 500 municipalities), Mindanao in the south is overwhelmingly dependent on fishery and agriculture exports. Incomes correspond thus, in part, with the country's 80 ethno-linguistic groups, and religion plays a part, with the Muslim minority clustered in Mindanao. There are also divisions between generations about ends and means, with the youth finding it increasingly difficult to 'talk politics' with their more conservative elders.[17]

Enter Rodrigo Roa Duterte, also known as 'Digong' or 'Rody', the winner (with 39% of the vote) of the 9 May 2016 election, the first president from the southern island group of Mindanao, projecting himself as an agent of change against the elites and 'imperial Manila'.

A lawyer by training, Duterte worked as a prosecutor for Davao City, before becoming vice mayor and, subsequently, mayor of the city for 22 years following the 1986 revolution. He is famously foul-mouthed and described as a 'populist' and a 'nationalist' on account of his support for radical crime-fighting measures, including the extrajudicial killing of drug users and other criminals. An anti-American and outspoken critic of the church, Duterte has both confirmed and denied his involvement in Davao death squads. During his presidential campaign, he promised to reduce crime by killing tens of thousands of criminals.

Former president Aquino says that the rise of Duterte is 'a complete opposite of what we tried to achieve.'[18] Yet, perhaps because of that, Duterte has offered a popular message for Filipinos, tired of worn promises from the political status quo. Even though they had come off their peak, two years into his presidency Duterte still had approval ratings of 65%.[19]

While his promises may be popular, perhaps inevitably they are too dangerous.

The dangers of Duterte-ism

High logistical and infrastructure costs add considerable premiums to doing business in the Philippines, estimated to be perhaps as much as 8% of GDP in lost productivity and wasted energy. The Japanese International Co-operation Agency, for example, estimates that US$70 million is lost every day to Manila's gridlock.[20] With a weak mass rapid transport system, the roads are paralysed with 2.2 million buses, cars and 600 000 anti-quated, if vivid and cheap (US$0.20 per 4 kilometres), Jeepneys.[21] 'It takes longer', laughs Senator Honasan, 'to travel across Manila City than it does to reach Hong Kong.' He is not joking though.

The paradox of Duterte is that, apart from the rhetoric, there has been, so far, a commitment to sound macro-economic policies and a focus on delivering infrastructure. The central plank of his administration is a US$150-billion Build, Build, Build strategy, involving 18 flagship projects from highways to airports, ports, bridges, water pipelines and container depots. This was to be funded by the Tax Reform for Acceleration and Inclusion, which sought to rationalise incentives, reduce corporate (from 30% to 20%) and personal income tax, and broaden the tax base through extending VAT. The tax to GDP ratio is at 16%, compared to the Organisation for Economic Co-operation and Development (OECD) member country average of 34%. Tax revenue increases are to be offset by widened plans for unconditional cash transfers to the poorest, with the aim of reaching half of 20 million Filipino households. Already, during Benigno Aquino's presidential term, some 4.1 million households benefited from the conditional cash transfer programme.

But populism worries persist, not just because of extrajudicial issues, but because it threatens to undermine the system of government and already fragile institutional checks and balances.

The Philippines ranks 99th out of 180 countries surveyed by Transparency International in 2018, with a score of 36 out of 100, below the regional average of 44.[22] Freedom House estimated in 2018 that Duterte's war on drugs has led to more than 12 000 extrajudicial killings, ranking the Philippines as 'partly free' with a score of 62/100 (where 100 is most free).[23] The country ranked as 'free' from 1997 to 2005.

This would suggest that democracy is not to blame for poor governance; on the contrary, worsening democratic conditions have corroded institutions and the rule of law. Transparency International, for example, placed the Philippines alongside India and the Maldives as 'among the worst regional offenders' when it came to threats against or murder of journalists, activists, opposition leaders and even staff of law enforcement or watchdog agencies. 'These countries score high for corruption and have fewer press freedoms and higher numbers of journalist deaths,' reports Transparency International.[24]

Conclusion: Upsides and downsides

Duterte's popularity also reflects ongoing fatigue with politics as usual in the Philippines, where his brand of populism presents an alternative to business-as-usual practices, an appeal to people over the political elite. The emergence of such 'hybrid regimes', which combine elements of electoral democracy with autocratic governance, centring around strong, populist personalities and thriving on the absence of strong, functioning state institutions, is not of course limited to the Philippines.[25] Autocratic China has become the world's second-largest economy, without recourse to basic liberties or free elections. Russia's Vladimir Putin, Turkey's Recep Tayyip Erdogan, and the late Venezuelan leader Hugo Chávez have all developed playbooks for anti-democratic control. While they won power through elections, each quickly moved to undermine institutional constraints on executive power and ensure loyalty through the deployment of partisans to key positions, including the judiciary.

The gap between social expectations, on the one hand, and state capacity and promises, on the other, is at the crux of this phenomenon. The cost is to liberal constitutionalism. Even if one forgets the cost to international relations of the president's outspokenness, for a country already weak in checks and balances, this is unlikely to be a productive path ultimately.[26] For the conditions that lend themselves to success in the Philippines, experts agree, are improving efficiency in the public service, institutional oversight, policy inclusiveness and predictability, a healthy relationship between government and business, and the reduction of various social schisms.[27] To align politics with these requirements, and to deal with poverty, requires a batch of local government and electoral reforms, including around campaign financing, in which few politicians would see immediate benefits for themselves.

*

Bad governance is a function of leadership and the nature of the political system. That is the lesson from the Philippines. Despite considerable wealth in natural resources and population size, the economy consistently performed below the levels of its region during the twentieth century. Slow growth has been a function of perpetual mismanagement and congenital corruption, reflecting weak leadership in a powerful presidential system. Things have picked up since then, particularly through the services sector and a manufacturing boom in more than 360 SEZs, with the economy among the top three regional performers. But politics remains snared between family dynasties and the populism represented by President Rodrigo Duterte – one consequence being that nearly one-quarter of 107 million Filipinos live in poverty.

These are lessons, it seems, for others beyond the Philippines.

Chapter 6

Malaysia
Managing Diversity

> We return to history not to seek refuge in nostalgia, because retracing
> our steps into the world of yesteryear is a painful experience ... So let
> history be our guide and our tutor so that we may never again suffer
> the pangs, suffer the humiliation of a divided people.
>
> — Tun Muhammad Ghazali bin Shafie, Malaysian minister of home affairs, 1973–81

The lobby of Proton's Shah Alam factory outside Kuala Lumpur centres on
a colourful line-up of the various models since the manufacturer's inception. The slab-sided Saga, launched in 1985, quickly became Malaysia's
most popular car, selling more than a million units, helping Proton to gain
a 55% share of the domestic market within its first decade.[1]

But Proton's early success offered false promise, illustrating just how
difficult it is to start a national car project from scratch, the idea of then
Deputy Prime Minister Mahathir Mohamad in 1979. The Asian financial crisis of 1997/8 saw domestic sales plummet to less than half of a
400 000-vehicle annual peak. This was not the only challenge. Despite
capital investment of US$5 billion since 1983, the presence of tariff pro-
tection and government subsidies ensuring price competitiveness, and
an early technology-sharing agreement with Mitsubishi along with the
acquisition of the UK sports car icon Lotus in 1996 and the Italian motorcycle legend MV Agusta in 2004, the creation of a sustainably profitable
business has proven elusive.

Today Proton's domestic market share is around 11%, behind the second national manufacturer, Perodua, essentially a rebadged Toyota, and Honda. But change is afoot. In 2017, recognising the need for a global partner with the withdrawal of Mitsubishi in 2005, 49.9% of Proton and a 51% stake in Lotus were sold to the Chinese Geely concern. The Chinese carmaker also owns Volvo and the company that makes London's black cabs, among other manufacturing businesses. Now Proton is focusing on the latest version of the low-cost (US$8 000) Saga, along with its MPV and a Geely-ised version of the Volvo XC SUV. The focus of production is moving to a new, larger, hi-tech facility at Tanjung Malim, with a potential of one million annual units.

Proton illustrates that success demands more than good ideas and intentions. Instead, it is a game of volume through global access and cost-sharing, realities that are out of sync somewhat with nationalistic car concepts. The story shows, too, how economic diversification demands a fine balance between national imperatives, such as training, upliftment, poverty alleviation, ownership, infrastructure development and wealth creation, on the one hand, and international demands of capital, technology and trade, on the other hand. It is all about the choices intrinsic to the notion of a political economy – that is, the study of who gets what, when and how (the core questions of the discipline of politics) in the context of scarcity (the issues or patterns of production and distribution in the setting of scarcity, the key questions of the discipline of economics).

Put differently, domestic political economy and the sometimes limited choices it offers set the boundaries for reform and growth.

Getting this balance right, appealing simultaneously to domestic and global constituencies, is never going to be easy, in spite of the intrinsic advantages Malaysia possesses. The most important of these has long been its historical openness to trade and capital, unlike other instinctively protectionist economies in Southeast Asia. This is epitomised by Penang, once the centre of colonial trade and today the heart of Malaysia's electronics industry.

The Penang factor

Penang, the Malaysian island 350 kilometres from Kuala Lumpur, has its modern origins in its leasing in the eighteenth century by the local sultan to Captain Francis Light, an employee of the East India Company, in exchange for military protection against expansionist Burmese and Siamese interests. This treaty was formalised in 1800 and extended over an area on the mainland denoted Province Wellesley – the future Duke of Wellington, Arthur Wellesley, having spent time on Penang co-ordinating local defences.

The British flag was raised on Penang on 11 August 1786. Light died eight years later from malaria, aged just 54 – young by modern standards. But this was an era, reminds Victoria Glendinning in her magisterial *Raffles and the Golden Opportunity*, of 'long everything – long journeys, long speeches, long dinners, long sermons, long poems, long scholarly papers, long book reviews, long personal letters, long reports – and long attention spans. Only death moved swiftly.'[2] Throw in a harsh climate and relentless working conditions, and things could unimaginably speed up, Penang soon earning the epithet 'the white man's grave' to accompany its other moniker, 'the pearl of the Orient'.

Light's white tomb lies in Penang's Protestant Cemetery off Jalan Sultan Ahmad Shah in George Town, behind the mouldy, low yellow and white wall, its red-brick walkway shaded by giant, twisted frangipani trees. He had originally landed on the island just up the road from his final resting place, on the spot where he erected Fort Cornwallis in the name of the governor general of the British East India Company, Charles Cornwallis. Many of the 500 tombs in the cemetery are those of young children.[3]

The risks were high, but so were the rewards. Penang was perfectly situated for trade, offering a halfway point between Madras and Canton, a place for British ships to load up with spices, tin and bird's nests demanded by the Chinese market, and to protect its Chinese monopoly, too, in tea and opium. It also provided a British bulwark to threatening Dutch expansion. Appointed superintendent of the island, Light created a free port to encourage trade, which grew to over US$30 million within three years of his arrival.[4]

Immigrants flocked to make their mark and fortune. From just 60 inhabitants that first year, by 1810 the population had grown to 22 000, and rapidly to 190 000 by 1890, including among them an influential Armenian community who consecrated the church of St Gregory the Illuminator. The four Armenian Sarkies brothers, Martin, Tigran, Aviet and Arshak, established the legendary Eastern and Oriental Hotel – the E&O – on the George Town Esplanade, still there in all its grandeur, as if straight out of a Wes Anderson film.

With the shift from sail to steam travel and the rise of its Straits Settlements trade rival, Singapore, Penang's importance declined, to be revived somewhat 150 years later in the 1970s with the development of one of Asia's largest manufacturing bases. On the island, clustered in four industrial parks, is a plethora of hi-tech giants from Plexus to Bosch, Motorola to Intel. The latter led the way in opening operations, establishing a US$1.6-million plant 'in a paddyfield' in 1972, the year after its initial public offering, its first offshore operation and second-ever factory. Then Intel president, Gordon Moore, the author of Moore's law, positing the doubling of computer power every two years with dramatic development implications, laid the cornerstone of the next Penang facility in 1978. The same reasons for Intel going to Malaysia nearly 50 years ago are still evidently true: location, workforce and local government support.

The Penang Development Corporation (PDC) was established in 1969 specifically to drive economic growth, urban renewal and the development of new townships, centring its activities on the establishment of a free trade zone, the first being created in 1972 on the southern side of Penang. The PDC can provide subsidised land or, in the case of start-ups, factory space for small and medium enterprises, and works with InvestPenang and the Malaysian Investment Development Authority, the latter offering tax and training incentives 'especially for hi-tech, strategic industries'. Fiscal incentives for hi-tech companies include tax holidays for the first five years, and deferments of as much as 60% of tax losses against future profits.[5]

Monthly salaries have risen in Penang as skills have increased and global demands changed, now averaging over US$500. Despite competition from lower-wage regional rivals in Vietnam, Cambodia and China, the reasons for businesses being in Penang remain: widespread proficiency in English, the free industrial zones (which have superseded the free trade zones), good international logistics (the one side of the airport, opposite the passenger terminal, is dominated by operations for TNT, UPS, Fedex and DHL, dedicated to moving out high-value electronics) and unions that are present but generally on side.

Electronics make up the bulk of Penang's manufacturing output, ahead of equally hi-tech medical devices, pharmaceuticals and food processing. There are unusual spin-offs. More than 300 000 medical tourists visited Penang hospitals in 2017/18 for complex procedures, including open-heart surgery, at prices around 10% of similar operations in the US.[6] All this reflects an impressive national achievement: with revenue of over US$90 billion annually, digital electronics and machinery make up 40% of Malaysia's total exports by value. As a result, Malaysia has become richer substantially faster than the global average, while Africa's share of per capita growth has steadily eroded.

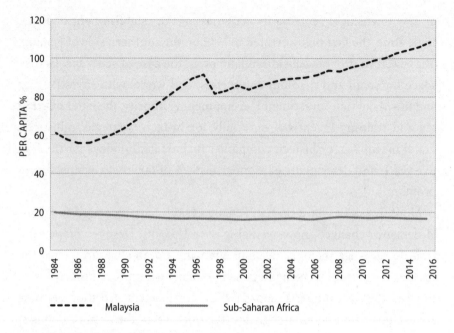

Figure 6.1: Africa and Malaysia: share of world GDP

Source: World Bank Databank, 2019; own calculations.

This is also evident from the apparent correlation between export growth and GDP growth for Malaysia (Figure 6.2).

Penang's transformation from colonial trading entrepôt to modern electronics centre is indicative of Malaysia's own economic transition over the last 50 years. It is one of the world's most open economies, its trade to GDP ratio averaging over 130% since 2010. Some 40% of jobs are linked to export activities. The country enjoys seven bilateral free trade areas (Japan, Pakistan, New Zealand, Chile, India, Turkey and Australia), along with the 11-member Association of Southeast Asian Nations (ASEAN). The success of this approach reflects in the thirteenfold increase in GDP since 1971, the year of the start of Malaysia's New Economic Policy (NEP).

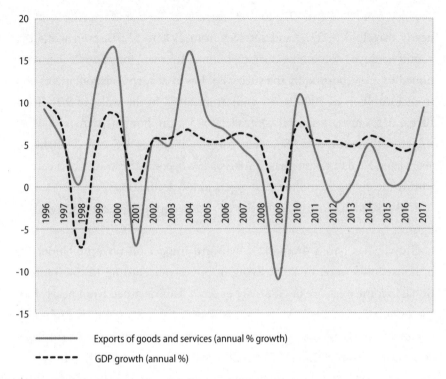

Exports of goods and services (annual % growth)

GDP growth (annual %)

Figure 6.2: Malaysia annual export and GDP growth (percentage)
Source: World Bank Databank, 2019.

The Malaysian diversification story

Malaysia has made considerable progress in diversifying its economy from a dependence on agriculture to manufacturing and services. Between 1971 and 2018 the economy grew at an annual average of 6.6%, with full employment being achieved in 1992.

As a measure of the extent of diversification, the share of agriculture to GDP declined from 32% in 1970 to 7.8% in 2018, even though the output of the sector went up fourfold in financial terms over this period, and palm oil, which represented 39% of agriculture production in 1960, moved to 83% in just 20 years. The proportion of mining to the overall economy similarly declined from 24.5% in 1970 to 7.9% in 2018, while manufacturing went up nearly threefold to 23%, and services from 29% to 55.5%, even while the country enjoyed something of an oil boom.[7] Tourism, for example, has continued to grow, buoyed by the success of low-cost travel, visitors increasing from 10 million in 2000 to 26 million in 2017.[8] In the wake of 9/11, Tony Fernandes, once a financial controller for Virgin, bought AirAsia, a debt-ridden airline, for one Malaysian ringgit (about 24 US cents). Eighteen years later, Kuala Lumpur-based AirAsia has become the lowest-cost carrier worldwide, flying 90 million passengers to 165 destinations.[9]

There is much more to Malaysia's growth record than just the impressive figures.

Growth has had a dramatic downward impact on poverty. Under 1% of households were, by 2018, living in poverty, according to the international income measure of US$1.90 per day.[10] This declined from nearly half the population in 1970. Moreover, while income inequality is high, it is declining. The Gini coefficient, measuring income inequality, has similarly come down from 0.513 in 1970 to 0.399 today. The World Bank reminds us that from 2009 to 2014, for example, the real average household incomes of the bottom 40 grew at 11.9% per year, compared to 7.9% for the total population of Malaysia, thus narrowing income disparities. This has been expedited, in turn, by a shift from the farms to the cities, and the provision of homes and opportunities, as the rural-urban split has flipped from 67:33 to 25:75 over the last 50 years.

Poverty alleviation has been driven by a competitive policy regime, especially in attracting foreign direct investment, improved planning, modernising infrastructure, and redistribution.

The country's development record and, indeed, virtually its entire post-colonial history have been difficult to separate from Mahathir bin Mohamad, who has dominated the political stage since the 1970s, both inside and outside the United Malays National Organisation (UMNO). By 2018 Mahathir was back in the leadership saddle as the world's oldest head of state at 92.

As the fourth prime minister, from 1981 to 2003, Mahathir oversaw a period of rapid growth and modernisation. This was most visible in dramatic infrastructure projects, including the 450-metre Petronas towers, which still dominate the Kuala Lumpur skyline, the building of a new government city outside Kuala Lumpur in Putrajaya, a modern airport and high-speed rail link, the Cyberjaya tech complex and the 770-kilometre North-South highway.

Growth by itself was not deemed to be enough. The government had received a wake-up call in the May 1969 racial riots. A Malay affirmative action policy – the Bumiputera – was put in place through preferential redistribution of the proceeds of growth to the indigenous population. This did not occur through nationalisation, though foreign assets were bought out and preferentially distributed to a new elite, as were government contracts and education opportunities. There was an overt political aspect

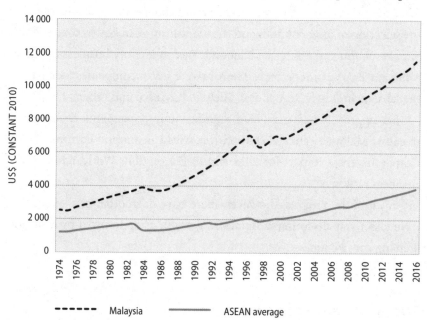

Figure 6.3: Malaysian versus ASEAN average GDP per capita

Source: World Bank Databank, 2019.

to this policy, since it helped to maintain Mahathir's authority within the UMNO, though, for all of its political advantages, it also increasingly had costs, as is highlighted below. The overall economic masterplan was implemented via five-year strategies (by 2019, the country was on its 11th such iteration), and appropriate government agencies and monitoring units. At a macro-level, Malaysia's Economic Transformation Programme was launched in 2010 with the aim of propelling Malaysia into a high-income economy (>US$12 000 GDP per capita) by 2020. It focuses on key sectors, and identifies 131 entry point projects. Since the start of the programme, GDP per capita has increased from US$9 000 in 2010 to US$11 500 in 2017, a much steeper increase than the ASEAN average.[11]

The Economic Transformation Programme has been managed by the Performance Management and Delivery Unit (Pemandu), an agency under the prime minister. Because the majority of investment (60%) was sought from the private sector, private sector companies were closely involved in the selection of opportunities and the identification of key sectors. For this aim, Pemandu had established 'laboratories' to identify business opportunities and entry point projects. Many private sector companies took part in the labs, including Exxon-Mobil, Shell, PwC, Tesco and others.

This approach has paralleled significant improvements in competitiveness. Malaysia ranks 25/140 on the World Economic Forum's Global Competitiveness Report for 2018 and 15/190 on 2019 World Bank Doing Business rankings.[12]

For all of the progress, however, there have been other challenges that have effectively discounted Malaysia's growth, as epitomised by a second 'Penang connection'.

The importance of governance

Anwar Ibrahim was, in the 1990s, Malaysia's uber-successful and popular minister of finance, the man expected to take over from Mahathir as his successor. Then came a spectacular fall from grace, Anwar being accused of corruption and sexual improprieties in 1998 by his boss, fired and then imprisoned. Few in Malaysian history have been prosecuted for their views and popularity as Anwar has been. His sentence was overturned under Mahathir's successor, Abdullah Badawi, in 2004, but new accusations surfaced in 2008. His acquittal was mysteriously dismissed in 2014 on the eve of a state by-election, which he was widely expected to win, and he was again imprisoned until the king of Malaysia pardoned him in 2018.

Such are the vagaries of politics and the need of broad support that by 2018, however, Anwar was back in favour. His return reflects the fractious, distinctly sectarian and occasionally violent nature of Malaysian politics. Mahathir made his surprising political comeback in the Pakatan Harapan coalition in the 2018 general election, becoming the first prime minister not to represent the Barisan Nasional. Prime Minister Najib Razak was unseated by adroit opposition politics. The plan appears that Mahathir will, in time, hand over to Anwar, whose People's Justice Party was central to the 2018 election victory. In politics, after all, there are no permanent friends or enemies.

While in agreement that Malaysia's growth has a positive story to tell in terms of poverty alleviation and the value of pro-market policies, Anwar is deeply critical of the costs to governance and 'rampant corruption', which he says has its roots in 'poor leadership, weak institutions and human greed', noting that 'a fish always rots from the head'.

The means of incumbent Prime Minister Najib Razak's defeat may have been Mahathir's return, but the cause was his involvement in the 1Malaysia Development Berhad (1MDB) scandal.

The book *Billion Dollar Whale* details the story of the Penang-born and Wharton-educated entrepreneur Jho Low, orchestrator of one of the greatest heists in history.[13] At the young age of 28, Low managed to convince Najib that he could use the 1MDB, a Malaysian sovereign wealth fund, as a financing vehicle by attracting major investments from the Middle East and other global markets. Goldman Sachs and other banks helped raise US$10 billion, before half of this amount disappeared from the fund.

Low was labelled 'Asia's Great Gatsby' for his extravagant parties, including one where Britney Spears allegedly jumped out of a giant birthday cake. His 300-foot superyacht, which gave its name to the book, and which was seized by the Malaysian government, was reported as sold in April 2019 for US$126 million, the largest amount of money to date that the country has recovered from the US$4.5 billion embezzled through 1MDB.

While Low has allegedly fled to China, Najib was arrested in July 2018 by the Malaysian Anti-Corruption Commission, which seized 1 400 necklaces, 567 handbags, 423 watches, 2 200 rings, 1 600 brooches and 14 tiaras in a raid on his home. He faced 42 criminal charges, including 27 money laundering charges, nine for criminal breach of trust, five for abuse of power and one for audit tampering.[14] Investigators allege that US$1 billion found its way into his personal bank accounts.

While the scale of the 1MDB bling may have shocked, as Anwar indicates, this was far from the first corruption scandal, the roots of which lie in the nature of the political compact at independence. Malaysia suffered heavily in the Asian financial crisis in 1997/8, partly as a result of over-borrowing by politically connected individuals in unproductive assets, notably apartment buildings. The ratio of non-performing loans was estimated at 14.6% at the time of the start of the crisis against an OECD average of about 3.2%, while the ratio of bank lending to nominal GDP reached as high as 138.5%, hinting at the extent of over-lending, the ease of access to finance for some and the frailties of oversight.[15] Real estate made up 35% of all outstanding bank lending, and the loan:deposit ratio was dangerously close to 100%, meaning that banks were lending more than they could raise with deposits.[16] Recovery, and Malaysia's international stature, were not helped by Mahathir's rants against international financiers, notably George Soros.

Institutions have, for a long period, been deliberately undermined in personal interests.

During his first term, Mahathir's children went into business. The eldest son, Mirzan, having been behind a conglomerate, was heavily in debt by the time of the 1997 financial crisis. Anwar's opposition to a state bailout of one of Mirzan's companies was reportedly 'critical to his falling out with the premier'.[17] Under Mahathir, unbridled personal authority came at the cost of institutional strength as the compliance of the judiciary was engineered and the Internal Security Act exercised to detain activists, religious figures and political opponents, including Anwar. The problem, it seems, was less the capacity of growth of the Malaysian economy than the way economic and institutional choices were shaped by politics – in essence, by the political economy.

The pros and cons of social redistribution

After independence in 1957, the arrangement between the Malaysian political and economic elites was 'sufficiently explicit', notes Joe Studwell, to be popularly known as 'the bargain'.[18] In terms of the traditional, colonial division of roles, the economy was dominated by the Chinese, the Indians populated the civil service, and the Malays were largely engaged in subsistence agriculture on the kampongs or in menial jobs. Or, as it was colloquially put: 'The Mercedes-Benzes were owned by the Chinese, driven by the Indians and washed by the Malays.'

In the immediate post-independence order, there was a greater effort to share the spoils, but mostly among the elite. As a result, throughout the 1960s, inequality increased, especially within the Malay group itself. As Mahathir admitted and endeavoured to justify in 1970:

> These few Malays ... have waxed rich not because of themselves but because of the policy of a government supported by a huge majority of poor Malays. But if these few Malays are not enriched the poor Malays will not gain either. With the existence of the few rich Malays at least

the poor can say their fate is not entirely to serve rich non-Malays. From the point of view of racial ego ... the unseemly existence of Malay tycoons is essential.[19]

As noted, following the race riots of 1969, the government accelerated the redistributive aspect of their growth strategy, which was designed to remove past barriers to economic participation and break down polarisation through Malay affirmative action. The NEP became known as the Bumiputera (literally, 'sons of the soil') programme, incorporating quotas to raise the percentage ownership of Malays in the economy to a target of 30%. Given that this only officially reached 18.4%, in 1990 the NEP was later supplanted by the National Development Programme.

Like South Africa's Broad-Based Black Economic Empowerment policy, the Bumiputera is an affirmative action programme, operating in favour of a 'politically dominant and economically disadvantaged' ethnic majority.[20] In Malaysia's case, the increase in the share of Malay economic wealth was 'largely achieved by state buy-outs of foreign (mostly British) businesses', using petrodollars that became available with the development of Malaysia's oilfields in the 1970s. There was no nationalisation of private assets, only redistribution in terms of new assets or expanded economic capacity. Both programmes have led to significantly increased representation of previously disadvantaged groups in targeted areas, but structural and qualitative backlogs have persisted despite the policies.

When interviewed in 2007, Mahathir had an interesting view of his own legacy: 'When I came into office, many Chinese saw me as an "ultra"[Malay nationalist]. But I was able to convince them otherwise and to stay and work within Malaysia.' His greatest failure? 'Not being able to change the mindset of traditional Malays sufficiently to change their way of doing things and objectives in life.'[21]

Other critics of the Bumiputera regime say that it has worsened governance by its focus on preferential contracts in the absence of strong institutions, and by political indifference and the creation of a strong sense of entitlement. Bumiputera might have been a success in terms of education and skills training for disadvantaged ethnic Malays, says Anwar, but it was 'disastrous' in its cronyism and corruption, which only enriched a few. 'Unfortunately,' he says, 'this is the lesson South Africa has taken away.'

After the 20-year term envisaged by the NEP expired in 1990, the Malay share of corporate equity was estimated to have increased to one-fifth from almost nothing, though the Chinese share, Studwell observes, had also doubled to two-fifths. The elite bargain, or tycoon consensus, was doing better than ever. The benefits of the NEP are widely seen as not filtering down to all Malays, but rather as benefiting a small, cronyist elite connected to the ruling UMNO, referred to thus as 'UMNOputras'. While wealth disparities between ethnic groups have narrowed, the gaps have widened within these communities, especially the Malays.

As Malaysia moves to high-income status, this stabilising political measure is increasingly becoming a constraint as competition among high-income countries is tougher, hence the need to fully leverage the country's talent. Failure to reform the policy could trap Malaysia in middle-income status, while it is also not foreign to the governance weakness of the country, as is highlighted above, and the less efficient civil service, as has been emphasised by the World Bank.[22] Regardless, there is no consensus on what to do today with the Bumiputera. As one former top civil servant has summarised, 'It has so many problems, and foments corruption, but when I see the conditions of poverty among indigenous Malay communities, I believe it has to be retained. But it does', he acknowledges, 'create a culture of dependency, for politicians as much as citizens.'[23]

Yet, few question the validity of the Bumiputera concept. For it is realised that, in the words of one government official, you 'can't build a nation with 55% of the people unhappy'. It also, adds another, 'enabled the country to get over an inferiority complex created by colonialism and change their mindset'.

Anwar says that 'it is necessary, but should not be based on race, but rather need. It should', he says, 'not enrich the few, the billionaires, but rather should address the plight of the poor, whether Chinese, Indian or Malay.' The misuse of 1MBD, which was intended as a development fund to invest in industries that could create jobs for all Malaysians, irrespective of ethnicity – hence the name '1Malaysia' – illustrates the extent of this enrichment. There is a connection, says the man-most-likely, between politics and such economic outcomes. 'We need to be clear that democracy cannot just be a concert of the rich and the famous,' he states.

This raises a more profound point about the nature of the overarching political economy and the elite pact that gave rise to it. It may also help to explain why Malaysia has struggled to achieve its targeted high-income status, being stuck in a middle-income trap, and why the hoped-for productivity gains have not been achieved. Between 2010 and 2015, per capita GDP in Malaysia increased from US$9 069 to US$9 766, or by merely US$700, in contrast with China, which increased per capita GDP from US$4 516 to US$7 925 over the same period. The ambitious target of 3.7% labour productivity growth between 2016 and 2020 remains out of reach as productivity growth reached just 2.2% in 2018.[24]

The failure to keep making gains has its roots, it would seem, in the compact at the heart of Malaysia's apparent stability and success.

Conclusion: Politics, policy and productivity

Countries get rich by making or doing things and selling them. Their ability to do so depends on a combination of 3 Ps: politics, policy and productivity. Together these components produce, as Malaysia has to a great extent been able to do, effective macro-economic management, investment in human capital, the opening up to private capital, security and the establishment of a productive regional environment, and political stability.

This is not news. The Asian export manufacturing success story is well documented, including how states have moved out of low-tech to higher value addition, rising wages and rising living standards. Where there are problems and failures along the way, this tends to relate to politics and a deficiency of leadership, where leaders are unwilling to use their mandate to make tough decisions in their country's overall best interest. Rather, they govern by dividing, by favouring elite interest groups, where identity triumphs over issues. 'Politicians have to balance loyalties between interests and groups,' reminded S.R. Nathan, the former president of Singapore. 'You also need a strong personality to stand up to counter the contradiction between the need to create jobs and the rights of workers [since] democracy implies a strong sense of responsibility and a strong sense of obligation.' As Nathan cautioned, 'the central point is whether leaders have the will to realise their vision – at the expense of being popular'.[25]

In Malaysia, a small elite has been able to exploit political and social fault lines for their gain, in so doing being more the beneficiaries than the instigators of growth.[26] The system has remained far too dependent on – and thus vulnerable to – individuals in business and in government rather than political and social institutions. Yet, this has come at a cost. The operations of the elite have not spurred higher productivity even if they ensured political buy-in. Rather they have been notable beneficiaries of the post-independence political compact with its protectionism and subsidisation – rent-seeking by another term. That most of the tycoons in Malaysia made their money out of preferences, monopolies, government contracts and trading rather than manufacturing, as elsewhere, tells its own story, rather than a system underpinned by the sort of competitiveness and productivity gains that drive sustainable economic development. That large areas of Malaysia and, indeed, Southeast Asia are still poor, where wage gains have slowed and are in need of redistributive policies, is a result of political failure and the related influence of a small elite on economic policy. Moreover, to continue to compensate through redistribution has other risks, not least the creation of a sense of entitlement, the perpetuation of cultural myths, and in missing the point that Anwar makes forcefully: 'The greatest tool for social access and mobility is education.'

The real Malaysian success story has been the growth of small businesses, the expansion of farming output and the increase in the numbers of workers in foreign factories. It is ironic that foreign investment has driven up employment where there are such strong nationalistic, even xenophobic, impulses. Such sources of growth have their risks, too, not least given the fickleness of foreign consumers and market sensitivity to labour prices. As Studwell notes, 'Centralised governments that under-regulate competition (in the sense of failing to ensure its presence) and over-regulate market access (through restrictive licensing and non-competitive tendering) guarantee that merchant capitalists ... will rise to the top by arbitraging the economic inefficiencies created by the politicians.'[27] This is more likely, he contends, in environments where the democratic process is manipulated to favour the interests of one group or another.

The limits of economic competitiveness and sustainable growth are products of a political environment. In Malaysia's case, until now, this same political environment, which once assisted the country's economic growth through stability, is now preventing it from reaching its full potential.

Put differently, to paraphrase Bill Clinton, it's the political economy, stupid.

Chapter 7

Indonesia
The Cost of Corruption, the Benefits of Growth

> Corruption is much more likely to flourish where democratic foundations are weak and, as we have seen in many countries, where undemocratic and populist politicians can use it to their advantage.
>
> — Delia Ferreira Rubio, chair, Transparency International, 2019

Kalibanteng Dutch War Cemetery in Semarang in Indonesia contains more than 3 100 graves, mostly of civilians who perished during the Japanese occupation between 1942 and 1945, many of them women and children. Fields of white crosses stand out on the beautifully tended site with its manicured grass, swept walkways and pruned shrubbery.[1]

That more than 24 000 Dutchmen and women are honoured in seven Second World War memorials across the country is indicative, among other things, of Indonesia's violent and turbulent political history, and lengthy and messy colonial one.

Nearly 450 years of Portuguese and, from 1595, Dutch imperial involvement took various forms. The trading empire of the United East India Company was converted, upon its bankruptcy in 1800, to a colonial one under the Dutch crown in 1816, not unlike what happened to the Congo in the transfer of authority from King Leopold to the state. A brief and bloody British interregnum occurred when, in 1811, following the annexation of Holland by Napoleon, Sir Thomas Stamford Raffles, considered the founder of Singapore city (and of the London Zoo), led a military expedition that captured Java in just 45 days. His subjugation of local powerbrokers infamously included the 21 June 1812 assault on the southern Javanese city of Yogyakarta, when the sultan's court (the Kraton) was plundered by British troops.

At the rear of the Kalibanteng cemetery lie the remains of Dutch colonial troops, distinguishable by their ornate Muslim tablets. Most of these date from 1949 when the Dutch cracked down on the nationalists, who were led by a young civil engineer, Sukarno. Possibly as many as 200 000 Chinese, Dutch, Eurasians and Indonesians died in the revolution between the bold declaration of independence on 17 August 1945 and the transfer of sovereignty from the Netherlands to the Indonesian republic in December 1949.

Sadly, this was not the end of the killing.

A further 500 000 or so died in the purges – famously depicted in *The Year of Living Dangerously*, also the translated title of Sukarno's 1964 National Day speech – which accompanied the enforced transition of rule from Sukarno to General Suharto in 1966, portrayed as an attempt to restore order after a failed communist-led coup (which Suharto, the head of the reserves, it is alleged may have had a hand in). Whatever the reason, it offered the pretext for settling all manner of scores.

Despite misty-eyed socialist mythology, Sukarno's rule was neither democratic nor did it deliver development. Instead, as corruption and inefficiency throttled growth, in order to get by he relied on a combination of personal charisma, anti-Western posturing, including the expulsion of 50 000 Dutch settlers in the late 1950s, the oxymoronic purchase of Eastern bloc weaponry while birthing the Non-Aligned Movement at Bandung, and grand-scale heroic architecture.

By the time he left government, inflation was at 1 000% and the country's infrastructure was wobbling.

Heroic architecture ≠ development

The name Bandung is up there in international political iconography, the Indonesian city that was the site of the 1955 Asia-Africa Conference, a symbol of the heady days of struggle and promise.

There, leaders of 29 developing countries met under President Sukarno's chairmanship in the former Dutch Concordia recreation hall, renamed for the occasion the Gedung Merdeka (or Independence Building), to accelerate the national liberation struggles underway across their continents. Prime Minister Jawaharlal Nehru of India, who attended along with Vietnam's Ho Chi Minh, Pakistan's Mohammad Ali Bogra, Egypt's Lieutenant Colonel Gamal Abdel Nasser and China's Chou En-lai, among others, described Bandung as the 'focal centre and capital of Asia and Africa'.

Other than a sepia-stained jamboree, and some theatre, the conference delivered the Ten Bandung Principles, including respect for human rights, sovereignty and territorial integrity, equality of all nations and races, abstention from intervention, the right of self-defence, refraining from aggression, commitment to the peaceful settlement of disputes, promotion of national interests and co-operation, and respect for justice and international obligations.

That most summits come up with the same list, or parts of it, even today shows either how far ahead of their time the boys of Bandung were (because the leaders were all men), or how little things have progressed since.

In the 'Paris of Java', as Bandung was known in the colonial era, given its café lifestyle away from the oppressive coastal tropical heat, the presidents and prime ministers walked the 100 metres down Jalan Asia-Afrika to the conference from the luxurious Savoy Homann Hotel, with its wacky interior and curvaceous art deco balconies, to the conference hall. For some delegate nations, however, it was just the start of a long and tough road to peace and prosperity: Pakistan, Cambodia, Laos, Lebanon, Syria, Iraq, Afghanistan, Iran, Ethiopia, Liberia, Sudan and Libya were all to suffer coups and, in some cases, serially so and even outright civil war, most within the decade. In the case of North and South Vietnam, present as separate delegates, by 1975 the latter had been swallowed by the former amid widespread destruction and loss of more than 1.3 million lives.

Sukarno himself was gone in ten years, removed in a coup d'état by the stubby General Suharto, but not before he had brought his country to an economic precipice. Just as the colonialists had gone in for grandiose architecture to make a statement, Sukarno did much the same to attempt to make up for his lack of economic substance.

Jakarta, too, is a monument to his follies. At one end of the Jalan Thamrin thoroughfare, along Jalan Veteran, is Merdeka (Independence) Square featuring the Monumen Nasional, or Monas, a 132-metre-tall statue with a carved flame on top (dubbed 'Sukarno's final erection') and nearby the 120 000-capacity national mosque, the largest in Southeast Asia, a Masjid Istiqlal (of which Sukarno was the technical chief supervisor); at the other end is the Senayan sports complex, host to the 1962 Asian Games.

Along the way are myriad other unsuppressed nationalistic urges, including the swish glass and aluminium Hotel Indonesia (now the Kempinski), Sarinah department store (promoted as the Indonesian Emporium), the Semanggi clover-leaf bridge interchange, and various statues, including, further south, the infamous Pizza Delivery Man – a figure holding a large, flat object aloft.

Such eccentricities were alone not the source of the economic problem. It was that Sukarno lacked a plan for the development of Indonesia. His attempt at a 'development' bank was illustrative of this failing. It did not promote export or, for that matter, any industries. Rather it lent to traders. At the same time, the government pursued an affirmative action programme known as Benteng (or 'fortress') to encourage indigenous merchants. Sounds familiar?

Trading was – and is – not, however, investment in making things to sell – the way countries get rich. As Joe Studwell has put it, by the early

1960s, with ramping political pressures caused by the worsening economic situation, Indonesia 'became a zero-discipline fiscal environment' with the Central Bank 'feeding the beast of credit demand unquestioningly'.[2]

It is not that nation-building was unimportant; it is whether it was best achieved through growth or architecture.

Today Semarang is a busy port on the coast of northern Java, the most prosperous and populated of Indonesia's 13 500 islands, where 60% of Indonesians live on 7% of the land mass. Still, the country's average density of nearly 130 people per square kilometre – nearly three times the global average and four times that of Africa's – highlights Indonesia's status as the world's fourth most populous nation.

Despite, or perhaps because of, the numbers and its dispersed archipelago, Indonesia's infrastructure is poor. Jakarta's inadequacies are compounded by its ten-million inhabitants, treacle traffic and suffocating smog. The government is constantly caught between investing in transport between the islands and on them, the result being unsatisfactory in both respects, worsened by the antics of ancient, smoking trucks and buses and some 80 million *bebek* (literally, duck) – the ever-present motorcycle.

The impact of poor physical infrastructure is amplified by a stifling bureaucracy and policy vacillation. Indonesia ranks 109th of 189 countries on the World Bank's overall Doing Business indicators, just below Kenya, including a lowly 173rd on the ease of starting a business.[3]

Changes in mining regulations, especially the stipulation around majority local ownership within a decade and equally clumsy stipulations demanding beneficiation, have created uncertainty among foreign investors. A dire record of land management extends to the government's handling of the palm oil-induced deforestation crisis, which has seen Indonesia lose nearly a quarter of its forests since 1990.[4] Half of Indonesia's greenhouse gas emissions come from deforestation and other land-use changes, not to mention rapid biodiversity loss. Palm oil companies (supplying some of the world's largest household brands) are the main culprits, yet their growth continues unabated as government fails to enforce its own logging moratorium.

Sound economic decision-making has also proven hostage to the vagaries of populist politics, such as with the subsidy of fuel and food, which consumes nearly one-third, says the UN, of the budget, money that could be put to better uses. Overall, with 34 government ministries, recurrent expenditure (debt, subsidies and salaries) sucks 90% of the budget.

Again, this sounds all too familiar in an African context.

Bureaucratic obstructionism is compounded by a lack of skills and a national fatalism. The term *begitulah* (that's just the way it is), a local variant of *mañana* meets *insh'allah*, seems, more positively, to have its roots in a collectivist approach, in the overwhelming need for accommodation at every level.

The 'Etc.' issue

There has been, after all, a formidable 'national issue'. Not for nothing is Indonesia's motto *Bhinneka tunggal ika* (Unity in diversity), shades of South Africa's *!ke e: /xarra //ke*, once, in more recognisable terms, *Ex Unitae Vires*.

The 'express' rail service from Bandung to Jakarta winds its way through the Tangkuban Parahu ('upside down boat') volcanic range, over lime-green rice terraces and muddy, brown rivers, pocked with the red roofs of countless settlements. There were significant improvements in the national Kereta Api railways during the tenure of its CEO Ignasius Jonan, later appointed by President Jokowi as the country's transport minister. But the journey still takes more than three-and-a-half hours. The basic rail infrastructure is still much the same as it was during the Dutch colonial period, hence ambitious schemes for a high-speed national network, and the commencement of the construction of Jakarta's underground and light rail systems in 2014.

While the Dutch brought railways, irrigation and potable water systems, ports and 79 000 kilometres of roads, which became the basis of the modern Indonesian state, these benefits went hand in hand with humiliation, founded on rigid caste and social politics and racial elitism. These strains have continued to confound Indonesia – explaining, in part, the African empathy.

The Dutch, perhaps inadvertently, helped to forge a sense of national identity on the anvil of colonialism, although like similar experiences in Africa (think Congo) the outcome is a geographic nonsense and ethnic potpourri made up of 360 groups and 719 languages. And although 90% of the population is Muslim (making it the most populous Islamic nation), they are themselves divided over the relationship between their religion and government, between a secular or Sharia state. The activities of the al-Qaeda-backed Jemaah Islamiyah group, including the 2002 Bali bombings, heightened this divide, with the government realising the need to crack down, on the one hand, not least to preserve its (2018) 15.8-million visitor, US$14-billion annual revenue tourism industry,[5] at the same time taking care not to appear to be attacking Islam itself. A constant among Sukarno, Suharto and subsequent regimes has been the pluralist ideology of Pancasila (five principles), enshrined in the 1945 constitution.

The national military museum is replete with dioramas depicting the gallant independence struggle, while outside bits of East bloc hardware supplied to Suharto moulder in Jakarta's steam. In the foyer is a copy of Sukarno's independence statement of 1945: 'We, the people of Indonesia', it reads, 'hereby declare the independence of Indonesia. Matters relating to the transfer of power etc. will be executed carefully and as soon as possible.' As Elizabeth Pisani notes, however, Indonesians 'have been working on that "etc." ever since' in attempting to 'mash' together all of the extraneous geographic and diverse ethnic bits cobbled together, as she notes, 'from the wreckage' of 'colonisation, kleptocracy and a war of independence'.[6]

Compounding the ethnic issue is the role of the Chinese. From the seventeenth century, they have operated as Indonesia's economic middlemen, akin to the Lebanese in West Africa or Asians on the eastern African sea-board, in the process taking over many of the biggest and most profitable businesses. Liem Sioe Liong, an immigrant trader from Fujian, epitomised this role, using connections with the government to prosper, and building his Bank Central Asia into the provider of capital to domestic monopolies in cement, flour, toll roads and other sectors of Suharto family interest. Liem was forced to flee during the 1998 Jakarta riots, which targeted the Chinese community, and which saw an estimated US$20 billion of mostly Chinese capital flee to Singapore, Hong Kong and the US.

During the 1990s, it was estimated that ethnic Chinese, now little over 1% of the population, controlled more than 70% of the shares of publicly listed companies. Such minority interests echo across Africa, not least in South Africa.

These schisms reflect high and, according to the UN, widening inequal-ity, notably between urban and rural areas, and between the smaller and larger islands. The 53% of Indonesians in the cities produce three-quarters of the national GDP. Yet, in West Papua, for example, poverty is three times the national average. More than six million Indonesians work in the dias-pora, reflecting the shortage of wage opportunities back home.[7] Still, they send home an average, at least, of US$1 000 annually, an important source of succour and start-up funding alike to relatives and friends.

It is a country full of contradictions. McKinsey, the consultancy firm, has predicted that, with the right policy interventions, Indonesia could rise from being the world's sixteenth to seventh-largest economy by 2030.[8] There are more than 290 million mobile phones, many Indonesians having more than one in their pockets, and Jakarta tweets more than any other capital. But whereas 64 million Indonesians use Facebook,[9] 80 million have no electricity, 110 million live on less than two dollars a day and, according to government, nearly 29 million live in poverty.

No surprise, then, that business has been tightly entwined with politics and elite interests.

Cronyism and corruption

Ninety minutes' drive north-east of Semarang is the town of Kudus, famous for the production of *kretek* – clove-flavoured cigarettes. Invented by a Kudus local, Jamhari, who claimed the cloves helped his asthma, the industry grew to more than 200 factories around the town, although this has consolidated today to a few big players. Suharto's favoured son, Tommy, gained a monopoly on the cloves used in *kretek*. That was not all. He also attempted to squeeze government coffers for US$1.3 billion to finance his Timor car project, essentially at the outset little more than the rebadging of Korean Kia vehicles. Fortunately, the wheels fell off the economy, and thus the car, as the Central Bank skilfully and successfully stalled before that loan was fully made.

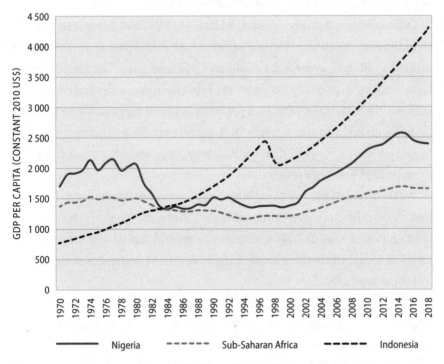

Figure 7.1: A tale of two giants: GDP per capita in Nigeria and Indonesia

Sources: World Bank national accounts data; OECD National Accounts data files.

It did not end with Tommy, although he was convicted of corruption charges and spent time in jail in the early 2000s. Suharto's wife, Ibu Tien, controlled the monopoly on the importation and milling of wheat, while daughter Siti Hardijanti Rukmana, aka Tutut, won the contract to build Jakarta's toll road. Mobutu Sese Seko would have been proud, if not a little jealous.

While the family made hay, the army ran thousands of businesses too. According to Transparency International's 2004 rankings, Suharto's was the most corrupt regime ever, embezzling perhaps as much as US$35 billion, or more than a billion a year from his 32 years in power.[10] Ultimately, his regime was undone by a combination of family and (military) institutional greed, along with its accompanying helter-skelter financial deregulation, permitting borrowing for the politically connected.

Little wonder that numerous academic studies have compared Nigeria to Indonesia.[11] Both were formed as one country, and nation, by Europeans around 1900, and governed by 'indirect' colonial rule. The economies of both once relied heavily on palm oil exports. Since independence, both suffered three decades of military misrule and corruption, the first coups being launched months apart – in September 1965 in Indonesia and in January 1966 in Nigeria. Their military regimes ended, too, at the same time, in 1998 and 1999 respectively.

While Indonesia is one-third larger in population than Nigeria, 265 million to 191 million in 2019, their administrations are similarly devolved, at least on paper. Nigeria has 36 states and a federal capital territory, divided into 774 local government areas. Indonesia has 34 provinces divided into 494 local regencies.[12]

In both, the impact of poor physical infrastructure is, for example, amplified by a stifling bureaucracy, discontiguous geography, violent history, ethnic diversity, widespread corruption and policy vacillation. And government in both has continuously struggled to get some of the basics right.

To top everything, like Nigeria, Indonesia has had to deal with an oil endowment. One of the reasons the Japanese coveted the Dutch colony, after the loss of more than 90% of its oil supply post the July 1941 US embargo, was its status then as the world's fourth-largest oil producer after the US, Iran and Romania. With the discovery of oil in the 1920s, Indonesia became the springboard for the creation of the Royal Dutch Shell Company.

Yet, for all of the above, Indonesia's development progress over the last 50 years has been, at least by African standards, nothing short of stellar.

But it works: Why?

In 1970 Indonesia's per capita income was less than Nigeria's, at just US$75 versus US$209. By 1990 it was up to US$516 (Nigeria's had shrunk to US$174), and by 2006 it was at US$1 308 and Nigeria's at US$733. As Figure 7.1 indicates, things have evened out since the oil price rise of the 2010s and as governance has improved in Nigeria, but Indonesians are today on average richer than Nigerians, while inequality in Indonesia is much lower comparatively, 0.381 to 0.488.[13]

One reason for this is sustained growth.

Between the years 1965 and 1997 the Indonesian economy grew at an average annual rate of almost 7%, graduating it from low-income to lower-middle-income status. Despite the Asian financial crisis, which saw GDP shrink nearly 14% in 1998, the economy picked up to average 4.6% growth from 2000 to 2004, and, thereafter, to at least 6%. Whereas Indonesia was able to diversify its exports to a large degree, Nigeria's dependence on oil had hardened.

This has had a dramatic impact on human development, with Indonesia's UN Human Development Index score improving by 45% from 1980 to 2013. In Indonesia, the life expectancy of a child at birth has more than doubled from 32 at independence,[14] to 69 years in 2017.[15] In Nigeria, life expectancy is just 54. Adult literacy, which was 10%–20%[16] at the time of independence in Indonesia, is now 95%;[17] in Nigeria it is 59%.[18] When Suharto took over, 60% of Indonesians lived in poverty. Sixty years later, it was just 9.8%.[19] In Nigeria, it has gone in the opposite direction, from 15% in 1960,[20] to an estimated 50%.[21]

That long-term growth matters is the first of five reasons separating Indonesia's development trajectory from Africa's and it explains why Southeast Asia has enjoyed a jobs-growth experience rather than just a growth one.

For all of Indonesia's excesses and failings, as one foreign business person based in Semarang put it, 'while developed countries would be happy for 5% (growth) anything less than that here and they are slipping back. It would be considered a disaster.'[22] The growth imperative has demanded having a plan for improved prosperity, which entrepreneurs can take advantage of, and its execution by the Suharto government brought results, reducing inflation at the start and steadily improving and extending governance. This was not a Soviet-style five-year industrialisation plan, however, since these seldom produce the goods, not least where the state is weak. Rather, the Indonesian plan for prosperity has been focused on providing the general framework for prosperity to occur, in this case through what is termed in Indonesia as MSMEs (micro, small and medium enterprises), which are responsible for more than half of GDP.

In Indonesia, during the colonial period, the agriculture sector had a relatively disappointing development history. Despite Dutch attempts to raise the living standards of Indonesians through improved agriculture methods and fairer land ownership in its so-called Ethical Policy in the early twentieth century, it remained an export-driven sector focused on coffee, indigo, tobacco and sugar, Europeans invariably benefiting more than the locals.

Under Suharto, the plan focused on improving agricultural yields, as has been a common first step across Southeast Asian countries, thereby increasing demand for services and goods and enabling the division of labour. Indonesia produced its first rice surplus in 1983.

This went hand in hand with the gradual liberalisation and internationalisation of the economy to secure international investment in setting up export-oriented manufacturing industries. As a result, by the late 1980s, Indonesia had not only become an agricultural exporter, but also an exporter of textiles, footwear, apparel and consumer goods.

The burgeoning domestic market, second, is a further factor in explaining Indonesia's success, not least given the size of its middle class, estimated at 75 million in 2013 and perhaps 140 million by 2020,[23] the biggest boom worldwide outside of China and India.

So, too, is the regional context: choose your neighbours, like your parents, carefully. Indonesia has – along the lines of the 'flying geese' development model – been able to pick up the pieces as regional economies have moved out of labour-intensive manufacturing. It is well positioned to become the next China as the neighbourhood behemoth moves up the value chain.

Third, whatever the problems with Indonesia's education system and shortage of skills necessary for future growth, the costs of labour still matter. While these are not a complete substitute for productivity, they are a good guide for foreign investors. In the furniture businesses clustered around Japara, for example, minimum monthly labour costs are at US$140, while comparable costs in Vietnam are up past US$200 and China is heading through US$500.

Fourth, while Indonesia's infrastructure is ropey and, along with all the other abovementioned constraints, may discount growth by as much as two to three percentage points annually, it has not derailed the economy.

Indonesia teaches that just as infrastructure is no silver bullet for success, it is seldom the sole reason for failure. Take Yogyakarta airport, scruffy, antiquated and analogue, where passengers are tripped up by touts and vendors. Yet, by making full use of what it has got, and it does not have much, its dinky terminal handles more flights and international visitors annually than Nairobi's Kenyatta airport, efficiently and without fuss or officiousness. Software in the form of officials and their attitude matters as much, it would seem, as the hardware. Thus, Indonesia's industrial parks – which have increased from 74 in 2014 to 87 in 2017 – have delivered jobs and growth,[24] whereas a legion of Nigerian industrial areas, such as Apapa, Ikeja, Ilupeju, Kirikiri, Trans Amadi in Port Harcourt and Ogba, have struggled and, in many cases, failed.

And finally, Suharto's downfall illustrates the most important reason of all for Indonesia's success – a commitment to popular welfare. Contrary to the notion that an authoritarian state is required for development, Indonesians were willing to accept that regime only when it delivered growth. As Peter Lewis notes, 'The comparison of Indonesia and Nigeria highlights the importance of developmental leadership in shifting the equilibrium of developing economies towards productive accumulation.' By contrast, the stability of Suharto's regime and 'his relatively consistent commitments to growth reveal a marked contrast to the sporadic tenure of Nigerian leaders and their strategies of clientelism, distributional politics, and economic predation.'[25] This enabled coalitions for growth to be established, in contrast to Nigeria where 'the polarisation of political elites and the weakness of central institutions gave rise to a more fragmented, competitive and anarchic realm of rent allocation and corruption.'[26]

Peter Cunliffe-Jones suggests in this regard that the reason for the difference between the two countries, Indonesia and Nigeria, is the degree of pressure that Indonesians put on their leaders to deliver.[27] They feared the consequences if they failed to deliver. When Suharto's excesses outweighed his successes and the nepotism proved too great a burden to bear, the old system of 'guided democracy' gave way to parliamentary democracy, given what Amartya Sen has stressed as the importance of the 'protective role of political democracy' in economic crises.[28] While democracy may, for some, be a messy system through which to navigate, its absence and the effect of weak institutions will, if Indonesia is anything to go by, ultimately be very costly.

Conclusion: Mixed bag, but better

Suharto was a mixed bag. Yet for all of his excesses, he dramatically improved matters. Not for nothing is he known as Bapak Pembangunan (Father of Development) to the polygamous Sukarno's Bung (Buddy). The general's rule fortunately coincided with the oil boom. But still much of this was wisely invested: in agriculture, education and infrastructure, especially roads. On the downside, his time in office represented the costs and benefits of big-man rule. While things got done quickly, there was endemic corruption with weak opposition and few checks and balances. There was little investment in institutions able to survive past his leadership.[29]

Whereas Suharto believed that Indonesia could continue in the same way, this model of 'do what the boss says' rule obviously did not work beyond a certain level of wealth and complexity.

His legacy of the twin problems of corruption and big-man rule continues to bedevil the country. In 2019 Indonesia was ranked 89/180 on Transparency International's Corruption Perceptions Index, in the company of Sri Lanka and Bosnia, and two places below China.[30] This contrasts with the country's changed circumstances: the stronger institutional and physical infrastructure, the larger, better educated and more assertive middle class, and greater integration with the global economy through, in part, the digital communications revolution.[31] The emergence of the mayor of Jakarta, Joko Widodo, popularly known as 'Jokowi', as president in 2014, from outside the established political and economic elites, may offer hope that the health of Indonesia, the giant of Southeast Asia on which so much depends, is improving. This will also require careful balancing of sensitivities between ethnic and religious groups, the economic interests of indigenous and Chinese constituencies, and central (Javanese) and regional government, all the while holding the diverse country together.

In this, Indonesia shows that the route to a more open and prosperous society is both fraught with difficulties and replete with opportunity.

Chapter 8

Thailand
Closed Politics, Open Tourism

One night in Bangkok and the world's your oyster
The bars are temples but the pearls ain't free
You'll find a god in every golden cloister
And if you're lucky then the god's a she
I can feel an angel sliding up to me.

— Murray Head, 1984

Boxing Day 2004. An earthquake measuring 9.1 on the Richter scale rips through the Indian Ocean. Just before 10 a.m. on Patong Beach in Phuket, Thailand, the water starts to recede from the shoreline, causing some curious beachgoers to wander in and see what is going on. The tsunami that follows takes 230 000 lives across 14 countries within a matter of hours.

Thailand received 11.5 million tourists that year, at that point its highest number ever. Some 5 400 people died from the tsunami, including 2 000 foreigners. More than 4 000 of these victims were never seen again.[1]

Patong Beach 15 years later bears little resemblance to its past, and few reminders apart from clearly indicated tsunami escape routes along the esplanade. The event also did not have a marked effect on tourism, as within two years Thailand's tourism numbers were up 20% to nearly 14 million. Perhaps tellingly, the number of annual tourists has since grown to 38 million, despite a multitude of tourist-sensitive events, including two coups d'état, political instability and terrorism attacks.

Thailand offers a paradox. It has maintained continued growth in the tourism sector in spite of political upheaval. While the country is open and welcoming, with a world-renowned service culture and paradise beaches, its politics is closed, stifling and somewhat vacuous.

One answer to this paradox lies in early and successful economic diversification; another in good macro-economic institutions. But riding on past glories without encouraging innovation means that inevitably, at some point, Thailand has become stuck. Thailand's lesson, and its warning, is that it always pays more to be open and welcoming – also to your own people.

Record and sources of Thai growth

Thailand has made, in the World Bank's view, 'remarkable progress in social and economic development' over the last four decades in moving from a low-income country to GDP per capita of US$6 500 in 2019.[2] This has been due to sustained high rates of economic growth, driven by both services and manufacturing, as a result of which poverty has been all but eradicated.

Between 1960 and the Asian crisis of 1997, Thailand's economy grew at an average annual rate of 7.5%, 'creating millions of jobs that helped pull millions of people out of poverty.'[3] Poverty declined from 67% in 1986 to 7.8% in 2017. While problems remain, including rural-urban inequality and education access, the range and pace of reforms have been remarkable, incorporating environmental sustainability, competitiveness, infrastructure and effective government.

As a result, Thailand has managed impressive macro-economic stability, low inflation and debt, and become one of the most economically open countries in the region, as measured by trade as a proportion of GDP. But it has got stuck, and fallen behind relative to others in the region. The country dropped from being ranked among the top 15 countries worldwide in the

World Bank's Doing Business Index between 2008 and 2012, to 49th in 2015. It has since recovered to the 27th spot out of 190 countries.[4] Value addition is low, poverty is increasing as inequality is widening, and educational outcomes are poor despite public spending of nearly 5% of GDP.[5] Moving further up the value chain will require greater effort and an altogether different set of capabilities, both from government and the labour force.

Thailand had early success at opening up and diversifying into manufacturing and industry, partly due to a stroke of good luck: in the 1980s, when the US was embattled in a trade war with Japan, many Japanese manufacturers were looking to move their manufacturing offshore, following the appreciation of the yen on the back of the September 1985 Plaza Accord to depreciate the US dollar in relation to the yen and Deutsche Mark. At the time, Thailand's government was under the visionary leadership of Prime Minister (and former General) Prem Tinsulanonda. True to messy political form, Prem had been appointed by parliament as Thailand's 16th prime minister to replace a predecessor who had been installed by a military junta. Prem's government saw the change coming and decided to take advantage.

With a planning team established within the prime minister's office as the National Economic and Social Development Board and headed from 1980 to 1989 by Dr Snoh Unakul, who was formerly the governor of the Central Bank and later deputy prime minister,[6] the government led a roadshow to Japan to convince Japanese companies to invest in Thailand. One of these was Toyota, which decided on Thailand based on generous foreign direct investment incentives and a liberal tax system and, of course, market size.[7]

Their vision paid off just as gas was discovered in the Gulf of Thailand in the early 1980s. The government established the Thai Board of Investment to attract foreign investment and expertise, and to offer tax incentives. The eastern seaboard special economic zone was established, which today includes a range of auto-manufacturers and parts suppliers, as well as a multitude of electronics firms.

The British-born (and Eton- and Oxford-educated) Abhisit Vejjajiva served as the leader of the Democrat Party from 2005 to 2019, and aged just 44 as prime minister from December 2008 to August 2011 – a time of great confusion in Thai politics. As prime minister, he attempted to promote a People's Agenda, focusing attention on the poorer sectors of Thai society, through two economic stimulus packages on infrastructure and cash subsidies.

'For light manufacturing and services,' Abhisit notes about the reasons behind the growth in the sector, 'the decision almost four decades ago to move from an import-substitution to an export-oriented strategy, with accompanying policies to reduce distortions (including necessary adjustments to the exchange rate) was crucial.'[8] Focus helped. 'Investment in infrastructure to develop the eastern seaboard project in order to set up a manufacturing base meant Thailand could take full advantage of the need for Japan to move its production base to the region.' As a result of these initiatives, 'the Thai economy continues to be well diversified', he notes. 'The agricultural sector has the potential for growth in food/alternative fuel/ agro-industry, [while] the existing manufacturing base in cars and electronics can be shifted to higher technology and value added.'

The export orientation of the economy has helped to bring about growth in the small- and medium-sized business community, given their role as parts suppliers to larger corporations, notes Somkiat Tangkitvanich, the director of the Thailand Development Research Institute (TDRI).[9]

One of the relative newcomers to the Thai manufacturing scene since 2000 is the British motorcycling icon Triumph.

The triumph of manufacturing

When Triumph Engineering went into receivership in 1983, the company was bought by English property developer John Bloor. For several years they kept boutique production of the venerable Triumph Bonneville ticking over, while the company designed a new model and recapitalised.

The original gamekeeper then turned poacher. Visits to Japan followed to appreciate modern facilities and manufacturing techniques, which were put into action with the opening of a new factory at Hinkley in the UK in 1991. It was equipped with the latest in computerised machine tools and manufacturing techniques.

Ten years later, Triumph opened another manufacturing site in Chonburi in Thailand, now one of three in that country, where it produces 80% of the 65 000 Triumphs sold worldwide annually. The Thai move inevitably led to concern among the 450 British workers that jobs would go abroad, but now there are 600 people employed in the UK, particularly due to growth on the R&D side. Triumph Motorcycles (Thailand) employs 1 220 workers.

The Triumph brand has been a motorcycling success story in recent years, with a rapidly expanding range of both modern and retro machines, which have resulted in increased volumes and profits. Rather than a threat to quality and the character of the Triumph machine, a critical part of that success has been transitioning production to Thailand.[10]

Triumph produces up to 300 bikes daily, six days a week in Thailand.

Triumph's Thai operation was born as a cost-effective supplier of components over which the parent company could retain control in terms of quality, price and lead times, as opposed to sourcing from third-party Indian or Chinese companies. A second good reason for the shift is that there are no import duties levied in bringing in machinery, components and materials from the UK. Moreover, by meeting a 40% local content requirement, Triumphs can be sold in the booming Thai market (Asia's largest for middleweight and large-capacity bikes) without a 60% import duty for foreign-made products, ensuring it is also well-positioned to supply the world's four largest powered two-wheel markets: India, China, Indonesia and Vietnam. As its CEO, Nick Bloor, summarises: 'Triumph chose Thailand over other markets ... based on a number of factors back in 2000, which are still relevant today.' In sum, 'the country has a very stable and supportive position on business that supports long-term investment, [and there is a] positive attitude of the Thai workforce towards education and learning new skills'. There is also 'a strong supplier base that supports the manufacture of our motorcycles'. All of this complements, he says, 'what we strive to achieve as a premium brand'.[11]

While Triumph is cagey about the exact incentives on offer, there is clearly something attractive in the package of cheap and industrious labour, liberal trade and tax breaks. Triumph is far from alone in Thailand. Honda's factory is ten minutes away, Ducati's an hour south, and Harley-Davidson 30 minutes beyond Ducati. Suzuki, Yamaha, Kawasaki and BMW also have factories, with a collective capacity of producing three million bikes annually.[12]

However, while Thailand's economy has benefited from the search for lower labour costs, the same imperative is driving some industries away. Textiles and garments, shoes and leather goods, and gems and jewellery have all been a major source of employment. For example, the textile and garment sector provided nearly 12% in total employment in 2012. As Thai wages have risen, its competitiveness in such labour-intensive industries has declined. This fell dramatically after the imposition of a minimum wage in 2013, causing these particular geese, to cite Kaname Akamatsu's well-known phrase, to fly elsewhere.[13]

A number of alternative strategies have been suggested and tested to reinvigorate competitiveness, including moving the production bases to low-wage countries, or moving up the value chain through design, branding and marketing.[14] Moving into higher-wage products, such as motorcycles, is, too, part of the answer. The three Thai Triumph factories are not simply trading on cheaper labour for assembly but produce sophisticated components, including injection mouldings and high-pressure castings. This explains the Thai government's next generation Eastern Economic Corridor plan, with its focus on so-called S-curve industries: autos, intelligent electronics, advanced agriculture and biotechnology, food processing, high-wealth and medical tourism, digital, robotics, aviation and logistics, health care, and biofuels and biochemical industries.[15]

Other sources, as former Prime Minister Abhisit notes, will have to plug this employment gap.

Agribusiness has helped. Mitr Phol is Thailand's largest sugar-processing business, contracting 40 000 farmers and employing 7 000 people directly. In addition to their successful sugar business, which produces three million tonnes per year, Mitr Phol has started a biofuels business to utilise waste from sugar processing. 'It is part of a positive cycle,' says Krisda Monthienvichienchai, president and CEO of Mitr Phol. 'The sugar processing produces waste, which we turn into energy, and ethanol, which we blend into fuel.'[16] The success of this has again, however, relied on government subsidies and the correct tariff pricing to incentivise the ethanol and energy businesses respectively. And, of course, it has also depended on being at the right place to farm this crop.

'You cannot be the best in every crop,' says Krisda. With Thailand's land and climatic suitability for sugar farming, this was a natural advantage. In addition to sugar, in which the country is the second-largest producer in the world after Brazil, Thailand is also first in rubber production, and a major producer of rice, palm oil and coffee.

There is a considerable upside in agriculture, in particular, given relatively poor rates of productivity and an increasingly ageing rural population. As the TDRI's Dr Tangkitvanich puts it: 'Agriculture comprises 30% of the workforce and just 10% of the value addition in the economy. Services is 50% in both measures and industry the rest.' And he argues that while Thailand has been successful 'in terms of economic diversification, we are now having to deal with relatively high-income disparity'.

Does politics matter?

Bangkok's Chinatown, known locally as Yaowarat, is now best known as a hustling and bustling tourist spot, with its smoking street food, lavish

temples and cheap curios. It is the epicentre of the modern Thai economy, from where Chinese Thais, today numbering around 15% of the total
70-million population, built their empires. Over 50 years in the late nineteenth and early twentieth centuries, around 20 000 Chinese entered the
country each year from southern China. Starting in menial tasks, such as
blacksmiths, labourers, rickshaw pullers, and rice and rubber farmers, they
quickly built up their wealth and influence, mostly through hard graft and
entrepreneurship.

But Chinatown is indirectly indicative of a fundamental disjuncture in
contemporary Thai society and in its economy. Thai Chinese dominate the
economic landscape out of proportion to their numbers. By the late 1990s,
Thai Chinese were estimated to own or control not less than 65% of Thai
banking assets, 60% of trade, and 90% of manufacturing investments.[17] As
a result of such power, the Thai Chinese have been the subject of repeated attempts to limit and redistribute their wealth. Little wonder they have
gained an influential presence among the political and military elite.

For Thailand, these issues are deeper than a sense of ethnic division and
widening inequality. It goes to the heart of how and by whom the country
is run. The commanding presence of a royalist and military elite is at the
centre of this political economy. The military have intervened to overturn
the government no fewer than 20 times in Thai politics since 1912, including on two occasions since 2000.[18] Thailand has strict lese-majesty laws,
which ban criticism of the monarchy, and shield the royal family from
public view and scrutiny. The royal family controls substantial assets, well
over US$30 billion, managed through the Crown Property Bureau, which
was established in 1938.[19]

This gulf of wealth has manifested in a volatile political environment,
especially since the removal of the populist prime minister, Thaksin
Shinawatra, in September 2006. Despite a democratic general election the
following December, the People's Power Party was unable to form a stable
government. Instead, Abhisit was sworn in as the 27th prime minister in

December 2008. By the following April, protests by the National United Front of Democracy Against Dictatorship (or Red Shirts) forced the cancellation of the Fourth East Asia Summit. The following April's Red Shirt protests resulted in 87 deaths and nearly 1 400 injured when the army attempted to disperse protesters. Then Prime Minister Abhisit was widely held responsible for the deaths and even charged with murder in 2013, although the case was later dismissed. Then, in July 2011, the opposition Pheu Thai Party, led by Yingluck Shinawatra (the younger sister of Thaksin Shinawatra), won the general election by a landslide. But the protests continued, demanding an end to the Thaksin regime.

In August 2014, Yingluck was replaced by army chief General Prayut Chan-o-cha. Elections have regularly continued amid this political turmoil, but they are hardly free and fair, by any objective measure. By 2019, Thailand was ranked as 'unfree' in Freedom House's indicators, with a score of 30/100 (where 100 is most free), placing it below Zimbabwe. Freedom House noted, 'Thailand is currently ruled by an unelected junta aligned with the country's monarchy and economic elites. Citizens are excluded from meaningful political participation.'[20] The freedom trend is constantly down, whatever the economic circumstances. During Prime Minister Abhisit's time, even while the stock market and the baht returned to their highest levels since the 1997 Asian financial crisis, Thailand's media freedoms deteriorated significantly.[21]

An oppressive state and limited freedoms ultimately impose a tax, no matter how 'open' and 'easy' it is to do business by conventional measures. One indication of this is that many of Thailand's largest domestic companies are investing increasing amounts abroad, other than in Thailand itself.[22]

Yet, just as the political environment has worsened, tourism has boomed, seemingly immune to political concerns – perhaps unsurprisingly, given that much of this boom is sourced from China itself.

More than one night in Bangkok

Tourists arriving at Bangkok's Suvarnabhumi Airport are welcomed by a colossal modern building with an impressive cantilevered roof, although few probably notice this. What they would notice, and this might be the basis for their decision to visit the country in the first place, is visa-free access – if you are from one of the 85 countries to which this exemption applies. What Thailand has realised, to their credit, is that convenience is king when it comes to tourism. So, try not to stop them, or even slow them down with unnecessary visa hurdles.

Tourists equal money. And in Thailand, they spend more money than anywhere else in Asia, with US$57 billion spent in 2017.[23] Travellers spend on average US$173 per day in Bangkok, according to Mastercard's Global Destination Cities Index, which has ranked Bangkok as the world's most-visited city every year since 2015.[24] The average daily spend, well below that of Singapore (US$286) and Paris (US$301), reflects Thailand's appeal to those at both ends of the spectrum: from backpackers on Contiki-type holidays, to big spenders doling out multiples more to stay in Bangkok's high-end hotels.

Tourism in Thailand has moved along a great deal in the past 40 years.

While the country acquired a reputation for sex tourism along the Patpong area of Bangkok, or in the seedy areas of Pattaya, much of it fuelled by the presence of large American military bases during the Cold War, it is now better known for its value-for-money family holidays. Yet, on the Big Mac Index,[25] at US$3.72 (in 2019) Thailand ranks as more expensive than Japan (US$3.60), China (US$3.05), Vietnam (US$2.80), the Philippines (US$2.67), Hong Kong (US$2.55), Indonesia (US$2.34), Taiwan, which is seventh cheapest (tied with South Africa), at US$2.24, and Malaysia (US$2.20).[26] Bangkok ranks at the 216th most expensive of 433 cities surveyed in cost of living rankings in 2019,[27] or 47/103 countries surveyed.[28]

Yet, in terms of tourism, Thailand is still known for its value. Average comparable hotel prices are well below other regions, at around US$90 per night (for a double room sharing), compared to the Caribbean at US$120, Latin America and North America at US$110, and Europe at US$105. Bangkok's price in June 2019 was €78, compared to Beijing at €97, Cape Town at €77, Kuala Lumpur at €58, Shanghai at €106, Sydney at €135, Tokyo at €137 and Singapore at €78.[29] Thailand is not cheap by international standards, but is competitive in Asia.

Similarly, as a top backpacker destination for many tourists, internal travel within Thailand is known to be relatively inexpensive.[30] Budget-friendly airlines, such as AirAsia, Bangkok Airways and Nok Air, have direct flight options across various cities in the country as well as international connections. In addition to air travel, Thailand has an extensive rail system covering over 4 000 kilometres and a road network that covers about 86% of country.[31] An average bus trip costs about US$4 and, comparatively, transportation in Bangkok is 5% cheaper than in Beijing and 66% cheaper than in Tokyo.[32]

Cost is clearly not everything: despite ranking relatively high compared to other Asian destinations like Malaysia and Vietnam on the Big Mac Index (one proxy measure for affordability), Thailand outranks every other Asian destination in terms of money spent by international tourists, according to data from the UN World Tourism Organisation.[33]

Abhisit adds that Thailand's tourism has benefited from (and made the most of) some natural advantages, such as beaches, and the Thais' service-mindedness, but that the shift to look outwards has helped.

Policy has certainly played its part.[34] For example, as noted above, passport holders of 67 countries enjoy visa-free access to Thailand, with another 18 countries receiving visas on arrival (including China, from where nearly ten million tourists arrived in 2018, or a quarter of Thailand's total arrivals).[35] Malaysia is the next-largest single source, at 12%. The whole of the Association of Southeast Asian Nations (ASEAN) accounts for 26%; Europe just 17%.[36]

Chinese tourists and the rise of the middle class in ASEAN

countries have been a source of great growth for Thailand, says Wiparat Tharateerapab, director of the Ministry of Tourism and Sports' Bureau of Economics. Another factor is its good geographical location and service culture – what Wiparat calls 'Thai-ness' – which has resulted in 60% of tourists returning after their first visit. All of this has required intra-government co-operation. 'Tourism is a complex issue,' she notes. The temples and beaches don't belong to the Ministry of Tourism. Temples are with the Ministry of Culture and the beaches with the Ministry of Forestry and Land. Roads are with the Ministry of Transport. The airports are with the Civil Aviation Authority. And,' she smiles, 'we also have to work with the tourist police.'

There has been a concerted marketing effort, starting with the 'Visit Thailand' campaign, again a product of the Prem regime in the mid-1980s, and progressing to the contemporary 'Amazing Thailand' slogan. The Thailand Tourism Authority (TAT) was created in its current guise in 1979. With 30 overseas offices, including five alone in China, it is focused on branding and marketing the Thai experience. TAT executives see 'over-tourism' as their major challenge, preferring a retreat to higher yields, which will, they plan, be achieved from 'better market segmentation'.

Careful management

Careful packaging, and an established service culture, help to explain why 90% of foreign visitors in Thailand are on holiday, compared to the 50% average in the rest of the world.[37]

Such slickness can be seen in the statistics. Whatever its political challenges, including the death of its much-loved king in 2016, Thailand's international tourism arrivals still grew by an impressive 9%, despite the sensitivity of this sector to traveller safety. Thailand ranks 11th among nations in international tourist arrivals, up from 18th ten years earlier. Only one Asian country is in the top ten: China.

Worldwide rank		
France	86 918	1
Spain	81 786	2
USA	76 941	3
China	60 740	4
Italy	58 253	5
Mexico	39 298	6
United Kingdom	37 651	7
Turkey	37 601	8
Germany	37 452	9
Thailand	35 381	10
African countries		
Morocco	11 349	32
South Africa	10 285	36
Egypt	8 157	42
Tunisia	7 052	45
Algeria	2 451	76
Zimbabwe	2 423	77
Côte d'Ivoire	1 800	90
Namibia	1 499	96
Mozambique	1 447	99
Uganda	1 402	101

Table 8.1: International tourist arrivals, 2017 (thousands)

Sources: World Tourism Organization; Yearbook of Tourism Statistics; Compendium of Tourism Statistics and data files.

With big numbers of tourists come fresh challenges and responsibilities. Following the 2004 tsunami, the country has also developed a skilled crisis communications capability, including early warning systems for tsunamis, diseases (such as SARS) and terrorism. The TAT has become known as a world leader in post-crisis tourism recovery, in which reputation management plays a major role.[38]

In part, this is down to the synergy achieved with Thai Airways, since 1991 a majority government-owned airline. With more than 100 aircraft in its fleet, and flying to 74 destinations, initially the national carrier was an asset, though decreasingly so as Bangkok has attracted more carriers as a regional hub, and Thai Airways became yet another loss-making national airline. TAT sees Thailand's central regional location as its key strategic tourism asset, along with the friendly service disposition of the Thai people.

Tourism now rivals manufacturing in terms of the sector's economic importance to Thailand, accounting for 11% of GDP. As the International Monetary Fund has noted, tourism is a key driver of growth and of the

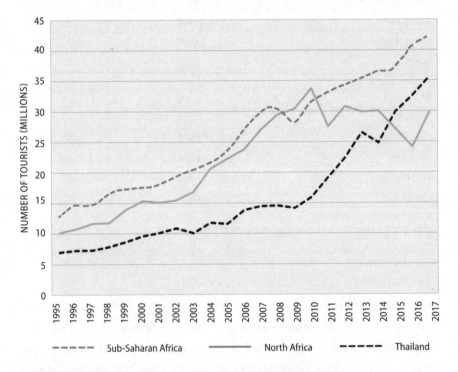

Figure 8.1: Comparing international tourism (number of arrivals)

Sources: World Bank Databank; World Tourism Organization; Yearbook of Tourism Statistics; Compendium of Tourism Statistics and data files, 2019.

large current account surplus, which stood at 10.6% of GDP in 2017. It helps to drive small and medium enterprise activity, including hotels, restaurants, wholesale and retail trade, and logistics, together accounting for almost 30% of GDP. These sectors are growing at over 3% per annum. In Bangkok and other major tourist destinations, some 40% of retail and wholesale trade is estimated to come from foreign tourists.[39]

These three sectors – hotels and restaurants, logistics and transportation, and trade – employ nearly 10 million Thais. It is estimated that a 10% drop in tourism would drag the Thai economy down by 0.9% of GDP growth.[40]

Suvarnabhumi was opened in 2006 to replace Don Mueang International Airport. Both are still in use as Thailand's tourism and its role as a regional aviation hub have boomed.[41]

Suvarnabhumi is the 21st busiest airport in the world, and ninth busiest in Asia.[42] It handled 63.4 million passengers and 95 airlines in 2018. Its growing importance reflects the increase in tourists to Thailand, from eight million to over 38 million in the 20 years to 2018. Don Mueang handles another 40 million annually,[43] 25% over its capacity.

Thailand has done well in tourism. Yet, imagine what might have been if it had acted sooner. Bangkok lost out to Singapore's Changi, ranked as the best worldwide in 2018,[44] with 65 million passengers.[45] Despite Bangkok being the natural hub geographically for flights into the region, Singapore moved ahead with developing Changi as a hub since Thailand was not progressing with its own plans.

Expansion plans due to finish in 2022 will see Suvarnabhumi increase capacity to 65 million passengers a year, and phase three to 125 million passengers by 2024. Yet, there have been challenges. The TDRI lists a number of reasons for slow progress at the airport, including lengthy immigration waiting times (at one time up to three hours);[46] transit day room issues; insufficient numbers of chairs and phone charging points; insufficient English-speaking staff; and poor information displays.[47]

Challenges are not limited to airport arrivals, however. While it is

Rank	Airport	Country	Passengers
1.	Hartsfield–Jackson Atlanta International Airport	United States	107.4
2.	Beijing Capital International Airport	China	101
3.	Dubai International Airport	United Arab Emirates	89.1
4.	Los Angeles International Airport	United States	87.5
5.	Tokyo Haneda Airport	Japan	87.1
6.	O'Hare International Airport	United States	83.3
7.	London Heathrow Airport	United Kingdom	80.1
8.	Hong Kong International Airport	Hong Kong SAR, China	74.5
9.	Shanghai Pudong International Airport	China	74
10.	Paris-Charles de Gaulle Airport	France	72.2
11.	Amsterdam Airport Schiphol	The Netherlands	71
12.	Indira Gandhi International Airport	India	69.9
13.	Guangzhou Baiyun International Airport	China	69.8
14.	Frankfurt Airport	Germany	69.5
15.	Dallas/Fort Worth International Airport	United States	69.1
16.	Seoul Incheon International Airport	Republic of Korea	68.4
17.	Istanbul Atatürk Airport	Turkey	68.2
18.	Soekarno-Hatta International Airport	Indonesia	66.9
19.	Singapore Changi Airport	Singapore	65.6
20.	Denver International Airport	United States	64.5
21.	Suvarnabhumi Airport	Thailand	63.4

Table 8.2: Top 21 airports worldwide by passengers (million), 2018 figures

Source: Airports Council International, 2018

Rank	Airport	Country	Passengers
1.	Johannesburg	South Africa	21.3
2.	Cairo	Egypt	15.9
3.	Cape Town	South Africa	10.7
4.	Addis Ababa	Ethiopia	10.2
5.	Casablanca	Morocco	9.3
6.	Algiers	Algeria	7.8
7.	Nairobi	Kenya	7.2
8.	Lagos	Nigeria	6.2
9.	Tunis	Tunisia	5.8
10.	Durban	South Africa	5.5

Table 8.3: Top ten African airports by passengers (million), 2017 figures
Source: https://qz.com/africa/1539984/south-africa-not-ethiopia-has-africas-biggest-airport/.

relatively easy to make travel bookings due to many online travel operators, low internet adoption among Thai small businesses creates an information barrier. The 2015 terrorist attack in Bangkok made a dent in visitor numbers, as did a boat accident in Phuket in 2018 where nearly 50 Chinese tourists lost their lives.[48] Safety has remained a concern, particularly road safety, and the risk of civil unrest and protest is also always beneath the surface.

Popularity at a cost

Maya Bay, part of the Phi Phi Islands near Phuket and the setting for drama thriller *The Beach* starring Leonardo DiCaprio, has been closed to visitors since mid-2018. 'Ecological recovery' has been ordered, due to the effects of mass tourism and yachting on the coastline and coral reefs. At its peak, the beach received 5 000 visitors a day. When it reopens by 2021, daily visitors will be capped at half this amount.[49]

This reflects the cost of tourism that is in disharmony with the environment. Thailand's animal tourism, which includes elephant, tiger and monkey encounters, has also come under fire recently for the unethical treatment of these animals.

According to Wiparat Tharateerapab of the Ministry of Tourism, environmental degradation is an inevitable cost of tourism growth, but in the interest of long-term sustainability in the sector, 'we must work to protect the environment for our own benefit'. Thailand must be more than just a cheap destination, she says.

There are ways to do it differently, even if the plastic litter and grimy streets of Phuket's beachside hints that this might be far off still. An association of some 70 hotels and resorts around the island has committed to phasing out some single-use plastics in 2019[50] – although this might be too little too late. Ecotourism, if done right, can be a game-changer, as it has been in some of Thailand's more progressive resorts, which serve a generation of environmentally aware travellers looking for low-impact holidays.

And this is not all. Bangkok's Chinatown is awash with shark fin soup restaurants. Despite growing international agreement that the shark fin trade is unsustainable and unnecessarily cruel (the fins are usually removed while the shark is still alive, and the rest of the animal is thrown back to drown to save space on fishing boats) and there is an official ban on this delicacy, this is in theory only. Ethical tourism has some way to go, yet offers greater future prospects, especially as the TAT's goal is greater market segmentation for higher-paying tourists.[51]

Conclusion: More than one night in Bangkok

Tourists in Thailand stay for an average of nine to ten days. Now the focus is on expanding the tourism sectors to include medical tourism (both for those seeking cheaper and better treatments); so-called MICE (meetings, incentives, conferences and exhibitions); developing new segments, such as film and sports tourism;[52] and developing new sites, including man-made attractions. The international market for medical tourism is estimated at US$36.9 billion and is projected to reach upwards of US$179 billion by 2026.[53] Thailand is the leading Southeast Asian destination for this sector. Both MICE and medical tourism growth will depend on boosting qualified human resources, with Thai workers seen as strong on service attributes but weak on languages. Along with concerns about a rickety transport infrastructure, notably connectivity to the public transport system, there are also fears about crime, safety and security. Of particular concern is Thailand's status as having the world's second-highest rate of traffic-related deaths.[54] And, as noted above, environmental sustainability is increasingly on the agenda, which requires at its core limiting the number of visitors. This will have to be balanced against the growing reliance on the tourist sector as manufacturing continues to decline.

The increasing number of Chinese tourists presents a great opportunity, but also a challenge, in that European tourists, in particular, are turned off by destinations that are busy and crowded. But as noted above, the trend is established: Asia's middle classes are increasingly the engine of tourist consumption, replacing Europeans and North Americans.

Overall, the lesson for Africa of Thailand's tourism growth is clear: focus first on your immediate neighbourhood, as the short-haul market is easiest to boost; maintain your natural resources well; segment the market in search of yield; establish an appealing narrative based on your advantages (in the case of Thailand, a widespread service culture and empathy); and, critically, ensure ease of access through visas and air flights.

But there is, too, a cautionary tale, just as there has been in manufacturing. Thailand's 'democratic deficit' has resulted not only in the loss of freedoms, but also a loss of innovation and dynamism. Tourism growth can only be sustained if infrastructure is strengthened, planning is improved, human resources are cultivated and developed, and ecological conservation is heeded.

Chapter 9

China
Cats, Mice and Cement

> In economic policy, I think we should allow some regions and enter-
> prises and some workers and peasants to earn more and enjoy more
> benefits sooner than others, in accordance with their hard work and
> greater contributions to society. If the standard of living of some peo-
> ple is raised first, this will inevitably be an impressive example to their
> 'neighbours', and people in other regions and units will want to learn
> from them. This will help the whole national economy to advance wave
> upon wave and help the people of all our nationalities to become pros-
> perous in a comparatively short period.
>
> — Deng Xiaoping, *Selected Works of Deng Xiaoping*, Volume II

'When I was a student in Shanghai in the 1980s, I had two ways of getting home [to Qufu in Shandong Province to the north],' recalls Professor
Changgang Guo of the Institute of Global Studies at Shanghai University,
while perusing Shanghai's twenty-first-century skyline from the perspective of the 150-year-old Bund on the other riverbank.[1] 'I could take a ship,'
he says, pointing at the Huangpu River in front of us, 'which would take
22 hours, and then a bus. That would cost 8 yuan. Or I could take a train
and then the bus. That would be 12 yuan. I would always choose to take
the cheapest option, just like I would take the normal bus over the air-
conditioned one, the difference between one or two yuan.' Guo's parents
were peasants, their farmland 'too small' to provide adequately for the

family, which only enjoyed meat 'five times a year unless we could catch a bird or two'. It was 'a very tough life' of subsistence and survival.

Since then, the world has changed for Guo and hundreds of millions of Chinese. Growth, in turn, has enabled modernisation, transforming society and global commerce. Per capita GDP has increased fivefold between 1990 and 2000, from US$200 to US$1 000. Between 2000 and 2010, average incomes rose again by the same rate, from US$1 000 to US$5 000, moving China into the ranks of middle-income countries. By 2018, China's per capita income had topped US$7 300 in constant terms.

The scale of change in China is unmatched worldwide. Since initiating market reforms in 1978 and changing from a centrally planned to a more market-based economy, China has averaged nearly 10% growth annually. The 'fastest sustained expansion by a major economy in history' has lifted more than 800 million people out of poverty, three-quarters of the global figure during this period.[2] Paradoxically, as one result of China's transformation, over half of the world's poorest now live in sub-Saharan Africa.

Statistics aside, the reduction in poverty, and increase in wealth, can be most visibly viewed in the changes in infrastructure, exemplified by the commissioning of two 600-megawatt power plants every week.

Shanghai illustrates China's infrastructural hyperbole par excellence. 'If you want to be rich, you must pave the roads first,' muses Zhu Jianhao, referring to an old Chinese saying as he surveys part of the city's skyline from the 37th floor, the home of the Municipality's Urban Renewal Team. He proudly points out the four-level, clover-leaf road intersection, virtually underneath the municipal HQ. As a young engineer, he had been responsible for the project in 1990, the first such intersection in Shanghai.

The city's first freeway was constructed in 1988, a 20-kilometre link to the nearby satellite city of Jiading, known as Hujia Expressway. Over the course of the following three decades, Shanghai, which has grown in population from six million in 1980 to 34 million in 2019, has installed more than 700 kilometres of metro, and 830 kilometres of highways among

13 000 kilometres of roads. The city's two international airports, Pudong and Hongqiao, handled 74 million and 43 million passengers respectively in 2018. Pudong was only opened this century. That Shanghai is today the world's busiest container port, moving 37 million TEUs (twenty-foot equivalent units) annually, is down to many things, not least its level of infrastructure: 125 berths, 4.7 million square metres of storage yards and more than 5 000 units of cargo handling equipment.[3] (China had seven of the top ten busiest ports in 2018; the exceptions being Singapore at number two, Busan in South Korea at number five and Dubai's Jebel Ali at number nine.)[4]

Housing supply in the city has increased ninetyfold since 1990, with Shanghai a field of cranes. Little wonder China consumed more cement in the three years from 2011 to 2013 than the US did in the whole twentieth century. In 2017, China produced more cement than the rest of the world combined.[5]

But it is not just the hardware that is seen as a great leap forward. Shanghai is a virtually cashless society, where Alipay, Baidu Wallet and WeChat are de rigueur and everything is done on smartphones. China has leapfrogged the PC age and arrived at a society that's connected by mobile apps only, where WeChat has 1.3 billion subscribers out of a potential market of 1.5 billion.

Yet, the infrastructure and connectivity narrative can be misleading in trying to understand what drove this remarkable change.

Justin Lin, the former chief economist at the World Bank, reminds us that China had frequent electricity blackouts in the 1980s when its industry was taking off, and comparatively speaking lacked adequate roads even as growth accelerated.[6] He also disputes the role of improvements to the business environment in driving success: China was only ranked 93/175 in the World Bank's Doing Business indicators in 2007, and scarcely climbed to 89/183 by 2010. The big ranking jump came much later between 2017 (78/190) and 2018 (46/190).

Beyond the statistical superlatives and infrastructure records, what lies at the heart of China's success, and can Africa take anything away from this experience? This is especially when culture, specifically Confucianism and the commitment to hard work and education, is sometimes anecdotally cited as a key reason for rapid growth in China as elsewhere across the region.

Confucianism, or something else?

Qufu, a three-hour high-speed train ride north from Shanghai, was the birthplace of Confucius over 2 500 years ago. At the heart of the tiny town centre, with willow-lined rivers and quiet streets, is the Confucius Temple, built to honour the sage shortly after his death in 479 BC. The 50-acre complex boasts a grandeur similar to Beijing's Forbidden City, with red walls and yellow roof tiles, the latter colour normally reserved for the emperor.[7]

Mao denounced Confucius, though he is now revered by China's leaders. While Mao's Red Guards smashed tombstones in acts of anti-Confucian vandalism, now China's leaders come each year on his birthday, 28 September, to lay flowers at the temple.

Confucius is known for making education available across China and for establishing the discipline of teaching. He devoted his life to learning and lecturing for the purpose of transforming and improving society, believing in the value of self-improvement. While he noted that learning was 'for the sake of the self', he also advocated public service as integral to a true education.

Today, Confucianism is taken to explain why Asia has enjoyed such dramatic development over the past three generations.

But it was not always seen this way. Confucius himself left for exile at the age of 56, when he realised that his political masters were uninterested in his policies and ideas. As recently as the 1950s, a number of international organisations had harsh views about the growth prospects of East Asia on account of the region's Confucian work ethic. The 1950 United Nations Human Development Report noted, for example, that 'economic progress will not be desired in a community where the people do not recognize that progress is possible'.[8] For many years China was similarly seen as hopeless.

Also, while Confucianism promotes diligence, education, commitment to the family and public service, it is less clear how it aligns with the mass consumerism that drives East Asia. Consumer items have grown well beyond the basics in the 1980s of colour televisions, refrigerators, washing machines and hi-fi systems to the proliferation of top-end sports cars and fashion brand names in the big cities.[9] There are more Bentleys and Porsches sold in China than any other market, and China is the single-largest emporium for Europe's luxury goods, confirming the 'Crazy Rich Asians' narrative. As Bin Zhao notes, 'looking around, one is more likely to see cut-throat competition than harmonious co-operation'.[10] Confucianism is no longer a search for the aesthetic essentials of life.

Rather than culture, as expressed by Confucianism, the reason for the success of the region and China specifically seems to be down to other factors, far less exotic and much more pragmatic.

A decidedly different path?

Analysts routinely cite two factors as key to China's success after 1976.

The first concerns the ability of the Chinese state to implement policy, to pull citizens in the same direction and to get its message across.

China has also never lacked strong government. Admiral Zheng He's expeditions to Africa and elsewhere in the early fifteenth century have been well chronicled. In the late eighteenth and early nineteenth centuries, the empire of the Middle Kingdom of China accounted for an estimated one-third of global wealth; today it is 16%. 'We have 3,000 years with a written language,' Xi Jinping reminded Donald Trump during the American president's visit to China in November 2017, as they walked through the Forbidden City's cobblestoned courtyards.[11]

Few would have argued that China under Mao Zedong was not strong: his great legacy to China was, it is commonly pronounced, an unprecedented level of internal political stability and a strong, unified state.

Still, it was not so long ago that China was a sick man of the global economy. By the mid-1970s, China had fallen way behind its Asian peers, mainly due to misguided economic policy, most notably during Mao's misnamed Great Leap Forward (1958–62) and the Cultural Revolution (1966–76), which saw production plummet to the point of famine, together causing the loss of perhaps as many as 40 million lives. Under Mao, China's share of the global economy hovered at 5%.

The problem was that there was little way of reforming the system in which Mao had become all-powerful on account of his role in China's liberation, and despite his failing record of delivery, he occupied a position of relative impunity, which has echoes of some African circumstances. While some – notably the president of the country, Liu Shaoqi (Mao was leader of the Communist Party of China), and then general secretary of the Secretariat, Deng Xiaoping – attempted to instigate a debate on market alternatives, they were dismissed and denigrated as 'capitalist roaders', a popular traitors' label during the Cultural Revolution.

This points to the second oft-stated reason: that China changed its policy direction with Deng, releasing market forces and the country's entrepreneurial talents. In so doing, the country employed its obvious organisational strengths towards a ruthless mercantilism. Deng brought an injection of market sanity as a relief to the ideological madness, epitomised by his 'it doesn't matter if a cat is black or white, so long as it catches mice'.

Deng had been influenced in the necessary steps by the exposure he gained in visits to Thailand, the US and Japan, where he 'saw exactly how large the gap had become'. This convinced him, according to Yang Guang

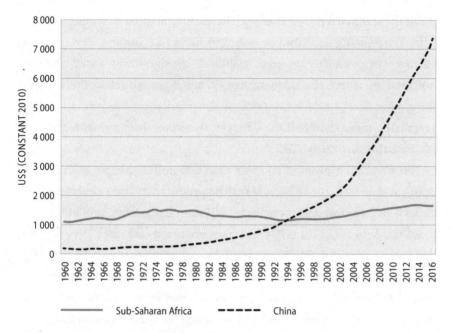

Figure 9.1: China and Africa: GDP per capita

Source: World Bank Databank, 2019.

of the Chinese Academy for Social Sciences, that the slogan of capitalism versus communism had become largely 'irrelevant' because the 'market and state were just tools for development', as the comment about the cat conveyed. There was also some pressure felt by the Communist Party of China. Yang recalls, 'I left high school at the time of the start of the Cultural Revolution. When I worked in the rural areas, farmers used to speak fondly to me of the "old society", the era of Chiang Kai-shek, when landlords would provide food to the peasants during the lean spring months. People wanted to be rewarded for their hard work.'[12]

This was complemented by a fierce focus on planning, starting with the regular five-year plans. At the same time, Deng also had to enhance regional stability, ending the border issues with Mongolia and Kazakhstan, the war in Vietnam, and negotiating the return of Hong Kong and Macau.

All of these initiatives, together with his economic policy changes, enabled what Yang Guang describes as 'a shift in focus to economic development'. Changes in productivity were facilitated by significant social changes, not least in where the Chinese live. When Mao launched the Cultural Revolution in the mid-1960s, 18% of the population lived in cities. Fifty years later, more than half the Chinese are urban dwellers, with a plan to increase this to 70% by 2035.[13]

This involved movement of more than 600 million people from its dirt-poor rural areas to the cities, where their productivity increased from 0.5% to 3.8% per annum and incomes by 8.5% annually, from US$307 in 1978 to US$2 381 in 2017.[14] In 1978 China's urbanisation rate was 17.9%; by 2014, this had increased to 54.8%, an annual average increase of 3.2%, the largest peacetime population movement in human history.[15] Moreover, this trend has lowered the dependency ratios,[16] and increased the rate of savings across the economy – so much so that government now believes that savings rates are too high and are trying to encourage consumer spending to stimulate the economy. China's household savings rate was 46% in 2019, contrasting with (and fuelling) high rates of government debt.[17] (South Africa's rate is, to take an example, less than three times this amount.)

In contrast to many other countries, China viewed urbanisation positively, as a source of growth and industrial development, says Yu Zhu, a professor of geography and demographics at Fujian Normal University.[18] The Hukou system of Mao's time, which strictly prohibited the movement of people through compulsory household registration, was gradually relaxed after 1978. Contemporary movement is unrestricted, apart from some restrictions in terms of access to social services, particularly government housing, for migrants. China has an estimated 240 million migrants (termed the *liudong renkou* or floating population).

As a result of this drive to the urban areas, today's 'supercities', such as Shanghai and Beijing, have property prices to rival London, Paris and Sydney, even while average incomes are lower by a factor of three.[19]

Government considered the resultant inequality between rural and urban areas 'a price worth paying' for growth. There was a willingness to focus on some regions first, notably Shenzhen in Guangzhou, before tackling other areas. This hints at the difficult trade-offs made in China's development. It was less a case of 'our turn to eat', as the Kenyan custom is, than 'wait your turn, and eventually everyone will prosper'.

Yet, rather than a sudden change of direction, China's development was an inevitable result of a much longer, ongoing process of modernisation.

The Shanghai effect

The basis of post-feudal modern China was cemented by the role of Sun Yat-sen. Influential in overthrowing the Qing dynasty in 1911, he had been born to poor farming parents. After a period abroad, Sun forsook his career as a doctor in 1894 to seek political fortunes, troubled by the way China had been humiliated by the technologically superior colonial powers. A 16-year exile followed a failed uprising in Guangzhou. Based in Japan, he founded the United League and continued to mobilise against the Qing regime. After a period of instability, Sun installed himself as generalissimo in 1923 until his death from cancer in 1925. He is still a symbol of Chinese modernisation.

When Sun came to Shanghai in 1912, he and his family set up house in a two-storey Western-style building in the former French concessionary area of the city. Even by his global standards, he would have found it a very modern, cosmopolitan city.

Once a small fishing village on the Huangpu River, Shanghai developed during the late Qing dynasty as a trading port. In 1842, following their victory in the First Opium War, the British opened a concession in Shanghai. Thereafter, the city entered a period of growth and transformation interrupted only by the Mao regime. French, American and Japanese concessions soon followed that of Britain.

By the 1930s, Shanghai had developed into the most important port and most modern city in Asia, as notorious for its licentious character as it was famed for its banks and business. Known as 'the wicked old Paris of the Orient', with 'as vivid a cast of chancers, schemers, exhibitionists, double-dealers and self-made villains as had ever been assembled in one place', the city was 'both glamorous and squalid, extremely rich and poor, unscrupulous and tough'.[20] Street names in Shanghai's Old City – Honglangan Jie ('street of the red banisters') and Hongzhuang Nong ('red hamlet lane') – invoke not the colours of Marxism-Leninism but the brightly painted facades of the legal and ubiquitous brothels. 'Tit-pinch lane', Monai Nong, was narrow enough, as the name suggests, to provide pedestrians with groping opportunities.[21] The term, to 'shanghai', lower case, now means to coerce or scam.

It was a city of what were, by the standards of the time, stunning mod cons. The Astor House Hotel was established in 1846 as Richards' Hotel and Restaurant near the confluence of the Huangpu River, where it remains. Enjoying the reputation as the finest hotel in China – Albert Einstein, Charlie Chaplin and Zhou Enlai have all stayed there – this was the site of the debut of the first telephone, first electric lamp and talking movie in China. The Peacock Hall ballroom was once the site of the Shanghai Stock Exchange.

The city's rise came on the back of commerce, but of a shady kind. By the 1830s, 24 000 chests of opium were imported annually from India at a vast profit (estimated at £100 per case), enough to feed two million addicts. When the Chinese authorities resisted, after lobbying by William Jardine, the Scotsman who later co-founded Jardine, Matheson & Co., the British parliament sent 4 000 troops to China in what became the First Opium War. By 1842, the troops had established Shanghai and four other coastal cities, Canton, Amoy, Foochow and Ningpo, as treaty ports, granting extraterritorial immunity from Chinese law to British citizens and some other Westerners.[22]

The world's largest banks and trading houses were set up along the area on the river known as the Bund.

The city was a prototypical export processing zone: no visas or passports were required. At its heart it was a trading emporium, a quality that Shanghai has perfected today. In the years leading up to the Second World War, Shanghai became a haven for Jews fleeing Nazi-controlled Europe, with more than 20 000 finding refuge.

This changed forever with the Japanese invasion in 1937, when foreigners were evacuated or interned. During the war, all territorial concessions were formally signed over to Chiang Kai-shek and the Kuomintang government. After the communist takeover in 1949, the city and its industry suffered, especially during the Cultural Revolution, as hundreds of thousands of Shanghainese were sent to work in rural areas throughout China. The advent of Deng Xiaoping's open-door policy allowed its contemporary phase to take place, signalling a renaissance for the commercial Shanghai of the pre-war years.

Liberal Shanghai eventually wove its way back into the Communist Party through Rong Yiren, the so-called red capitalist and vice president from 1993 to 1998, whose family were well-known industrialists in Shanghai pre-1949. Although he 'did time' as a janitor during the Cultural Revolution and his assets were confiscated, he was rehabilitated by the rise of Deng. At the end of his life he had accumulated a fortune through the CITIC Group, which, although a state-owned investment company, operates like a listed multinational – the 45-storey ultra-modern CITIC Square on Nanjing West Road is testimony of its might.

Shanghai has been an open, modern city for 170 years, and it remains so. In this sense, Shanghai is also a microcosm of China's development. It was not sudden at all, but rather a gradual shift, a piecemeal move to liberalisation, as Justin Lin observes below.

Lessons to emulate, things to avoid

Some 80 000 Africans visit China every year to study the country, 6 000 of them as full-time, full-scholarship students. What good lessons might they learn? The first of these is counter-intuitive. 'Don't try and imitate China,' says Kobus van der Wath, who established The Beijing Axis, an advisory and trading operation, in 2002.[23] 'Its success is not down to export to GDP ratios, or the extent of accumulation of foreign direct investment, or the statistics on infrastructure. Rather,' he notes, 'it is about having sound policy, a good and continuously evolving plan to implement it, and discipline in so doing.'

Justin Lin seconds this view, noting that to get to China's level of performance, African countries should not aim too high and attempt to imitate its high-income example, but rather adapt to their own set realities and discover their comparative advantage. He highlights the difference between what China and East Asia did in utilising low-tech, labour-absorptive industries and gradually moving up the value chain, and what Africa attempted in the 1960s through income substitution. The latter approach failed as it created 'white elephants', which could not compete without government subsidies.

China, by contrast, learnt from the Mauritius example, says Lin, in creating 'enclave' conditions through export processing zones, which enabled policy changes in patches to encourage industry while 'leaving domestic institutional reforms for later'. He adds that 'you need an honest assessment of your capacity – people, skills, resources, constraints, advantages – in trying to develop. All successful countries start with what they have rather than with what they don't have.'

There is also, however, much more to the Chinese model than just economic liberalisation. It involved significant and ongoing bureaucratic reforms to ensure efficiency and accountability. This enabled continuous improvements in productivity, which were fuelled by entrepreneurship. This was, in the words of Lin and his African Development Bank counterpart as chief economist, Célestin Monga, 'facilitated by an enabling government that provides appropriate infrastructure and institutions and encourages learning and knowledge sharing'.[24] Or as one senior Chinese diplomat put it: 'The critical part of the Chinese experience is in getting the right people in the right place to enable government. This ensures reform, opening up, governance and delivery,' he notes. 'And discipline is key.'[25]

This relates to another good lesson: the institutionalisation of 'management by objectives'. Performance targets are routinely monitored. Any failure to achieve set goals leads to poor evaluations, and lower incomes and negative career prospects, reminds Professor Guo. Poor bureaucratic performance has consequences.

On the other side of the lessons ledger, there are several aspects that suggest caution in attempting to apply the China example.

Unlike most African circumstances, China is virtually a mono-ethnic society. Whereas there are more than 50 classified ethnic groups, 91.5% of the population is regarded as Han. Africa's national make-up is more complex and reliant on consensus more than diktat as a mode of government, as Ethiopia has recently shown, for example.

Next, there is a danger in believing that China's success is down to authoritarianism. As the University of Michigan's Yuen Yuen Ang cautions: 'For other authoritarian governments keen to emulate China, their leaders should not pick up the wrong lessons. China's economic success is not proof that relying on top-down commands and suppressing bottom-up initiative works. In fact, it's the exact opposite: the disastrous decades under Mao proved that this kind of leadership fails.'[26]

There is, moreover, little evidence that Africans would stomach the Chinese means of ensuring rules-based development, moving people around from the farms to the cities, or even the methods to end corruption. More than a million Communist Party officials have been disciplined for corrupt practices in recent years,[27] and thousands executed annually. Moreover, Africans have fought for and won democracy and government's respect for human rights over the last 30 years, and they are unlikely to give this up easily.

Similarly, African attempts to pursue a business-party-government 'iron triangle', of the sort that dominates the Chinese polity, have generally ended in failure. This model may work in a market large enough to fire investment through local demand, but is unlikely to succeed in fragmented and much smaller African environments. Even though the performance of state-owned enterprises, which account for 70% of all corporate borrowing and roughly a third of the economy,[28] has lagged behind the private sector, reforms have been halting, especially in strategic sectors – known as 'national champions' – such as aerospace, telecoms, power generation, carmaking, and ship-building.[29] Deng's policy of separating party and government, and government and business, has seemingly been officially abandoned.[30]

While China's high growth has been sustained for over 30 years, it has been largely infrastructure- and consumption-driven. As a result, government has stacked up its debt as high as its towering skyscrapers, perhaps touching as high as 300% of GDP in 2019 (if central, local, commercial and state-owned enterprise debts are lumped together). The so-called Pudong model of growth, with LGFVs (local government financing vehicles) that enable lightning-speed infrastructure growth, certainly has its limits. Attempts to diversify into tech, for example, have been successful, but the returns to hi-tech are significantly lower than those to bricks and mortar (or concrete and glass). The high costs of real estate, compounding debt, falling growth and rising inequality look like a perfect storm for China. Even as government controls all information and communication channels, banning sites like Google, Facebook and WhatsApp, the risk of a popular insurgency is not out of the question, as youth unrest in Hong Kong in 2019 has shown. China's Gini coefficient has risen by 15 points since 1990, to 0.50 (where 0 is perfect equality) in 2018.[31]

Consumption-driven growth is capped by physical limits – whether the continued availability of natural resources, population growth, continued increases in disposable income, or the allowances China sets itself in terms of carbon emissions. Already, government's push for cleaner development has increased the price of cement. But when China's own resources have run out, and its domestic consumption and population growth (the latter already a cause of great concern to government) have slowed, it will have to turn to other sources of growth. This might explain its fast-growing presence on the African continent and the push behind the Belt and Road Initiative.

Related to this, there is an environmental downside to such consumption-fuelled growth. While it is not as bad as India (which has the seven most air-polluted cities worldwide), China has 60 of the world's 100 worst. This much was acknowledged by Xi Jinping in professing that 'clear waters and green mountains are as valuable as mountains of gold and silver' (*lüshui qingshan jiushi jinshan yinshan*),[32] a theme he first picked up on in 2005 as party secretary for Zhejiang. China's lights – and its industry – are kept on primarily by coal, supplying 70% of its energy needs,[33] already making China the world's largest energy producer from coal, though there are plans to increase this by a further 20%.[34] This does not mean, however, that China is stuck on this path – on the contrary, it can lead global change. To do so, it will have to manage vested interests, such as in the construction sector and related industries.

Conclusion: A chance to do it differently, again

Volkswagen has run a joint venture with the Chinese government since 1984. By 2019 it had captured nearly 10% of China's 23-million vehicle market, the largest in the world, turning over €30 billion annually, accounting for 40% of the VW Group's profits, and employing 35 000 people directly across eight vehicle and two engine plants. The Anting III plant in Shanghai, which produces 300 000 cars a year, is a highly automated modern factory with just a sprinkling of staff operating the giant presses that clank, bang and squeeze out panels and the whirling and spinning orange robot arms that weld them together.

The level of automation reflects a big change in China, from a low-cost sweatshop in the 1980s and 1990s to an increasingly technologically sophisticated market, from US$1 per hour in 2004 at VW to over US$15 on average 15 years later. This, too, is evident in the relative productivity of Volkswagen's Chinese plants, all ranking at the top of the 120 worldwide. And while VW's Chinese operation was once a technology 'taker' assimilating European-sourced R&D until the 1990s, from the 2000s it has increasingly become a tech provider, with over 2 000 staff focused on developing specific local and, increasingly, global solutions. China is planned to become a major centre for VW's e-mobility project, which will commit over €100 billion worldwide, and more than half of this to China, in finding solutions to digitisation, autonomous vehicles and new power systems.

Like other carmakers, VW acknowledges that the future is about software and not hardware, where connectivity is the critical element in the vehicle's performance, and where the competitors are decreasingly in this regard solely other car manufacturers but rather data and tech companies of the likes of Amazon, Facebook and Google.

Hence, the VW focus on creating a platform that marries skills in IT and manufacturing, at both of which the Chinese workforce, in VW's words, 'excels'.

This is a metaphor for a future economic model, says Yang Guang. China cannot, he observes, rely on cheap migrant labour from the rural areas to plug the low-wage gap, not least because this source of labour is drying up, and also because of the environmental impact of this model, premised as it is on increasing consumption. And, Yang points out, the cost of development naturally increases as you move up the production ladder: 'Huawei spends billions on R&D, for small margins; makers of textiles and shoes don't have to do this.' China's economy has in recent years moved into tech and services, with its three largest public companies – the mammoths Alibaba, TenCent and the Industrial and Commercial Bank of China – all falling into this category.

Whatever the model, in all likelihood China – and the world – will have to get used to a lower rate of growth, more in the 3%–4% margins, than 6%–10%. Three per cent growth still means adding an economy every year of some US$400 billion, the same size as the economy of Argentina, South Africa, Ireland or Israel. But this portends other challenges.

Xunlei Li is, in his day job, an economist at Zhongtai Securities. He also serves as an adviser to the Central Committee and the Standing Committee of Shanghai's Municipality. He warns that China is 'facing a structural problem. The focus on creating profits has created social inequality, which could create long-term problems in the pattern of growth.'[35] There is also an 'asset bubble', especially in property prices, in which 'people have the majority of their personal investment'. Such problems, he reflects, of high prices, low wages and the high cost of property particularly affect young people, hence the social disquiet seen in Hong Kong.

There are valid questions about whether a consumption-driven economy of this nature can continue unabated, for reasons relating to the global order and environment as much as the housing market and debt situation.

China emits more carbon than the US and the countries of the European Union combined. It is fraught with paradox. Even though it is still building coal-fired power plants, it is also the world's biggest investor in renewables and has the largest solar capacity. Renewables constitute one-quarter of its energy mix, most of which is from hydro.[36] Radically changing this mix will likely require altering consumption patterns, especially in China's burgeoning cities, which produce an estimated 85% of the country's emissions, with the country overall creating more than 27% of the world's total. No country has, in living memory, made a bigger, more positive impact on poverty and global growth. So, too, however, no country can make a bigger impact on climate change if it were to get renewables right and reduce its carbon emissions.

China remains caught between relatively poor rural and affluent urban areas, and within the latter between its Tier I cities (such as Guangdong,

Shenzhen, Beijing and Shanghai), Tier II (Nanjing, Hangzhou, etc.) and the rest. It is the difference between a consumer-driven cashless society with Western real estate prices – where per capita incomes are over US$25 000 and American accents and overseas college degrees are the norm – and incomes less than a third of this amount.

China is fraught with such paradox. Few states have displayed China's ability to make the change from a command economy to market socialism and from Mao's totalitarianism to today's conditions of relative openness. The development of a surveillance state employing big data, artificial intelligence and facial recognition intent on shrinking the space for individual freedoms contrasts with a relentless pace towards the globalisation of China.[37] Given the scale of China's socio-economic transformation over the past 40 years, it would be reckless to rule out a move to greater individual freedoms, of the sort that Africans have won, though it is difficult to imagine on the current trajectory. Whether it changes, or not, the decision is sure to be China's alone.

Perhaps the environmental and political issues raised hold China to a different standard from others in Asia, or indeed farther afield. Yet, China's extraordinary success and example beget this focus and expectation. Bridging these urban, rural and intergenerational worlds and maintaining growth to do so is as much a political as an economic policy challenge – another lesson for Africa.

*

China's great change this century was down to a policy shift towards openness, towards global markets and capital. But the pattern of development had started much earlier in the mid-nineteenth century with Shanghai's enclave economy, which drove international connections, however perverse and skewed these may have been. Chairman Mao's period reflected both continuity in state consolidation and an aberration in a continuous process of economic openness and expansion. The ascent of Deng Xiaoping and his cats and mice ensured it got back on track. Many Africans aspire to 'be like China'. But China also tells a cautionary tale of the cost of such rapid growth and the increasing costs of maintaining it.

Chapter 10

Vietnam
Making Better Development Choices

It was patriotism, not communism, that inspired me.

— Ho Chi Minh

In the last 30 years, Vietnam has become one of the world's great development success stories, rising from the ranks of the poorest countries. On the strength of a nearly 7 percent average growth rate and targeted government policies, tens of millions of people have lifted themselves out of extreme poverty.

— Jim Yong Kim, president of the World Bank, 2016

Hanoi's Opera House provides the maudlin opening to Pierre Schoendoerffer's cinematic masterpiece *Dien Bien Phu*, the film taking its title from the site of the French defeat in Vietnam that led to the Geneva armistice in 1954, setting the stage for the American intervention. The film portrays brilliantly the schizophrenic world of colonial France, or for that matter Germany, Italy, Portugal or Britain. While young men were fighting and dying in Dien Bien Phu just 300 kilometres away to their north-west, the life of classical opera and sophisticated soirées carried on virtually regardless in refined Hanoi.

General Vo Nguyen Giap, the hero of Dien Bien Phu, is considered as 'second only to Uncle Ho [Chi Minh]' in the minds of many Vietnamese. The self-taught soldier met Ho in China after the Vietnamese leader submitted an article to a newspaper Giap was editing. Asked to raise a fighting army, he set about the task with a tiny nucleus of just 34 guerrillas, armed with flintlock weapons. The 'Grand General', the son of a rice grower, created a force that defeated the French in 1954 and the Americans who followed. Thousands of Vietnamese paid their respects on Giap's death, aged 102, in 2013.[1]

Following his victory at Dien Bien Phu, General Giap spent the next 60 years living in a former French villa, now alongside the Congress building, and just across an expansive green lawn on the other side of which lies Ho in his stern, Soviet-style mausoleum. Giap experienced immense hardships along the way. His first wife had died in a French prison along with an infant daughter; his wife's sister had been executed by a French guillotine. 'He would sit there with his commanders,' says his son Nam, 62, pointing at a concrete table and four chairs at the back of the house, 'and they would spread out the maps and discuss the war.' Overhead was a pergola whose uprights were made from shell casings welded together. '155 mm,' smiles Nam. Under the house was a bomb shelter, necessary during the various American air offensives on Hanoi. Just inside was the spare room, which has been turned into a shrine, with his image, medals and two urns of sand, one from Truong Sa (Spratly Islands), the other from Vi Xuyen, the site of the border battle against China, among the exhibits.

Nam spreads out maps of Dien Bien Phu in the conference room where the elfin-like Giap would host regular meetings with foreign dignitaries, his main occupation after his retirement as defence minister in 1981 and from the Politburo the following year.

Without a formal military training – 'he learnt from real battles,' says Nam – Giap's crucial skills were in managing the logistics and politics to sustain the war in the South. His enormous losses of troops must call into question the wisdom of his military tactics, yet serve to highlight the disparity of the stakes between the Vietnamese nationalists and various foreign armies. Put differently, the end justified the means.

Dien Bien Phu was testament to his fortitude and ingenuity. Much to the surprise of the French, Giap's forces were able to haul artillery pieces, many of which had been supplied by the Chinese from stock captured from the nationalist Kuomintang and in the Korean War, up and over the never-ending series of mountains and install them in burrows on the hillsides, making them virtually impervious to French counter-fire and air strikes.

Likened by Giap to a rice bowl, with his forces on the mountainous rim and the French at the bottom on the plain and its hillocks, Dien Bien Phu proved indefensible, despite carefully dug French trenches and fortifications. Unlike earlier battles, where Giap had squandered his forces in costly frontal attacks, he cautiously amassed his troops and supplies before the battle commenced. Viet Minh artillery rained down on the French troops from the surrounding hills. After the airfield was closed, provisions and reinforcements could only be parachuted in. By the time the French realised they were in a trap and could not win, it was too late to get out.

On 7 May, the day the French surrendered, talks opened in Geneva to end colonialism in Indochina. Liberation took a generation longer still with the temporary division of the country along the 17th parallel and the creation of a South Vietnamese government with American support.

Giap's diplomatic skills were also crucial in keeping open supply lines from China and the Soviet Union. At home, he organised the movement of troops and matériel down the Ho Chi Minh Trail, where thousands of porters cycled and shuffled their way down the border with Laos and Cambodia. 'People should not be overawed by the power of modern weapons,' Giap wrote. 'It is the value of human beings that in the end will decide victory.' And so was born his concept of a 'people's war'.

During the 21-year struggle that followed against the Americans and their South Vietnamese ally, Giap's star waned as that of his hardline rival Le Duan, the general secretary of the Communist Party, rose. After the disastrous cost of the Tet and Easter offensives, Giap again took military centre stage. By 1982, however, he was once more frozen out by the hierarchy, nominally a deputy prime minister in charge of science and technology, heading a national birth control campaign. He preferred, in his twilight years, to spend time hosting visitors and chatting about the war, as the numerous gifts in his banner-bedecked reception hall testify. Despite calls from former comrades to engage again in politics, he avoided being drawn into criticisms of the regime.

There were differences, however. Some contend he was unreconstructed, and dismissive of the market reforms made after 1986. Others say Giap was interested in retaining the South's capitalist-based system at the end of the war in April 1975 alongside the command economic model of the North, but was overruled by his colleagues, notably Le Duan. This explanation may, *ex post facto*, be an excuse to avoid personal responsibility for the economic disaster that followed unification.

By the early 1980s, the country faced food shortages as a result of the lack of incentives for farmers to produce a surplus in a collectivised agriculture system. Inflation touched 800%. There was no private sector or capital, no foreign trade outside of the state, no banking system while the Treasury controlled all finances and set prices, no flow of goods even between Vietnam's 63 provinces, and no foreign exchange. The Soviet Union, Vietnam's main barter trade partner, also provided one-third of its budget through aid. When Moscow throttled back on its assistance to deal with its own internal crises during the mid-1980s, Hanoi wobbled.

More than this, the mentality was one of old Soviet ways. 'The mindset', says Vu Khoan, 'was most difficult of all to change.' Khoan, 81 in 2019, served in various ministerial portfolios, as a member of the Politburo and as a deputy prime minister.[2] 'In 1957', he remembers, 'after the Geneva agreement was signed, we carried out a socialist transformation in the North. We invited Chinese and Soviet specialists to help work out a plan. As an interpreter, I accompanied the Russian delegation. We were told', he smiles, 'that we should calculate the requirements of cloth by multiplying the number of women by the metres required to sew a dress, never mind the colour or type of cloth.'

Doi Moi – or starve

Doi Moi, or renovation, started in 1986 first in the agriculture sector. All tools of production – land, capital, working assets – had been collectivised and owned by the state since 1975, and peasants were paid in rice and other produce, which 'the state bought at a predatory price', says Khoan. Collectivisation was especially resisted in the principal rice-producing areas of the South, around the Mekong Delta, given that many had benefited from land reform undertaken earlier by the Saigon regime (before reunification), and had subsequently been dispossessed. 'We wasted ten years,' says Nguyen The Dung, a land reform expert who has worked with

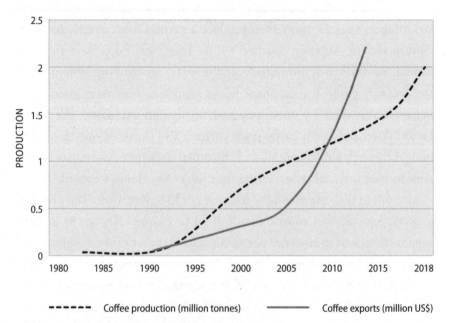

Figure 10.1: Vietnam coffee production and exports

Source: Food and Agriculture Organization, 2019

the World Bank and the Swedish International Development Agency among others, 'by not making market reforms earlier'.

After 1986, farmers were allowed to keep their surplus at a market price. The flow of goods across internal borders was encouraged, and other goods were to be marketed on the basis of supply and demand. Foreign trade was spurred by an end to the barter system between socialist states.

The result of the shift from collectivised to a 'contract' system of agriculture was staggering. With more secure and tradable property rights and market-based pricing (rice had been trading at one-tenth of the market price in 1988), households leapt at the opportunity to sell surpluses. The value of agricultural exports surged from US$500 million in 1986 to US$40 billion in 2018, an average annual growth rate of over 15%.[3] Today, Vietnam's coffee producers have the highest yields in the world.[4]

In this way, land reform boosted Vietnam's transition from an agricultural

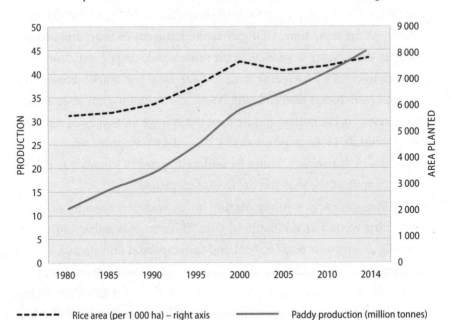

— — — — — Rice area (per 1 000 ha) – right axis   ▬▬▬▬▬▬ Paddy production (million tonnes)

Figure 10.2: Vietnam rice production and area planted

Source: Food and Agriculture Organization, 2019

to an industrial economy and from an informal to a more formal economy. It provided the capital base for subsequent developments. With new seed types and private sector extension services, rice production was boosted to yield as much as eight tonnes per hectare (compared to 4.5 tonnes in Thailand), the Mekong Delta producing four crops annually, ensuring not only self-reliance in staples but providing the foundation for exports.

While quantity, as Marx would have it, has a quality all of its own, inevitably other problems have followed, not least the price achieved by the farmers and widening inequality between the rural and urban areas, with the consequence that many young people no longer see an attractive future in farming.

Regardless, compared to the situation in the 1980s, this is a better problem to have.

A foreign investment law followed in 1987, with foreign direct investment (FDI) growing steadily from US$320 million in 1990 to US$130 billion by 2018.[5] At the same time, GDP per capita has leapt 25 times from under US$100 in the 30 years since 1989, in the process reducing poverty from 58% in 1993 to under 5%.[6] Vietnam's trade to GDP ratio is at 200%, second only to Singapore. Between 1986 and 2018, Vietnam's economy grew at an annual average rate of 6.4%, notably higher than the average for Southeast Asia and all lower-middle-income countries at 4.2% and 4.8% respectively.

The human dimension cannot be underestimated. Vietnam was able to prosper in spite of the past and because of its people.

John Musgrave was a young Marine in the war, permanently disabled by his third wound at the battle of Con Thien in November 1967, later becoming an anti-war activist, poet and spokesperson on veterans' affairs. He features in Ken Burns' epic documentary on the war. He speaks of the Vietnamese as 'survivors in the truest sense of the term and their ability to adapt is nothing short of extraordinary. All one needs to do is look at where they are today compared to where they were in 1975 to understand that there is something very special in their approach to life.'[7]

Pete Peterson was shot down on a bombing raid on Vietnam in 1966, spending six years in Hanoi's infamous jails with colleagues, including John McCain, who went on to become a prominent US senator. After serving as a congressman, Peterson returned to Vietnam in 1997 as America's first ambassador. Of all of the 'contributing factors that led to the success of the Vietnam economic development model', he writes, 'first and foremost is Vietnam's tradition for placing a very high value on education. At the time the Doi Moi policy was announced in 1986, even though the poverty rate in Vietnam was over 70%, its literacy rate was nearly 90%. That was a key factor in Vietnam's ability to quickly absorb large foreign investment by providing the educated workforce required for economic development.'[8]

Managing donors

The role of donors in supporting education, health and infrastructure spending, in particular, was successful given the extent of local ownership of both the solutions (as articulated through their five- and ten-year plans) and the initial problems faced. 'The Vietnamese had fought', Jonathan Pincus reminds us, 'for land reform, to rid the country of a feudal class, not for collectivisation.' Pincus served as the country economist for the United Nations Development Programme (UNDP) in Vietnam. 'Of course, there are lots of suggestions from partners to build trains, and ports, and other "big ticket" items,' he says. 'But Vietnam has largely been successful in steering donors towards their own needs.'

Total donor disbursements over the period 1993–2000, for example, amounted to nearly US$7.6 billion. This increased significantly during the 2000s, to over US$5 billion per annum, with Japan consistently the largest donor, followed by the World Bank, Asian Development Bank (ADB), Korea, France and Germany. Most of the aid has been spent on infrastructure, and specifically rural roads and expressways, urban development, education and health care, and technical assistance. The key items in 1999, to take a specific year, were capital investment programmes (over 50% of total official development assistance, ODA), mostly in energy and transport; human development (16%) focusing on health and education; and rural development (14%).[9] Loans formed just 10% of ODA in 1993, though this had climbed to nearly 70% by 1999 as Vietnam neared and broke through the middle-income barrier in 2010.

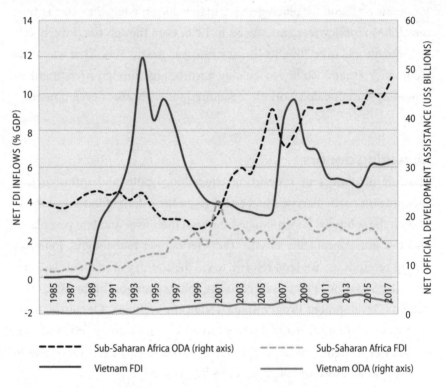

Figure 10.3: Vietnam and Africa: flows of aid and investment

Source: World Bank Databank, 2019.

Aid has in this way 'catalysed' development, as is evident from Figure 10.3, which shows that in sub-Saharan Africa aid had a 'crowding-out' effect on investment while Vietnam had the opposite experience. Moreover, the Vietnamese government has, according to the ADB and

UNDP, been open to policy advice from donors. The export orientation of Vietnam is cited as 'key evidence' of such influence, as are improvements to the business environment around logistics, the financial market and trade standards – as enabled through the development of the industrial parks.

From fire zones to free zones

The city of Biên Hòa, just 25 kilometres from Ho Chi Minh City in Dong Nai Province, is one of the key industrial centres of Vietnam, a multitude of Industrial Development Zones (IDZs), factories and warehouses dominating the local economy. The nearby province of Bình Duong has, however, become the epicentre of investment in the country, attracting 3 444 new foreign businesses from 64 different nations, with a total registered capital of US$331 billion, employing 450 000 out of a provincial population of 2.1 million. Little wonder Bình Duong's economic growth rate was at 14.5% during 2011–15, and the per capita income over US$5 100, 2.4 times the national average.

The Vietnamese Singapore Industrial Park (VSIP) is, as the name suggests, a joint venture with a Singapore consortium headed by that government's Temasek fund and a standout facility in Bình Duong. Started in 1996, it now encompasses several parks in the area and farther afield, with US$11 billion invested by 800 tenants, providing 200 000 jobs. With more than 6 000 container trucks leaving the VSIP facilities daily, Route One towards Ho Chi Minh City, just 25 kilometres away, is a slow-moving mass of rattling, ducking and diving trailers and trucks.

It was not always this way. In the 1960s and 1970s, Route One was a focus of National Liberation Front attacks against American convoys. The area around Biên Hòa suffered especially badly during and after the war, with the settlement of large numbers of refugees worsening an already severe humanitarian situation.

Biên Hòa was also the site of the main US airbase. By the early 1960s, it had become a joint facility for the US Air Force and the Republic of Vietnam Air Force, one of the last bases to fall to the advancing North Vietnamese troops before the collapse of the Saigon government on 30 April 1975.

The costs of conflict were massive. Just off Route One is a South Vietnamese army cemetery, where some 18 000 are buried, 10 000 in unmarked graves, part of some 250 000 South Vietnamese military dead. Once neglected, more attention is being focused on the gravesite as the wounds of the war heal, the change in its name from Bình An Military Cemetery to the People's Cemetery reflecting a change in spirit. Similarly, the US government has committed more than US$200 million to the decontamination of the land around the Biên Hòa airbase from the notori- ous Agent Orange. For a decade from 1961, US forces sprayed 80 million litres of the defoliant over 78 000 square kilometres of southern Vietnam in attempting to create a demilitarised zone and reduce the cover for their Vietnamese foe.

But the country has put the conflict behind it, despite the enormous loss in life, as many as 3.4 million, including two million civilians. There are now more than 320 industrial parks across the country. The first, Linh Trung, was created in 1993 within Ho Chi Minh City as a joint venture between the Vietnamese government and a Chinese state-owned company, one of 17 IDZs now in the city. There are 133 factories in the various phases of Linh Trung, with 75 000 employees. Annual exports totalled US$2.9 bil- lion in 2018, with a stake of US$1.2 billion invested.

So why did they come to Vietnam?

'In 1993, this was a very poor place, more like a village than the city you see today,' says Linh Trung's president, Yang Kai Yong. Originally from Guangzhou in China, he admits that the main advantage of being in Vietnam is the comparative costs of labour.

Labour costs in the major cities (Hanoi, Da Nang and Ho Chi Minh

City) average US$200 per month, and some US$180 in Bình Duong, against US$500 in China in comparable industries.

But it is not all about the cost of labour. 'Vietnam made a decision to open up quite early on. Their policies have learnt from the experience of other countries. It is also a stable society,' Yong observes, 'since the first thing that an investor considers is security.'

Export industries pay no VAT and corporate income tax is at 20% (compared to 33% in China), and there is a 10% incentive for an initial 12 years. Electricity rates are 50% lower than in China, though logistics efficiencies are around 20% less.

Most important, these factors together meant that investors 'made money, which is why we stayed, and why we reinvested. Vietnam has been good for us, and its trade with China good for Vietnam.' Given that other countries also offer low wages and incentives, something more was required. Hence the stress is still on making it easy to invest to this day, with one-stop shops and a welcoming attitude the norm.

And the parks did not wait for investors to knock on their doors. In 2018 alone, VSIP staged 30 seminars and promotions for potential investors around the world. They have a waiting list of nearly 70 investors wanting space in their parks in Bình Duong.

While many African countries are hung up on concerns about local procurement and value addition in such parks, often forestalling these initiatives before they even take off, the Vietnamese approach has been different. They saw the principal value in growth terms, both of employment and in the economy. For example, the average income to labour at VSIP has increased sixfold over the last 20 years. These industrial parks, which number on paper more than 300, now employ over three million Vietnamese, from just 86 000 in the late 1990s. That government is not clear about the exact number in operation tells its own tale about IDZ proliferation and the lack of government interference and demand on the state's resources.

It is a labour revolution, but not the one imagined by the country's revolutionaries back in 1945.

There will be challenges, of course, as Vietnam's labour costs inexorably rise and machines become cheaper and more efficient. Investment in manufacturing is notoriously disloyal. This can be offset by increasing local content (and thus adding more value domestically) or by improving productivity.

While there are some three million Vietnamese working in the textile and apparel sector spread across 7 000 premises,[10] the IDZs contain far from the caricature of cut and trim, sweatshop garment industries. On the contrary, many of the businesses are relatively hi-tech. In Linh Trung, for example, less than one-third of the 133 factories are in garments or shoes. Misumi, the Japanese engineering firm, for instance, arrived 20 years ago, and now employs 3 000 CNC machine operators across three factories.

And neither are these businesses a story of the big, bad Western multinational. The vast majority, some 90%, are Asian. This explains the government's concentration, too, on securing free trade agreements with the Association of Southeast Asian Nations (ASEAN), Japan, Korea and China, along with the US and the European Union. Vietnam, government officials proudly recount, joined the World Trade Organization in 2007. Vietnam is a member of 17 bilateral and multilateral trade agreements, driven both by the need for market access and new sources of foreign investment. The US is the largest trade partner, accounting for nearly 23% of Vietnam's total exports, followed by the European Union, China, ASEAN, Korea and Japan. Since 2015, Vietnam has become the fourth-largest exporter in ASEAN after Singapore, Thailand and Malaysia. Its total share in ASEAN exports has expanded markedly to nearly 17% in 2018 from 6.8% in 2010.

The IDZs have so far been a triumph in Vietnam because the government has been responsive to the needs of investors and Vietnamese workers alike. Vietnam has outperformed the region in two ways: it is not only a cheaper labour market, but one that is more open and politically stable. As one seasoned journalist put it, 'Vietnam is cheaper than China, and they have Facebook, Twitter and Google.' The workers, too, have reciprocated with enthusiastic alacrity. There are no magic ingredients to this success, being founded less on innovation than blood, sweat and policy. As one investor put it, 'The economy is the economy. You invest because of the conditions, not because of how you might like them to be.'

There are challenges, inevitably. Vietnam faces a 'triple transition': from a command to a market economy, from a low-middle-income to an upper-middle-income country; and from a labour-intensive to technology-intensive economy, especially in the rural areas, where the pattern of production is expected to shift from staple (rice) to higher-yield (vegetables and fruit) production, from agriculture per se to agro-industry.

Not all easy

The gulf of efficiency between domestic and foreign capital illustrates the challenge of skills and the unfavourable bureaucratic environment. By 2019, foreigners provided 20% of total capital, but accounted for half of GDP and 75% of exports. While the IDZs have been successful in attracting FDI, the criticism is thus levelled that 'Vietnam has not yet industrialised', since there has been limited technology transfer and limited insertion of Vietnamese domestic entrepreneurs in global value chains.

As the FDI in the IDZs illustrates, foreign capital will go wherever the margins are highest and incentives are best. The longer Vietnam relies on foreign capital, the more dangerous it becomes for Vietnam given the unfaithful nature of such investors, and the more imperative it is to strengthen domestic competitiveness. Domestic pressures will add to this imperative, as seen in the widespread 'anti-Chinese' riots that broke out in mid-2018 after government proposed increasing leases for foreign companies in special economic zones from 70 to 99 years.[11] Toyota's launch in 2003 of the Vios entry-level sedan, manufactured in Vietnam, illustrates some of the market challenges. Makoto Sasagawa headed the company's Vietnam operation. At the time, Vietnam was a small car market of 42 600 units annually, shared between 11 companies and 14 brands, of which Toyota enjoyed a quarter. By 2018 the market had grown to 252 000, shared between 19 companies and 21 brands. Per capita income had gone from US$420 to US$2 385 in these 15 years.

Some 98% of cars were by 2018 sold to private citizens, and just 2% to government, highlighting the shift in the balance of market forces. It was not all easy going, however. The introduction of a special consumption tax (essentially a sales tax) went up tenfold to 80% as the government sought to extract from foreign investors. It became difficult to increase volume in the circumstances, and thus to achieve the goal to improve the extent of local content in production. Instead, production was halved between 2003 and 2004, before the government throttled back the consumption tax to 40%.

There are other concerns about politically connected individuals and a small number of firms dominating the economy,[12] of the need to improve the business environment for the half a million small- and medium-sized businesses that dominate Vietnam's employment and have to deal with the distortions created by government support for state-owned enterprises (SOEs), and of the challenge of improving productivity.[13] There is also the need to manage the increasingly divergent trends across the country's 63 provinces, where the ten largest provinces account for 75% of the country's export-import value.[14]

Some gains can be made through privatisation of the approximately 700 SOEs that remain under state control. Some 11 000 have been 'corporatised' or 'equitised', either through amalgamation or privatisation since Doi Moi began in 1986. In a remorseless process, the number of SOEs was halved between 1990 and 2000 to 5 800, and again further to 3 135 by 2013.[15] By 2015, SOEs officially employed 1.3 million (or 2.5%) out of a total workforce of 52.2 million, falling from 1.5 million the previous year. By comparison, by 2019 Vietnam had more than 21 000 FDI projects, with a total registered capital touching US$300 billion.[16]

Other ways of encouraging domestic competitiveness will include a focus on education and skills-building, as well as a concerted effort to make it easier to do business for locals.

Education remains a challenge in 2019, despite the widespread literacy to which Ambassador Peterson refers. The higher education system faces a quality crisis, linked to outdated curricula and large-scale graduate unemployment.[17] Far from the socialist dream, only primary schools are subsidised by the government, by 50% of the total tuition cost. High enrolment rates mask low quality and high dropout rates, with less than two-thirds of primary school students enrolling in secondary school.[18] Meanwhile, for Vietnam's fast-urbanising population, stimulating businesses to create jobs is critical. Vietnam ranks 69th out of 190 economies in the World Bank's Ease of Doing Business Index, behind only Malaysia in the region, but registering a business can take 17 days.[19] No wonder then that the majority of the urban poor set up informal shops on sidewalks.

Around 1.2 million people migrate to cities every year, where about a quarter of the workforce now make up informal street vendors selling traditional *pho* and *bun cha*, or the now famous Vietnamese *banh mi*, a twist on the French baguette.[20] A clean-up campaign in 2017, which failed to make even a dent in the number of vendors, resulted in the resignation of Ho Chi Minh City's District 1 deputy major and 'Captain Sidewalk', Doan Ngoc Hai.[21]

Despite an image of stern governance and anti-corruption values, there is a lack of transparency and integrity in the system, with Vietnam ranking 117th out of 180 countries on the Corruption Perceptions Index in 2018 with a score of 33/100,[22] and sitting among the least free countries in the world as rated by Freedom House for civic and political liberties.[23]

Politically, Doi Moi has ushered in a new, younger leadership along with streamlining the country's more cumbersome bureaucracy, including through the one-stop shops within the industrial parks. There is a new language, at least, on corruption, with officials openly admitting it is a serious problem. Vietnam is thus today a 'hybrid': an increasingly free market economy under one-party rule, with private business operating alongside state-owned companies.[24] There is still a lack of openness in the mass media, with more than 100 people arrested in 2017 for criticising the government, protesting or joining unsanctioned religious or civil society organisations, according to Human Rights Watch.[25] Arrests, criminal convictions, and physical assaults against journalists, bloggers and human rights activists have also continued. In the face of the stresses produced by economic growth, including the resurfacing of development tensions between the North and the more laissez-faire South, the challenge for the Communist Party is whether it possesses the capacity to persist with economic reforms through the myriad political and

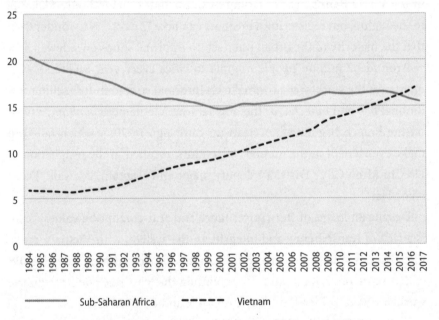

Figure 10.4: Vietnam and Africa: shares of global wealth (% per capita)

Source: World Bank Databank, 2019.

administrative changes required. For free enterprise, economic activity is inimically pluralist, at least in the long run.

Yet, while per capita income is growing and consumer spending increases by about 10% per year (well above the global average), concerns of governance are secondary to the question of further growth and foreign investment, at least from the perspective of government.

Services have expectedly taken an increasing share as the economy has changed. As one measure, the number of foreign tourists has risen from 2.1 million arrivals to 15.5 million just this century,[26] alongside some 80 million domestic traveller trips, which quadrupled during the 2010s.

According to the World Economic Forum's 2017 Tourism Competitiveness Index, Vietnam ranks 32nd globally (out of 120 countries) in terms of the volume and attractiveness of its natural and cultural resources, and third within the Southeast Asia region (behind Indonesia and Thailand). By 2017, tourism accounted for 8% of Vietnam's GDP, the country's single-largest services export, accounting for 68% of the services total with considerably positive impacts on low-skilled, rural and youth workers.[27] The sector directly employed 750 000 workers in 2017 (around 1.4% of Vietnam's total employment), up from roughly 450 000 in 2013. But more, too, can be done in this sector, not least since the share of repeat international visitors to Vietnam is under 40%, compared to key regional competitors, such as Thailand and Indonesia, where over 60% and 55% respectively of international arrivals are returning visitors, and the GDP and employment multipliers of 1.6 and 1.7 remain low by regional (2.4 and 2.5) and global (3.3 and 2.6) benchmarks.[28] This, in part, relates to a relative weakness in tourism transport and logistics infrastructure.

Conclusion: Why this path?

The most interesting question is why Vietnam's leadership took the free market reform path, if the route of others (Venezuela, Zimbabwe, Laos,

North Korea and Myanmar) suggests that they could equally have doubled down on ideology?

Khoan explains this in terms of a long struggle. 'We think that communism is still the future of mankind. That objective may be very long. We are in the first phase. That is why we use the term "socialist-oriented market economy" to explain our path.' Some younger members of the audience where he was speaking said later they had to stifle their laughter at this comment, seeing it as an ideological fig leaf to justify past failures.

On the contrary, in part the answer is down to the numerical dominance of a 'highly aspirational' youth, with two-thirds of the population under 35. They have little connection with the past, and their grandparents' struggles. Their lives are defined by the world outside, even though the war continues to shape external perceptions. As one thirty-something who runs a start-up in Ho Chi Minh City put it, 'In my generation, we didn't grow up with a war. Yet, the only thing that everyone I met at business school [in the UK] knew about Vietnam was the war.'

And, in part, the answer lies in the attitude, too, of the older generation, even those steeped in ideology. While Giap remained a committed communist, more than that he was a committed nationalist. One foreign ambassador expressed it optimistically thus: 'Malaysia's constraints are around race, and the governance problems this engenders. Vietnam's constraints are around ideology. It's much easier to get rid of communism than race.'

And even within a single generation. The executive mayor of Hanoi, Nguyen Duc Chung, served as a policeman in the city's investigative bureau for 30 years before moving into government. Now a senior member of the Politburo, his focus is on reducing pollution for the capital's ten million inhabitants, improving waste management, reducing the clog of traffic from the six million motorbikes and 750 000 cars by providing public transport, and improving water quality.

Such are the preoccupations of a middle-income country. There is no doubt that the generation that followed the 'liberators' (Giap, Ho and others) have seen a monumental improvement in living conditions. Vietnam's life expectancy surged from 66 in 1978 to 76 in 2018, while child mortality dipped over the same period from 48 per 1 000 live births to just 16. Through an almost stubborn focus on social welfare, poverty was reduced from over 75% to below 10% over this period.[29]

Now there are other things to focus on. Giap's son, who left the army in 1994, is now working in information technology. Where his father's struggle centred on unification and liberation, the son's generation has been more interested in wealth creation. To make the same sort of difference to Vietnam's fortunes, the next generation will have to be preoccupied with environmentalism and quality of food production, among other issues, if the Vietnamese are to keep their success going.

Vietnam's income aspirations (mainly through industrialisation and urbanisation) will perhaps inevitably run up against the limits imposed by land degradation (especially in the Mekong River Delta) and pollution of water and air, which will negatively affect the budding tourism industry. Similarly, Vietnam has been ranked one of five countries to be most affected by climate change, estimated to cause a reduction in national income by close to 3.5% by the year 2050.[30] With large vulnerable communities along its 3 444-kilometre coastline and projected sea level rises of 18–38 centimetres over this time, climate change ought to be high on the development agenda, especially as significant economic activity occurs in lowlands and deltas such as the Red River and Mekong Delta.[31]

What they might learn from the success of the Doi Moi is that a healthy dose of pragmatism and flexibility and a focus on homegrown reforms are imperative. With the valour of the 'liberators' against their foreign enemies, and the grit of the 'reformers' who came after them in carving a way out of poverty, this generation will again have to look inward to solve their domestic politics and environmental degradation issues. It depends, of course, on what they would want to be known for.

Overall, Vietnam shows that a development trajectory is by no means the inevitable result of forces outside of national control. On the contrary, they are very much within the power of political leadership. They simply have to possess the courage to make the necessary changes and, in so doing, in Vietnam's case, alter the fortunes of generations.

PART TWO

FIVE KEY LESSONS FOR SUCCESS FROM ASIA

Chapter 11

The Premium of Leadership and Institutions

> Hacker: Humphrey, do you see it as part of your job to help ministers
> make fools of themselves?
> Sir Humphrey: Well, I never met one that needed any help.
>
> — *Yes, Minister*

What drives the difference in performance and delivery between Asia and
Africa?

One answer is given as East Asian political authoritarianism, which has
enabled decision-makers to enjoy relative autonomy from electorates and
public opinion, free to make tough, if unpopular, decisions because they
did not have to be tested at the polls.[1]

Of the ten Association of Southeast Asian Nations (ASEAN) states, in
2000 just two were classified as 'free', three as 'partly free' and five as 'unfree'.
In 2019 this picture was only slightly changed: the movers are Philippines
and Myanmar, which are both now only 'partly free', and Thailand, which
turned completely into 'unfree'.

China falls squarely in the 'unfree' category, though Japan, South Korea
and Taiwan are all classified as 'free'. South Korea and Taiwan moved to
'free' in 1988 and 1996, respectively.

Africa is on a different path. Since 1980, the number of 'free' democratic
regimes in Africa has increased from two to ten, while there are an equal number, in 2019, of countries in Freedom House's 'partly free' and 'unfree' categories.

The reason for this change in political mood has been driven by the self-interest of African electorates. Democratic regimes in Africa not only better safeguard human rights than their authoritarian counterparts, but perform better economically. As shown in *Democracy Works*,[2] and highlighted in Figure 11.1, there is a correlation between conditions of economic openness, judicial effectiveness, transparency and democracy.

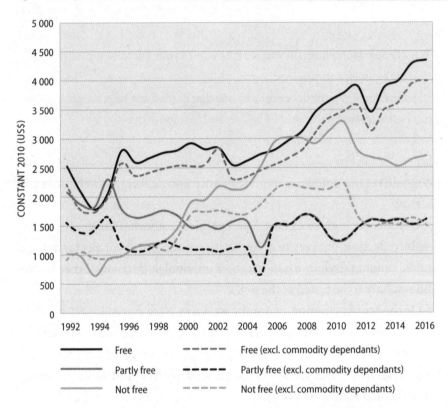

Figure 11.1: African countries' GDP per capita across Freedom House indicators

Sources: Freedom House Index of Freedoms, 2018; World Bank Databank, 2018.

For these and other reasons, Africans are unlikely to surrender these hard-won freedoms anytime soon.

Authoritarianism can just as much be a reason for failure as for success, depending on which examples are cherry-picked. Rather, the difference between East Asia and Africa appears to lie in other factors, not least the strong attachment Asian leaders have displayed towards the popular welfare of their people, and despite the lack of obvious advantages, at least at independence.

What underpins this commitment in the absence of democracy?

The roots of comparison

Daron Acemoglu and James Robinson argue in *Why Nations Fail* that the difference between development success and failure is down to the difference between extractive and inclusive institutions.[3] In inclusive institutions there are, they note, secure property rights, law and order, freer markets and the correct type of state support, the upholding of contracts, and the right overall environment for business to prosper. In short, this creates incentives for investment and innovation across a level playing field.

By contrast, in the extractive model, politically connected elites have preferential economic access. The playing field is not level, and the checks and balances are not there, with weak and unbalanced political institutions. It follows that prosperity is more likely where power is more broadly distributed, and where government is accountable and responsive to the needs of citizens.

What causes one system to prevail?

Asia can claim no special legacy of good institutions, or a less damaging colonial past. Despite the divergence in their respective development trajectories over the past 50 years, Southeast Asia and Africa enjoy prominent historical parallels.

Traditional Southeast Asian societies were characterised by ethnic disunity, frail institutions and limited governance outside of the capital, weak democracy, fragmentary external trade linkages and acute social stratification – indeed, many of the conditions prevalent in weak states, especially those in Africa.[4] Both regions share a history of commodity and colonial exploitation, where the conquerors were sharply divided from the conquered by race. 'Settlers' were in both cases imposed on the local populations, arousing particularly intense hostility.[5] This left them not only with unnatural borders and poor terms of trade, but their people were suppressed and, with their personal agency undermined, hostile towards outsiders yet suspicious of their fellow country people.

In their traditional pre-colonial world, in most cases the authority of Southeast Asia's various rulers, for example, was only absolute in and around the seat of power, and their control 'diminished in proportion to the distance one moved away from the capital'.[6] Equally, state borders were 'uncertain and porous', reflecting the lack of close links between these centres of authority and their outer periphery. As a result, the Southeast Asian region was not made up of the ten states that comprise the twenty-first-century ASEAN variant, but rather a more diverse and fragmented mosaic, of not less 'than forty states', comprising kingdoms, principalities and sultanates.[7] Their authority was delegated through a combination of alliance-making and simply allowing some regions to get on with matters in their own way.

Southeast Asia's twentieth-century economic transformation has its origins in the end of this traditional system. The spur for this was in the industrial revolution elsewhere, which accelerated the search for colonial possessions and their commodities. It also changed the focus and methods of production, and of political organisation in these territories.

With European involvement, Asia transformed quickly, in less than 100 years, from being a region where exports played a relatively minor role and where subsistence farming was dominant, to one driven by external demand. 'As Southeast Asia's export economy developed,' Milton Osborne reminds us in his magisterial account of the region, 'so did more general economic and social change penetrate into almost every level of society, leaving only the most remote regions and populations untouched.

The growth of the great metropolitan cities, the rise of exports and the development of a cash economy, the institution of new communication systems – all of these are products', he observes, 'of economic change in a period beginning only 150 years ago.'[8] With burgeoning exports of rice, rubber and tin, among other new commodities, to fuel the industrial demands of faraway economies, came improvements to road, rail and port networks to get them to these markets. With such increased trade, changes occurred in society: instead of seeking to migrate to the cities to escape the hardships of rural life, 'peasants methodically set to work to grow more and more on what was, proportionately per capita, less and less space'.[9]

While most East Asian countries had to accept a complex ethnic make-up as a result of colonial involvement, as with Africa, this has not in most cases resulted in endemic instability. Most, too, have had to cope with weak human resources, yet they have quickly, as noted, turned their people into an asset through investment in education. Though institutional capacity is similarly cited as a structural impediment, some countries (not least some in Southeast Asia) have grown economically with institutions at independence far worse resourced than in Africa. There are geographic discontinuities on a par with African states, with difficult topographies and, in the case of Indonesia and the Philippines, a vast archipelago complex.

This applies equally to the argument about the 'curse' of natural resources, which includes the apparently deleterious effect they have on the potential for economic diversification. Yet, such a curse does not apply to countries in Asia, such as Malaysia, Indonesia or Vietnam, although they possess a significant store of natural resources, greater than most African countries. Problems arise where the systems of governance are not inclusive but rather fractured, fragmented or elitist, and characterised by rent-seeking, often along ethno-political, racial or religious fault lines.[10]

The drivers of difference?

Several other reasons might be considered as to why Asian countries have retained a comparative commitment to popular welfare.

In *Power and Prosperity*, Mancur Olson distinguishes between 'stationary' and 'roving' bandits as the difference between systems that incentivise investment (a tyrant who wants to remain in power thus protects citizens and ultimately establishes government) and those that simply steal and destroy.[11] A 'roving bandit' has an incentive to maximise short-run plunder by stealing everything from victims. A 'stationary bandit' has an incentive to maximise long-run plunder by stealing just a portion of what victims produce every year. Most African regimes, by this measure, are roving, even though they tend to stay a long time. In the words of Zimbabwe's former finance minister (and opposition leader), Tendai Biti, a stationary bandit 'feeds and milks the cow' but the roving variant 'eats it'.[12]

But what made them stop or roam?

A first factor relates to the interrelated nature of settlement and state formation. Daron Acemoglu, Simon Johnson and James Robinson show that in those African countries where European colonialists were able to settle more comfortably (based on settlers' mortality rates, as an indication of the disease environment), and intended to stay longer, they generally set up better institutions, which translates into higher income per capita in the present.[13] Africa had more cases of indirect rule than Asia, where indigenous power structures were used by a far-off colonial empire to suppress and control local populations.

In *Political Order and Political Decay*, Francis Fukuyama explains how institutions and states develop in different countries.[14] Larger communities – and thereby larger armies – are a key step in the state-building process, one component of stable political order, the others being the rule of law and accountable government. A successful modern liberal democracy balances all three components to achieve stability. Of Africa, Fukuyama has this to say: 'States that make heavy use of overt coercion and brutality often do so because they cannot exercise proper authority.' They have 'despotic power' but not 'infrastructural power' to shape society. He notes, 'This was true of both the colonial African state and the independent countries that emerged after the end of colonial rule.'[15]

In the Pulitzer Prize-winning *Guns, Germs, and Steel*, Jared Diamond argues that the gaps in power and technology between Eurasian and other societies originate primarily in geographic differences, driven by necessity, including climatic and topographic conditions, which served to favour certain types of species and trade.[16] The plentiful supply of food and the dense populations that it supported made division of labour possible, permitting the freedom to pursue other functions, thereby driving technological progress and economic growth and, ultimately, conquest.

Africa's relative lack of population density may also have played a role; although the problem with Africa was not so much its population density (or lack of it) but rather, as David Lamb observes, its uneven nature.[17] Fewer than one-third of Africans live in countries around the continental average. While there are 44 Africans per square kilometre living across the continent (compared to the global average of 50 per square kilometre, or the East Asian average of 145 per square kilometre),[18] there are 440 Rwandans per square kilometre (about the same as the Netherlands, South Korea and India), 401 per square kilometre in neighbouring Burundi and just 35 per square kilometre in the Democratic Republic of Congo.[19]

In this vein, Jeffrey Herbst's *States and Power in Africa* argues that African failure to provide public goods, such as law and order, defence, contract enforcement and infrastructure, has its roots in the distribution of African population concentrations and the pre- and post-colonial political orders.[20] Without the high population density of Europe, Herbst shows that, as Charles Tilly points out with feudal China,[21] African rulers did not need to secure their power base by focusing their efforts on consolidating power in the hinterland, and building infrastructure, raising armies and establishing the tax and other fiscal institutions that went along with this.

The virtual absence of fighting over borders during the colonial period by European powers and the moratorium imposed by the Organisation of African Unity on post-colonial boundaries diminished the need to invest in defending territory beyond the key population centres.

While Africa has a very long history of state-building, in the pre-colonial era a significant portion of African people lived in small-scale societies in which government was dependent more on consensus among the entire adult population than rule by an elite. This is related, too, to population density. Africa's sparse populations have not lent themselves to this extent of control. Instead, parts of Africa were characterised by what anthropologists refer to as 'segmentary lineage' societies – those tribal units operating outside of state formations where authority is derived from lineage, not the state, where family is part of a larger 'segment' of more relatives and their families. Historically outside and frequently marginalised from the state and the formal economy, these groups were – and are still, in places like South Sudan – often pastoralist and nomadic.[22]

A cultural dimension?

Secondly, there may be a cultural dimension. This is not, however, the argument sometimes used of Asian thrift and sweat compared to the lack of African labour and discipline. There are few who toil harder and for less than the female African farmer. The culturalist arguments about work ethic are equally subjective and erroneous in the East Asian context, even though such differences have long been seen anecdotally as obstacles and assets to development. As it turned out, the British had false cultural impressions about Germany in the nineteenth century, while the Allies had very negative (and entirely fallacious) views about the political and economic sophistication (and constraints) of the Japanese in the first half of the twentieth century. Britain, like the US, had not appreciated the pace and extent of Japan's transformation from a samurai shogunate to a sophisticated and urbanising industrial power, which led them to misinterpret the growing Japanese appetite for resources. Equally, they misread the fighting ability of the Japanese soldier. 'They would not make good pilots because of their poor eyesight' was the commonly held view about the Imperial Japanese Army before the Second World War. Pearl Harbor and the skilfully flown Zeros soon proved this caricature costly and untrue. On the contrary, the defeat of Western powers at the hands of the Japanese during the early stages of the Second World War quashed once and for all the myth of European cultural and military superiority, at least among East Asians, setting the stage for what was to follow.

After the war, Japan's economic transformation, too, proved an important regional trendsetter, putting in place an East Asian 'formula' for rapid growth, while illustrating that Asians could outperform the West at their own game.

Culture, too, has less to do with apparently shared values, such as Confucianism, than commonly asserted, as highlighted in Chapters 4 and 9 on South Korea and China respectively.

Asia is so big and diverse that it is difficult to generalise about common values – supposedly, obedience to authority, both family and government; an emphasis on education; and always placing community above individual – across the whole continent, just as it is about Africa. As Joe Studwell notes, 'discussion of Confucianism fails to distinguish between the theory of a roster of vague moral precepts and the implementation of ideals so utopian as to be far more honoured in the breach than in the observance'.[23]

Rather, this cultural dimension is linked to the presence of large immigrant Chinese communities across the region, which spurred commerce and competition. Driven outwards by instability in China from the time especially of the Opium Wars in the middle of the nineteenth century, by 1850 around half a million people of Chinese extraction were settled in Southeast Asia. Facilitated by technology, notably the steamship, by the time of the First World War, this number had increased to four million people. In contrast to the grim Malthusian setting they left behind, migration was eased, too, by the relatively underpopulated territories in which they settled, around one-tenth as large as they are today. But the success of the Chinese immigrants had less to do with cultural values per se, Studwell reminds us, given that they were far from a homogeneous group and were rapidly assimilated, than their self-selecting nature with a greater willingness to take risks and work harder than those left behind.[24]

Yet, for all of the debate on the value of culture in Asia, it is the primacy of pragmatism over principle, whether religious, racial, ethnic or political, and the ability of East Asians to operate successfully within and without their own cultural context, which are central to explaining their development success.

The differences in performance thus have less to do with culture per se than the culture of leadership. As Biti, again, puts it, 'Africa's leaders celebrated at independence; Asia's took this moment as a call for renewed focus.'[25]

Security and agriculture as drivers

Thirdly, there is a security dimension. 'You see,' says President Muse Bihi Abdi, pointing to an area to the east on the giant map of Somaliland covering the one wall of the presidential briefing room in Hargeisa, 'in this area, clan members think "I have a gun, I am the government"', explaining why the area is spotted with al-Shabaab fighters and his government continues to battle to establish governance, and in sum the cost of war and, in Somaliland's particular case, of the absence of international recognition.[26] Those countries that remain with insurgencies, or at war, such as Myanmar in East Asia and in countless African examples, pay a heavy developmental price.

Fourthly, the richness of African agriculture has also, in some cases, proved a hindrance to the development and extension of government and the state, where the ease of subsistence for many rural Africans has let government off the hook in providing services and opportunities for them, although this relative wealth does not apply to all. Only 8% of the continent's land has a tropical climate, and only half receives adequate rainfall to support regular agriculture in the absence of other systems of irrigation.[27]

Landholding structures are a linked impediment to growth where land value cannot be collateralised through individual ownership and mortgage schemes. There has been very little interest among the leadership for such reform – quite the opposite in Zimbabwe, where land has been seized and redistributed based on political allegiances. In 2009, for example, over 80% of land across Africa remained in customary tenure, while in some countries, such as Mozambique or Tanzania, no private ownership of land is permitted.

Elements of Asian countries' successful land reform are discussed in more detail in Chapter 13.

Not a cheap date

Fifthly, aid has been used better – or at least it has not given Asian leaders another option but to pursue development through better choices.

Take Vietnam. At one point, the World Bank had their largest representative office outside of Washington in Hanoi. Vietnam was the poster child of development through foreign aid, receiving on average over US$5 billion a year for 20 years. Compared to Africa, where aid has a track record that is dismal at best, with donors pushing various agendas that are not always in the interests of the recipients, Vietnam succeeded in using aid to its advantage.

Experts at foreign policy since they fought their 'people's war' against America, Vietnam was able to play donors against its own needs. Vietnam benefited from being a global focal point in the early 1990s. 'Donors were incredibly eager to have a part in the Vietnamese success story,' says Jonathan Pincus, former chief economist for the United Nations Development Programme (UNDP) in Vietnam. Government had their pick of donors and funders.

'Western donors in Asia learnt from the Marshall Plan,' notes Jordan Ryan, who headed the UNDP in Vietnam and was the deputy special representative of the UN secretary general in Liberia, 'which had three important criteria: the moneys committed were large enough for the problem to be solved; it had a limited time frame; and there was local co-financing'. By comparison, there is acute donor fragmentation in Africa, and a lack of prioritisation by African partners, as exemplified by the Liberian experience 'where everything was a priority'.[28]

The Vietnamese government set clear targets through various five- and ten-year plans, applying a lot of thought to compromises among competing national interests. These national interests included big-ticket

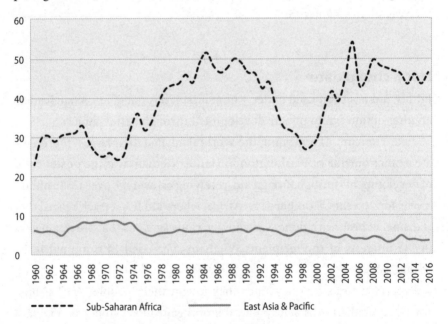

Figure 11.2: Per capita net aid inflows (constant 2015 US$)

Source: World Bank Databank, 2019.

infrastructure, education, health care and irrigation for agriculture. Under such clear directives, donors had no choice but to comply.

This seems to be a common success factor across East Asia. While aid has flowed into the region at a lower rate than in Africa, it has been comparatively well used, in part because the recipient countries have been clear about their own development agenda, and because aid has not been the dominant funding aspect. Whereas aid to East Asia has not exceeded 0.5% of gross national income in the last 60 years, in Africa it reached over 6% in the 1990s and remained at 3% in 2018.

Overall aid was successful because the economies of Asia were growing, with aid being used to supplement rather than supplant internal initiatives. By 1996, just four of the 40 countries eligible for debt relief under the Heavily Indebted Poor Countries initiative were in sub-Saharan Africa; none were in East Asia.

Aid, Asia teaches, works where it promotes internal, accountable governance, macro-economic stability, and the ability to engage with the global economy. In sum, the great paradox of aid has to be confronted if it is to be useful: to ensure independence out of dependency.

Bureaucratic institutionalism

The sixth and final factor relates to the tradition of bureaucratic institutional capacity in Asia. This is what we would, in effect, describe as 'governance'. One proxy measure would be the Doing Business indicators of the World Bank, where nearly two-thirds of East Asian countries fall into the top half of performers globally, and 60% of Africans in the last quartile. This illustrates governments' readiness to embrace the private sector. Another, as will be seen later in Chapter 15, has to do with the frictional challenges of investing. The World Bank governance indicators and Human Development Index are further measures. Figure 11.3 highlights the correlation between governance and wealth.

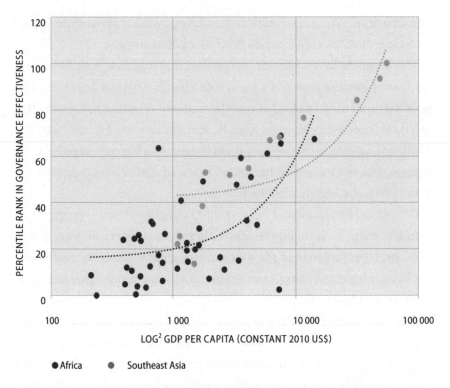

Figure 11.3: World Bank governance scores and GDP per capita (logarithmic scale)

Sources: World Bank Governance Indicators; World Bank Databank, 2019.

What are the reasons for weak governance?

We believe that the most important explanation relates to capacity and continuity in the public service. Rather than a 'yes, minister' environment where the civil service provides a check and balance for political excesses, and also an independent, professional and effective arm of delivery, African bureaucracies are characterised by high levels of deliberate politicisation and selective discontinuity, driven in part by the need to satisfy different constituencies.[29]

By comparison, there is a competitive tradition of institutional meritocracy in East Asia. In Japan, Taiwan and China, among other Asian examples, civil servants undergo rigorous examination where only the best and brightest are selected.[30] This is the result of a system that traces its roots back 1 300 years to the selection of government officials in China. As far back as AD 605, mandarins (or public officials) were selected by merit through thorough imperial examination. This went hand in hand with a long tradition of literature, with Chinese script first being used in the late 2nd millennium BC, which spawned other East Asian written languages.

For Africa, this explains why it is so challenging to establish a national project – one that is driven by strong leadership – the more fractured and decentralised a state is.

Conclusion: *Vuta pamoja* – development as pulling together

Africa has not lacked sincerity among its leadership cadre. On the contrary, there have been ambitious and well-intended development programmes, from free primary education in Nigeria in the 1950s to Julius Nyerere's attempts to modernise through Ujamaa in the 1960s and Africa's welter of mega-projects in the 1970s. Policy misdirection and corruption have indubitably played a part in failure, but what has been missing, overall, at least by comparison with Asia, is the ability to pull together a complex package, involving internal and external resource mobilisation, including freeing up capital, accessing markets, encouraging inflows of technology, improving logistics, and deepening and widening skills. It has not been possible to rely on good intentions alone.

Development failures in Africa seldom reside in single factors alone – geography, leadership, the extent of identity and religious fault lines, ideology, skills levels, the colonial legacy, and so on – but rather how they act in combination. Put differently, it is not one thing; it is everything. Single-issue explanations – and their corollary, magic bullet, one-thing solutions – can thus easily be dismissed.

What can be done to create the institutions necessary to promote development?

The answer seems to reside, at least over the long term, in establishing a tech-nocracy, enabling a process where long-term development trumps short-term populist and elite urges. East Asian countries partly owe their development success to the role of such technocratic expertise and a meritocratic culture that underpinned it. The role of the Ministry of International Trade and Industry in Japan, or the mandarins of Taiwan, Singapore or China, provide illustrations of such a technocracy that the political system sought to nurture and shield. While Lee Kuan Yew – 'a long-sighted genius with a ruthless streak' – is, for example, often singularly credited with taking Singapore from a failing state to a global hub, he was just one man within a bigger system, the extent of which is indicated by policy and governance continuity after his demise. Instead, while leadership was important, Singapore's success 'came from its system of expert rule, focus on meritocratic talent and long-term thinking'. Our system, said the Singaporean prime minister (and Lee's son), Lee Hsien Loong, in 2005, 'shielded civil servants from political interference, [giving them] the space to work out rational, effective solutions for our problems [so they can] practise public administration in almost laboratory conditions.'[31]

Dollops of pragmatism were required. Toyota executives describe the com-pany way: PDCA – Plan, Do, Check, Adjust. This pragmatism has infused policy solutions: economic processing zones were, for example, established as a means to focus infrastructure and progressive tax regimes on an isolated area or sector so as not to rock the domestic political or ideological boat, as the former World Bank chief economist, Justin Lin, argues in Chapter 9 on China. This could, for example, focus on municipal governance, where institutions are geographically circumscribed and thus more amenable and less expensive.

If development depends on the ability to work – *and pull* – together, leadership is critical in setting this direction towards a laser-like focus on growth and jobs to the exclusion of much else, setting it out as a prioritised plan, and evolving this over time. East Asia's leadership cadre was success-ful because they knew what to prioritise, and knew that the state could alone not be the driver and beneficiary of growth.

Chapter 12

Don't be a Prisoner of the Past

> Businesses have a way of going out and finding opportunities, and we have to provide [only] the environment that is conducive to this. Investment demands leaps in governance [along with] predictability and certainty in regimes and laws, including labour laws.
>
> — Tharman Shanmugaratnam, finance minister of Singapore, August 2014

Goh Chok Tong succeeded Lee Kuan Yew as prime minister of Singapore in 1990.

Goh's office is on the third floor of the annexe to the classical Istana, meaning 'palace' in Malay, designed by colonial engineers on a 106-acre nutmeg plantation and built by Indian convict labourers.[1] Completed in 1869, today it is an oasis of calm off the bustling commercial centre of Orchard Road. Istana is the official residence and office of the president of Singapore, and also serves as the working offices of the prime minister.

The adaptation and modernisation of the colonial Istana is evidence of the pragmatism of Singapore's leadership. The island was set in a direction looking forward from the time of independence, unwilling to look back. Singaporeans seldom mention history as an excuse. Albert Winsemius, an adviser to the Singapore government, suggested that the new state keep the statue of its colonial founder, Sir Stamford Raffles, as a 'precondition' for success. As Lee Kuan Yew wrote, accepting this advice 'was easy … Letting it remain would be a symbol of public acceptance of the British heritage and could have a positive effect', especially given Singapore's need for 'large-scale technical, managerial, entrepreneurial, and marketing know-how from America and Europe'.[2]

On the banks of the Singapore River stands Raffles' white marble statue at the site of his original landing. The inscription reads: 'On this historic site, Sir Thomas Stamford Raffles first landed in Singapore on 29th January 1819, and with genius and perception changed the destiny of Singapore from an obscure fishing village to a great seaport and modern metropolis.' With the river and skyscrapers to his back, Asian Civilisations Museum on his right shoulder and parliament to his left, arms folded, he is apparently gazing out to sea. This effigy is not, however, the original, unveiled on Jubilee Day on 27 June 1887. That bronze statue is 100 metres away in front of Victoria Memorial Hall where it was moved on Singapore's centenary from its earlier location at the Padang, between the fields of the (emphatically once white- and male-only) Singapore Cricket Club and (originally Eurasian) Singapore Recreational Club.

The symbolism is important. By retaining Raffles, by building on the past, Singapore has shown what is achievable with better choices in little more than a generation. 'There is no point', said Singapore's former president S.R. Nathan (1999–2011), 'in harping on the evils of colonialism – no point at all. It's over, you're in charge now. By talking about it, injustices will not become justices. This is in our hands. Instead, get on and go ahead with the job you have to do, and put money in the pocket of your people.' He added: 'Until you solve your problems yourself, they will not be solved.'[3]

Singapore's example is the East Asian pragmatic norm.

Vietnam: V-Day

Thirty years of civil war and more than 1 000 years of colonial intervention were ended when, on 30 April 1975, Tank 390, a North Vietnamese T-59 under the command of Captain Vu Dang Toan, crashed through the gates of Saigon's presidential palace. Inside, South Vietnam's last president,

General Duong Van Minh, better known as 'Big Minh', along with some 30 members of his team, waited to surrender to the North.

Vietnam was poised, at least, to transform from a war to a country. But the struggle was not over.

As we saw in Chapter 10, in 1989, 14 years after Toan's tank went through the gates, Vietnam had a per capita GDP of just US$94.[4] This was the result of failed socialist policies that had removed any incentive to produce, leading to stagnation and shortages. Rather than the joy of peace, Vietnam experienced a dark age of doctrinaire government, collectivisation and near famine, the loss of civil liberties, isolation, wars with Cambodia and, then, China, endless suffering and deprivation.

The Sixth Party Congress of December 1986 formally adopted the policy of Doi Moi (or renovation). This was provoked by the death of the wartime leader and hardliner party secretary, Le Duan, in July 1986 and the growing influence of technocratically minded pro-market reformers. As a result, since then, average income has multiplied many times to over US$2 500, driven by an average annual growth rate of 6%.[5]

But growth is an outcome of what were ideologically contentious policy changes, starting in the rural areas. From ruinous collectivised farming, the country shifted to allocating long-term leases to farmers with a better productive record. But the cities have delivered even more. With more than 8.5 million people, Saigon in the South (after 1975, officially Ho Chi Minh City), for example, has experienced 9.6% average growth between 2010 and 2015.[6]

Vietnam's transformation has been based on two fundamental choices.

The first has been Vietnam's ability to put the past behind, remarkable given the level of devastation during the last century, including four periods of foreign intervention (Chinese, French, Japanese and American), more than three million casualties of war, and the devastation caused by the communist economic folly that followed.

The second, related aspect is a wholesale recognition of the importance of foreigners in this process, in spite of the colonial experience.

	1978	2019
Population	63.5 million	97.48 million
GDP per capita	$134	$2 564
Share of global GDP (% global share of population)	0.2	0.5
Inflation %	411	3
Life expectancy (years)	69.9	76.2
Child mortality (per 1 000 live births)	58	21
Poverty %	±75	9.8
Literacy %	87	97.3

Table 12.1: Vietnam then and now

One Vietnamese worker put it thus: 'We grow with foreigners.'[7]

This has led to a revolution in attitude.

In Saigon is the War Remnants Museum. Opened in 1975 in the former US Information Agency, it was originally labelled the Exhibition House for US and Puppet Crimes. In 1990, as relations between the US and Vietnam improved, it changed to the Museum for Crimes of War and Aggression. It adopted the current title in 1995 when diplomatic ties were renewed and US sanctions were dropped.

Since 2007, US warships have frequently visited Vietnamese ports. The Vietnamese military conducts regular joint exercises with its American counterpart. When the then US defence secretary, General James Mattis, made his second visit in October 2018, he stopped off at the Biên Hòa airbase outside Saigon to reaffirm a US commitment to dioxin remediation, a toxic legacy of a ruinous war. Biên Hòa is now the site (see Chapter 10) of one of the largest industrial parks in Vietnam.

It is not forgotten that US forces dropped twice the tonnage of high explosives on Vietnam that the Allied side did on both Europe and Asia together during the Second World War. But the Vietnamese do not want to be defined by their past.

The US stake in Vietnam has grown quickly to one of its biggest trading and investment partners, despite its low starting point in the mid-1990s, a result of the US embargo and the poor health of the Vietnamese economy. US-Vietnam trade totalled US$451 million in 1995.[8] Since then it has increased a hundredfold to US$45 billion, making the US Vietnam's single-largest trade partner.[9] Between 2010 and 2015, Vietnam was the second-fastest growing of America's top 50 export markets. US investments topped US$12 billion by 2019.[10]

Why do African countries not pick up such lessons? After all, South Africa's ruling African National Congress (ANC) learnt in the past from the Vietnamese.

The ANC's Vietnam

In 1978, facing internal competition from the Black Consciousness Movement, Inkatha and the South African Students Movement, and with Umkhonto we Sizwe battling to make a sustained military impact, Moscow advised the ANC to visit the newly unified Vietnam. There they could learn from Vietnamese strategists like its military supremo, Senior General Vo Nguyen Giap – the 'Red Napoleon' – and the technique of a 'people's war'.

A delegation, led by the ANC president, Oliver Tambo, and including Joe Modise, Joe Slovo, Chris Hani, Alfred Nzo, Cassius Make and Mzwai Piliso, spent two weeks in Hanoi in October 1978. Despite obvious differences between the situations in South Africa and Vietnam, not least given the scale of superpower involvement and the intensity of the respective conflicts, the ANC delegation left, as Russia's Africanist veteran Vladimir Shubin has observed, feeling 'deeply impressed by the Vietnamese methods of underground armed struggle, especially the co-ordination between illegal en masse activities'.[11] In the process, they learnt that a revolution 'must walk on both feet: one military, and the other political'.

They concluded that 'the Vietnam experience reveals certain shortcomings on our part and draws attention to areas of crucial importance which we have tended to neglect'. In Tambo's words, it also exposed the ANC as having 'fallen into a bad strategic situation, in which too much emphasis had been placed on the armed struggle, at the expense of political mobilisation, making for an impossible equation'.[12] The delegation's findings were brought together in 'The Green Book', what ANC doyen Govan Mbeki referred to as a 'highly significant document in the evolution of the ANC and the South African struggle'.[13]

'The Green Book' enabled greater co-ordination of the ANC's political efforts, including the creation of a 'popular front' in the form of the United Democratic Front, the strengthening of a propaganda wing and the importance of international diplomatic efforts.

Another key lesson was that the Vietnam War was 'won' in Washington, and not just in the trenches. General William Westmoreland, the local US commander, referred to it as 'the first war in history lost in the columns of the *New York Times*'.[14]

Vietnam taught that if the ANC was to succeed in overthrowing the apartheid regime, it would have to gather a broad front of international support, increase media coverage and rally local youths to build a political movement that could outlast the then South African Defence Force. The armed struggle would have to become 'secondary' to armed propaganda.[15] Upon their return from Vietnam, the ANC took a decided ideological turn from socialism as a matter of tactical caution.[16]

The strategic impact of the ANC's 1978 mission to Vietnam on the course of ANC and South African history cannot be overstated. Howard Barrell has termed it a 'Damascus moment', a watershed between an exclusively militant (and likely unsuccessful) ANC and a multiracial, unified ANC.[17]

This pragmatic change of direction begs the question: if the ANC could learn in the past, why not now?

If the party took the same care in visiting Vietnam today, it would find a country transformed, where its party cadres are au fait with free market principles and institutional responsiveness, and where they don't just preach the importance of investors, but act to create space and the necessary guarantees.

For all of the drawbacks of a single-party state, including widespread corruption, and the rhetorical adherence to the ubiquitous hammer and sickle and socialist banners, the contemporary thinking is both liberal and pragmatic enough to realise the need for the state to relinquish its role in the economy. It was the outcome, writes journalist David Lamb, of putting 'Karl Marx and Adam Smith into an economic blender'.[18]

The number of state-owned enterprises, as described in Chapter 10, is one measure of this process. Public listings are another. The Ho Chi Minh stock exchange was launched in 2000 with two companies. Eighteen years later there were 396 counters with a US$148-billion market capitalisation, with another 376 on the Hanoi bourse.

The revolution is not limited to the world of finance and listings. 'The difference between now and then,' says Le Phuoc Minh, the director of the Institute of African and Middle East Studies, 'is that we have food where there was once only hunger, and the hope of becoming a middle class where previously everyone was just poor.'

This was the result of the state getting out of the way. Instead of state-led growth, as favoured by many African governments today, Vietnam relied on the private sector to provide the growth necessary for development. If Vietnam, the country of a die-hard socialist like General Giap, could put its ideologies aside and move on from history, anyone can.

Yesterday is another country

Giap died in 2013, aged 102. His passing signalled changing generations. The wartime leaders have all faded away, South and North, and some in exile. While Giap remains a national hero, by the 1990s Vietnam had moved on from his brand of leadership, loosening the reins of state control and making room for private enterprise. While the 17-member Politburo and the general secretary of the Communist Party were still firmly in charge, the country was now interested in prosperity, not just revolutionary rhetoric, political independence and economic survival. You could not eat ideology or ride it to work. If the first liberation struggle had been against the Americans and French, the second was in the transition through Doi Moi to a market economy and global integration. A third might still come, as Lamb puts it, in the political domain, the more likely if the party proves unresponsive to the aspirations of a globalising youth.[19]

Innovate, don't look back

Not getting stuck in the past also applies to the need to innovate, no matter how successful. That is the lesson of two of Asia's regional business icons, Fujifilm and Acer.

Fujifilm was established in 1934 and became the second-largest producer of photographic film worldwide behind Kodak. It was in a race to surpass Kodak and finally did so in 2000, just in time to witness a global fall in the sales of film so drastic that it brought the industry to its knees. When Jun Ito, an operations manager at their headquarters in Tokyo, joined the company in 1994, 90% of the business was film.[20] Within three short years, film had become unprofitable.

Were it not for some forward thinking and recognition of the changing times as early as the 1970s, Fujifilm would not have been able to develop its first digital camera in 1988, and position itself as the market leader in digital, with 30% at the end of the 1990s.[21]

Even so, with the advent of digital technology, Fujifilm suffered dramatic losses. Film and film cameras were by 2019 less than 1% of its US$20-billion turnover. But their losses were nothing compared to that of Kodak, which failed to believe that the digital era signalled the need for dramatic change. Kodak, which had employed 145 000 people at its peak and held billions of dollars in assets, filed for bankruptcy in 2012.[22] It had been blinded by its own success.

Testimony to a culture of innovation and reinvention, Fujifilm now invests more than 6% of its annual turnover into R&D. As Shigetaka Komori, the CEO who successfully steered the company through the difficult times, has stated, 'Fujifilm today is engaged in such a wide variety of businesses that it's difficult to summarize everything we do. But you can say one thing with certainty: this company is technology-oriented.'

Acer has also had to innovate quickly to stay in business. The company founded by Stan Shih in 1976, one of Taiwan's very few recognisable brands, was the world's second-largest producer of PCs in the early 2000s, but rapidly lost market share to competition in a saturated market. With the widespread rise of smartphones in the early 2010s, the company's prospects and core business looked weak, the resignation of its CEO Gianfranco Lanci in 2011 a low point.[23]

Change came in 2008 when Acer partnered with Google to develop Chromebooks, specialised laptops that run on Google's Chrome operating system. Early entry and a wide product offering have helped Acer become the leading Chromebook manufacturer, the majority of which are bought by schools.

Acer has again had to reinvent itself as a specialised gaming and design computing manufacturer, building high-resolution machines for a specialist market – the first mainstream PC company to do so. This move has been designed to take advantage of the nearly US$140-billion global gaming market, one that is predicted to balloon to US$300 billion by 2025.[24]

Innovation and occasional directional change are not only essential in terms of products, but also in terms of production methods. This much is illustrated by Toyota's revolution in manufacturing techniques, which have prompted an entire scholarship looking at the 'Toyota Production System', 'Just in Time' and other 'lean' factory-related lexicography. By learning from abroad (particularly the US), Taiichi Ohno developed the *genchi genbutsu* (literally, 'go and see for yourself') method, which takes engineers directly to the production floor, rather than relying on assumptions or previously held ideas.

We have been asked whether a company like Acer would invest in Zimbabwe – essentially, whether establishing a hi-tech sector could regenerate an otherwise defunct economy and create jobs. The reason why it won't is that Zimbabwe lacks the basics: electricity, a supply chain of electronic products, a cohort of locally based engineers, financing structures and institutions, sufficient collateral, government subsidies, the rule of law, policy predictability and ease of market access – in fact, any kind of comparative advantage that would make them a better bet for investment than an East Asian country. These 'rules' of investment apply to those sectors where investors are not bound by the presence of commodities. You cannot easily leapfrog the basics, as the next chapter argues.

Conclusion: Looking ahead

In Vietnam, pragmatism runs deep. Ho Chi Minh was, for his iconic revolutionary status, always the realist. During the Second World War, when the Viet Minh received assistance from the Office of Strategic Services, the secret precursor of the Central Intelligence Agency, Ho praised Washington as a champion of democracy that would help them end colonial rule. His independence speech on 2 September 1945 started by invoking the words of Thomas Jefferson: 'We hold these truths to be self-evident, that all men are created equal, that they are endowed by their Creator with certain unalienable rights, that among these are life, liberty and the pursuit of happiness.'[25]

After Saigon's fall in 1975, the Viet Cong did not put up a flag over the US Embassy as they did in other locations. 'We are not authorised to raise one,' said a soldier guarding the premises. 'We do not want to humiliate the Americans. They will come back.'[26]

The popular notion that Vietnam's growth success is just about incentives or cheap wages is a crude caricature of the difficult policy choices Hanoi has had to make, not least the commitment to liberal change, however bumpy and strenuous that path. It also shows that, no matter how important the goal of independence, it is necessary to have a plan to meet the aspirations of those who have fought for freedom beyond statist and redistributive impulses.

It shows that looking forward – with some sensitivity – always reaps better results than looking backwards, and casting blame.

Chapter 13

Get the Basics Right for Growth

It doesn't matter how slowly you go, so long as you do not stop.

— Confucius

When the atomic bomb exploded about 600 metres above Hiroshima on the morning of 6 August 1945, a group of children had just assembled in the schoolyard of Honkawa Elementary School, less than 500 metres from the hypocentre of the blast. They were awaiting roll call before their school day would start. Except that it never would, as nearly 400 of them would die when, at 8.15 that morning, the course of the world was changed forever.

The Hiroshima Memorial Museum displays parts of their incinerated clothing. Those who weren't killed immediately died slow deaths of pain and illness. Burnt by the intolerable heat from the explosion, which caused the ground temperature in the city to briefly rise to 4 000 degrees Celcius, some started drinking the sticky, black rain that begun falling from the sky. The rain was radioactive.

It is difficult to imagine any city – and people – that had to recover from such trauma. But as Chapter 1 illustrates, Hiroshima did, as did Japan.

Three days after the bombing, the city's trams had started running again. 'Blue sky schools' were convened in the open air, and teaching commenced at the soonest possible date. Just four months after the bomb fell, Hiroshima's biggest manufacturer, Mazda, had resumed its production line. Within a generation, Japan had rebuilt itself from the ground up, growing at 10% per year from 1950 and 1973, and reaching high-income status in 1977.

But post-war Japan was not built in a day. It rather came about as the result of reforms that had taken place much earlier, with the Meiji Restoration in the late nineteenth century to be exact.

This is the lesson from Hiroshima, Japan, and many other Asian countries: if development is underwritten by the 'basics', there is little that the hand of fortune can do to halt it.

Essential stages of economic growth

Why were some Asian economies harder hit by the 1998 financial crisis than others?

The obvious answers relate to exposure to financial markets and level of household and government debt. But there are other factors, not least the level of economic diversification, and the strength of underlying industries. This is what is called sustainable growth, and it explains partially why the economies of Japan, Taiwan, Singapore and South Korea were able to bounce back after the crisis and escape the middle-income trap, while others, such as Malaysia and Indonesia, were harder hit. They did not have their basics in place as well as they could have.

Most economies develop in stages. While development is not a destination, there were signposts along the way, which included agricultural reform, frequently catalysed in the case of East Asia by large-scale investment in agriculture. Land redistribution was premised on increased productivity, alongside (or followed by) universal access to education.

This was often followed, in the case of Japan, Taiwan, Korea and China, by urban growth and the rise of light manufacturing, spurred by agro-processing. Textiles and plastics came next, eventually displaced by heavier industries, and then followed by more modern industries such as hi-tech and services. Political and economic liberalisation followed, which also came with greater civic freedoms and a shifted focus to the environment.

Every successful Asian country described in this book has found itself at some stage of this ladder during the last half-century. Many are still ascending: Vietnam moving through the light manufacturing phase, along with Bangladesh and Cambodia, while China is nearing the end of its heavy industrial phase and entering hi-tech, as Taiwan and Japan had done in the late 1980s.

But this progression is not necessarily the model for the future, particularly with regard to industrialisation. A jump ahead, past plastics, fast fashion and heavy fossil fuel-based energy, is not just desirable, but a necessity if we want to leave an inhabitable planet for the next generation.

Problems emerge, however, when essential steps – particularly agriculture and educational reforms – are skipped. In *How Asia Works*, Joe Studwell recounts how the experiences of the unique city-states of Singapore and Hong Kong were for a while misinterpreted by the World Bank, leading to a prescription for economic growth that started and ended with laissez-faire government. This missed a fundamental point: free markets and economic liberalisation alone might lead to some years of rapid growth, but this will not withstand a storm. As Studwell puts it:

> What the Asian crisis clarified was that a consistent set of government policy interventions had indeed made the difference between long-run success and failure in economic development in East Asia. In Japan, Korea, Taiwan and China, governments radically restructured agriculture after WWII, focused their modernisation efforts on manufacturing, and made their financial systems slaves to these two objectives. They thereby changed the structures of their economies in a manner that made it all but impossible to return to an earlier stage of development.[1]

Malaysia, Thailand and Indonesia, meanwhile, had tried to develop by attaining high growth through their financial systems but without the necessary 'underlying fundamentals', to borrow from financial terminology.

This proved to be unsustainable, and left them in a middle-income trap.

'Telescoping' describes how Japan achieved within about 60 years a level of development that had taken Britain 150 years, while the tigers did so in just 30 years.[2] This is different from 'leapfrogging', which implies sidestepping essential reforms. In Africa, as in Asia, growth will be limited by skills levels, which are the brakes on productivity, and the absence of other basic elements, identified here as agriculture reform, infrastructure and the systems that enable efficient market access.

Rather, Japan shows the importance of incremental development and making sure the basics are in place.

A thick layer of human capital[3]

'The Meiji period defined how Japan does it,' says Kenichi Ohno of Tokyo's National Graduate Institute for Policy Studies.[4]

The foundation for education had been established during the Edo period (1603–1868) with the proliferation of some 20 000 Terakoya (private primary schools), which taught writing, reading and arithmetic – 'one of the key reasons', reflects Ohno, 'why the Meiji period could industrialise so fast'. These reforms included universal and standardised access to education, narrowing the gender gap as early as 1910.[5] The official literacy rate in Japan today is 99.9%, and nearly half the population possesses a tertiary education, the fourth-highest proportion in the world after Russia, Israel and Canada.[6] Japanese fourth and eighth graders consistently rank in the top five globally in mathematics and science.[7]

Japan's neighbours followed closely. The gap between these five East Asian countries and territories (Singapore, Japan, Taiwan, Korea and Hong Kong) and the next highest-achieving country tested by Trends in International Mathematics and Science Study (TIMSS) is 23 points.[8] Moreover, some of these countries achieved this standard in a shorter time than Japan, with Korea and Singapore reaching near-universal primary

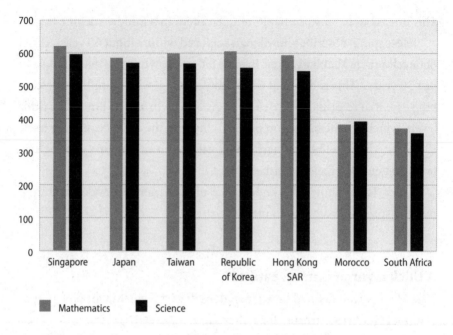

Figure 13.1: Eighth grade maths and science (TIMSS) scores, 2015

Source: TIMSS, 2015. The TIMSS achievement scale is based on the combined achievement distribution of participating. Fifty-seven countries and seven benchmarking entities (regional jurisdictions of countries, such as states or provinces) participated in TIMSS 2015.

school enrolment within 25 years, compared to the century it took Japan.[9]

'Education is our most important economic and social strategy,' says Singapore's senior minister, Tharman Shanmugaratnam.[10] 'From the early days the paradox was that we depoliticised the substance of education, yet we took a great political interest in creating an ethos of performance and autonomy in so doing.' Singapore 'moved educators around continuously as an organising principle to enable the spread of success and isolation of failure, never permitting entrenchment in one place. Every principal moved after five to six years. This created a performance ethic in the key arena of action, the school, and not the ministry.'

In the 1990s, Singapore took the bold step of instituting a performance-based pay system. 'This was highly contentious, and took more than five years to get it fully bedded in. Moreover,' Shanmugaratnam notes, 'the metrics are so difficult. As a result, we overnight had to make qualitative judgements. But now the culture is fully established, taking care that this is not a commercial setting and we don't want the teachers to impress the wrong attributes.'

'Education has been', he emphasises, 'absolutely central to facilitating social mobility in Singapore. Our public schools are regarded as our pinnacle, not the private system. Admission is not based on the parents' means but on geography, which stems from our social housing policy, which aimed to mix people up. Also, our metrics are not limited to exams alone, but are rather focused on demonstrating the individuals' abilities. We have found that this performance-based ethic motivates parents, linking parents with the teachers, motivating them.' This is also backed up by the rewards. 'We pay teachers the same as other professionals in the civil service, which keeps them highly motivated and well rewarded.

'Our experience at education shows', concludes Shanmugaratnam, 'that the system itself and governance count.'

There are shorter-term means of improving skills, not least by importing talent. This measure has been adopted by Singapore and South Korea among others, the former principally through its openness to foreign capital and multinational companies. In the case of South Korea, aid was used for the development of human capital, especially in the areas of agriculture, forestry, engineering and ICT. Between 1962 and 1971, for example, over 7 000 Koreans received training abroad, and more than 1 500 experts were sent to Korea by donor nations.[11]

Africa would do well to plan for the long-term educational needs of its people and act with alacrity by attracting talent, starting with the diaspora. Literacy levels in sub-Saharan Africa are the lowest of any region worldwide, at under 60% for adults. This reflects the state of primary school participation, which remains very low, only 77% of children of school-going age being enrolled in 2017 against a global average of 90%.

If fixing Africa's broken education systems is key to sustainable development, so too is the need to take farming out of subsistence and survival to commercial, agribusiness operations, as the example of Malawi shows.

Farms that produce for people

According to traditional economic theory, à la Walt Rostow, an agricultural revolution is an essential step in the path towards economic growth, as this allows for greater productivity and the division of labour in areas other than subsistence agriculture.[12] The importance of agriculture is not lost on African politicians, at least rhetorically.

The first half of the first Presidential Debate in Malawi's 2019 election, which took place at Lilongwe's Bingu wa Mutharika International Conference Centre in front of a crowd of around 1 000 and a live television audience, was dominated by questions on agriculture: land ownership (where women are unable to own land in some parts); climate change; environmental management; the Green Belt Initiative; the effectiveness of the Farm Input Subsidy Programme; the inclusion of women; and the future of tobacco, Malawi's principal export, which one of the candidates, Atupele Muluzi, said was 'our gold', an unusual statement perhaps for a minister of health, but one that illustrates Malawi's development plight and paucity of options.

The prominence of agriculture is hardly surprising for a country where 84% of the population lives in the rural areas, and where, in the estimation of the Reverend Lazarus Chakwera, the leader of the Malawi Congress Party, some 80% of them are dependent on farming.

The tobacco farmers are the lucky ones, linked into the global economy and to a system of governance where, given the nature of the product, there is intensive scrutiny of farming practices. It is the ideal crop in other ways. It is hardy, lasts for a long time, and is, in the case of Malawi's burley, air-cured, thus requiring no electricity, and very labour-intensive.

One hectare of tobacco produces 375 000 leaves. Each of these is picked and tied individually. The country produced 160 000 hectares (or 163 000 tonnes) of burley tobacco in 2018 – a lot of planting, picking, drying, tying and sorting.

The majority of Malawians remain, however, locked into subsistence farming, eking an existence from a plot of maize with occasional soya or groundnuts on the side. Their problem is not too much, but too little, globalisation.

Malawians enjoy, if that is the right word, an average per capita income of just US$420, just twice that at independence in 1964. And this is an average: many of the 2.5 million farmers countrywide earn little more than US$75 every year, the sort of levels of their Vietnamese counterparts pre-reform. Malawi ranks with the likes of Burundi, Niger, Democratic Republic of Congo and the Central African Republic as officially one of the world's poorest countries in terms of per capita income.

This reflects Malawi's population increase from four million to 19 million by 2019. In fact, GDP had increased tenfold in real terms in the 55 years since 1964, though the population increase has nullified half of the gain. By the start of 2019, more than half the population was under 18. And the projection of a 45-million population by 2045 does not give heart, nor do the bands of young men lounging around, village to village. The population is increasing faster than opportunities.

Such population growth will place considerable pressure on land. In the central region, the average farm plot is around one hectare. In the richer farming areas of southern Malawi, it is half this size, where population growth is, in the words of one commercial farmer, '15 years ahead of the central region'.

The morning following the Presidential Debate, we encountered Serious Chimpanje cycling along the Chitukula Road, northwest of Lilongwe, notable for his bright green and yellow Australia cricketing shirt and 20-kilogram bundle of tobacco strapped to his bicycle's carrier. He was taking them to the local trading centre 'because I need food', he said. He was likely to get just 220 Malawian kwacha per bag – about US$0.30 – and about one-sixth of what a farmer on a procurement scheme might expect, a price at which only the middleman could be profiting from his toil.

Sub-Saharan Africa still has more than 50% of its workforce in agriculture, double the global average, though they produce just 15% of the sub-continent's income.[13] Thus, boosting agricultural productivity should be a priority. But most African countries are not doing this. Most are caught in the (adverse) cycle of neglecting agriculture, which leads to intensified rural poverty, pushing people into the urban areas. This strips resources away from rural development, thus accentuating the adverse cycle of rural poverty and out-migration. Unlike their Asian counterparts, African leaders have not successfully promoted an African Green Revolution despite their rhetorical commitment to the concept.

African agriculture has to commercialise and diversify. If government cannot make the necessary investment, then transformation will require a private sector willing to invest. And this will, in turn, demand stable and favourable policy and macro-economic conditions. The results can be spectacular. For example, Vietnam was able to transform coffee production from virtually zero in 1980 to 27.5 million bags (or 20% of global production) in 2018, fundamentally because the government opened up the market. Until then, the government bought all production at a fixed price. The sector now employs 2.6 million people, working more than half a million smallholdings.[14] This sort of rapid transformation can be achieved in Africa. Better extension services in Uganda have seen that Central African country double its coffee yields and production within a decade to five million bags. Kenya's coffee production has by contrast fallen by two-thirds to just 800 000 bags, due to a shrinkage of areas under production and the use of poor varieties. Ethiopia has perhaps the greatest coffee potential, but so far has been hamstrung by an overvalued exchange rate, which undermines competitiveness in export markets and discourages increased investment and production.[15]

Make the right changes and choices and the upside is obvious, and huge for a poor country, where a small uptick in wealth is relatively large. There are notable advantages, including rich soils and plenty of water. Malawi can offset the disadvantages of location by employing an underutilised rail network, where transport costs are half as much as road. It has the basis of a usable and replicable agriculture extension and market system in the tobacco business, but translating this into other crops and sectors will require a government willing to adjust their interests and policies to the needs of Malawi's burgeoning population rather than elite interests. Get agriculture right and much else can follow.

Yet, for all of the fine speeches and statements at the Presidential Debate, the eventual winner of the May 2019 election, the incumbent president, Arthur Peter Mutharika, did not pitch up. Politics continues to remain frustratingly estranged from practical realities and the people's needs.

From Asia, Taiwan offers some further clues about allowing farmers to succeed.

Food for thought

'If the nest is overturned, there won't be whole eggs left.' So goes the Chinese saying, which served as the philosophical basis of Taiwan's model land reform programme of the late 1940s and 1950s.

Before land reform, Taiwan consisted of a feudal system, in which tenants paid as much as 50% of their harvest to landlords. When two million Chinese nationalists came ashore on the island in 1947, they were outnumbered by locals four to one. Very soon, pressure was building on the self-appointed government to equalise Taiwanese society, starting with the landholding class.

The impressive land reform project, dreamt up by Sun Yat-sen, took place in three distinct stages: first, rents to landlords were capped at 37.5% of harvests, giving tenants an incentive to work harder and keep more of the yields. From 1948 to 1951, agricultural yields increased by more than 47%.[16] This gave rise to a generation of wealthier farmers, suddenly able to buy oxen (labelled '37.5 oxen'), send their kids to school ('37.5 kids') and build houses ('37.5 homes').

Next came the release of public farmland to smallholder farmers, which the government did on a grand scale from 1951. They released about 140 000 hectares to the benefit of more than a quarter of a million households, making an immense improvement to land access and ownership, again driving productivity increases on these farms.

The third step, land to the tiller, was executed in 1953, when landlords were forced to sell their land to the government for a fixed price (2.5 times the value of annual yields). Landlords were paid through government-backed land bonds (70%), which tenants, in turn, paid off over a period of ten years, and shares in state-owned enterprises (30%). In this way, government incurred no debt from redistribution.

While these policies caused great disruption to the landholding class, this was a trade-off that government was willing to make, particularly because it kept the political nest upright. But land was not enough. They also had to increase the number of eggs.

Since the 1950s, Taiwan has had an extensive agricultural support programme, assisting farmers through extension officers, farmer associations and co-operatives. Today, Taiwan is the world's largest exporter of orchids and produces rice worth more than US$1 billion annually, still on small farms, with farmers able to make a living through high yields.

Agriculture reform ultimately had a further bonus in releasing 'energy from the villages to the cities', according to Shih-jung Hsu, professor and chair of the Department of Land Economics at the National Chengchi University in Taipei.[17] The cities were exactly where large-scale economic growth and development would then take place, including the establishment of bicycle factories like Giant and Merida, or tech companies like Taiwan Semi-Conductor Manufacturing Corporation and Acer. Across the Taiwan Strait in mainland China, a similar story unfolded, as described in Chapter 9.

Turning the urban areas into engines of growth also requires a series of reforms, without which they risk becoming sites of desperation, homelessness and unemployment, as Lagos all too clearly shows.

A city must work for its people

China viewed urbanisation positively, as we saw in Chapter 9, as a source of growth and industrial development.[18] China has more than 100 cities with populations of over one million.[19] Its positive attitude towards urbanisation is exemplified by the scale of infrastructure development in cities, from housing to roads and rails connecting 'supercities', all in the interest of productivity.

Africa's most populous city, Lagos, represents both the promise and the

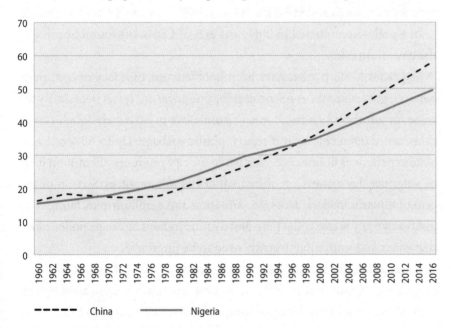

Figure 13.2: Urbanisation rates (%) in China and Nigeria, 1960–2017

Source: World Bank Databank, 2019.

fear at the intersection of demographic change and urbanisation. Lagos has grown a hundredfold, from under 200 000 people to over 20 million in just two generations. This rapid growth has placed inordinate strain on already faltering infrastructure, especially housing, transport and electricity. Fixing these legacy problems will not be easy; anticipation of future growth magnifies these challenges.

With an astonishing rate of influx of 18.6% since 2000, the fastest rate of any city in the world[20] (with Istanbul in second place at 11.7%), it is unsurprising that some two-thirds of the city's people live in slum conditions. Meanwhile, Lagos is estimated to double again in population in the next three decades.

Attempts to reduce the housing deficit, estimated to be at least two million units, are made more difficult by mortgage interest rates of some 38% – this a reflection both of heavy government borrowing in the market to fund its own needs and high risk. Around 60% of mortgage holders default.

In a poll we conducted in 2017, just 21% of Lagosians found housing in the city affordable.[21]

Upgrades to slum areas have been hobbled, too, by a lack of continuity between governments. A pet project for one governor is not necessarily the same for another. As a result, many people live in extremely tough conditions, amid open sewers and strewn plastic garbage. Up to 60% of Lagos State experiences floods each year, while the city produces 210 million litres of water per day against a requirement of 794 million litres. Sixty-nine per cent of households lack access to sanitation and a million-plus families do not receive any waste collection. Nearly nine in ten Lagosians polled agree that water and sanitation urgently need to be improved.

Lagos is the site of both dearth and excess, where vast wealth lives side by side with chaos and poverty. This fuels mistrust, compounded by episodic slum demolition. Many people prefer to remain put in the absence of visible alternatives; as one community leader put it, 'we are frightened that we will lose what little we have'.

Take the Makoko community in their stilt houses on the edge of Lagos lagoon, long a centrepiece of Western poverty porn. The nearly 100 000 people, most of whom are children, live in appallingly unhealthy conditions, where malaria and typhoid are rife. The water is a petrol black, full of faeces and much else. Yet, the community retains a strong attachment to the area and each other, partly because of its ethnic homogeneity (most are Egun), its shared fishing dependency, its 100-year history and the absence of viable options for improvement.

A poorly integrated transport system, and a failure to fully employ the city's numerous waterways, mean that Lagosians spend nearly three billion hours in traffic annually, an average of four hours each per day. The main port of Apapa is hamstrung by work to upgrade the access road, requiring trucks to queue for up to a month, instead of the normal two to three days, to collect containers.

The former governor of Lagos State, Akinwunmi Ambode, who served a four-year term from 2015 to 2019, had an ambitious agenda to transform the city into the continent's third-largest economy. Equally, his government had a bold plan to improve electricity payment collection rates and add 3 000 megawatts of capacity, through the use of independent power providers delivering directly to the distribution network.

But even the most well-intentioned plans fail against a backdrop of weak governance, widespread corruption, a time-consuming legal system, and anaemic economic growth highly vulnerable to the vagaries of oil prices.

Nigeria's growth remains limited by the structure of its economy – where elite interests have served to trump the reforms that could lead to much-needed diversification and job creation, which explains the limited benefit of the country's oil wealth. Developing a healthy manufacturing sector – uncaptured by monopoly interests – could help to put some of Nigeria's youthful energy to work. But, more importantly, entrepreneurs must be allowed to operate, and this will require infrastructure, particularly electricity, as is discussed in Chapter 14.

Conclusion: No single model

Asia's rapid development, as we have seen, has not relied on a single model.

In some cases (Japan and Taiwan), this was built on the break-up of feudal land ownership, and the incentivisation of farming talent and labour through ownership. In others (the Philippines and Malaysia), the elites were co-opted. In the case of Vietnam, which experienced the triple trauma of colonialism, a violent and ongoing liberation war, and the folly of a command economic experiment, the insertion of free market profit incentives in agriculture drove a change in policy throughout the economy. In South Korea and Japan, large companies, the *zaibatsu* and the *chaebols*, drove growth and employment, while in Taiwan this was down to small- and medium-sized, often family-owned, businesses. Singapore relied on multinational companies bringing skills, capital, technology and logistics chains, while China succeeded through (or in spite of) central planning. Some countries were more democratic than others but nearly all were ethnically or racially diverse, with difficult histories and a poor infrastructure inheritance. Nearly all were poor, in fact poorer than the African average in 1960.

Despite these differences, there are common threads. In each and every successful case, the 'basics' were put in place as a matter of priority. Farms were made to produce, ensuring self-reliance wherever possible, while moving into higher-value exports and education improved the productivity of workers. Cities were crucial as incubators of growth and opportunity.

Such reforms are a consistent theme across the region's development performers. They are the foundation of subsequent improvements, including logistics and electricity, discussed in the next chapter. The examples are clear: for growth to be sustainable, it must be based on the fundamentals of a national project, centred on education, agricultural reform and urban planning to benefit the many, not the few.

Chapter 14

Build and Integrate

No single entrepreneur or private firm can credibly overcome an infrastructure gap ... and no country in the world has the administrative
and financial resources to blindly build all the airports, roads, railways
... that entrepreneurs need. What is needed is selectivity, identification
and targeting of industries in which an economy has a comparative
advantage.

— Justin Yifu Lin and Célestin Monga, *Beating the Odds*

Some 1.3 billion people are without electricity in the world. Half of them are
in Africa. Even though sub-Saharan Africa has been growing its installed
electricity capacity at 7.5% per annum since 2010, it is not enough given the
backlog and the 2.8% annual rate of population increase. At such slow pace
of electrification, most African countries will fail to reach universal access
to electricity even by 2050.[1]

And there are wider developmental costs. African leaders often lament
the export of raw materials and import of manufactured goods from China.
Hence the call for beneficiation – processing that adds more value. Take
copper-exporting Zambia, for example. Copper is refined in the country
through combinations of chemical leaching and smelting. As much as 600
tonnes of earth have to be moved, separated, crushed and refined to produce one tonne of copper. The copper is then exported as plates to the
major consumers, in the case of Zambia overwhelmingly to China, which
takes half of its production. China turns the copper into insulation, wire
and pipe, among other things.

Zambia is short of power, given the demands of an increasing population and its overwhelming dependency on hydro and the premium on rain and careful water management. The national power company, ZESCO, produces on paper 2 250 megawatts, but in reality probably closer to half this amount. A mine smelter, which is necessary to refine concentrate into copper plates, taking it from 25% to 99.99% purity, is power hungry, as are the refining tanks. There are four of these smelters across the country, each drawing 40–60 megawatts. Competitive pricing for commodities is a function, in part, of scarcity, but also of skills, logistical efficiencies and input costs, particularly electricity and labour.

The continent's chronic power problems negatively affect no fewer than 30 countries and exact a heavy toll on economic growth and productivity, and therefore job creation, not to mention quality of life and the spread of wealth. As McKinsey notes, 'whether people can obtain electricity, and if so, how much they are able to consume are the two most important metrics that can indicate the degree to which the power sector is supporting national development.'[2]

Africa needs better infrastructure, which is modelled on people's needs and funded smartly. The lesson of infrastructure in driving development is that there need to be matching hardware and software to make it work.

How Asia did it

Diversification requires energy. Whether this be adding value to minerals or to power sewing machines or agro-processors, or even powering computer coding labs and tech start-ups, not much can happen without a reliable and inexpensive supply of electricity. It also has positive effects on health care, nutrition and education.

The problem is, Africa is energy short.[3] Africans receive one-quarter of the power resources available to Southeast Asians on a per capita basis, and a tenth of that consumed by South Americans.[4] Africa's total installed

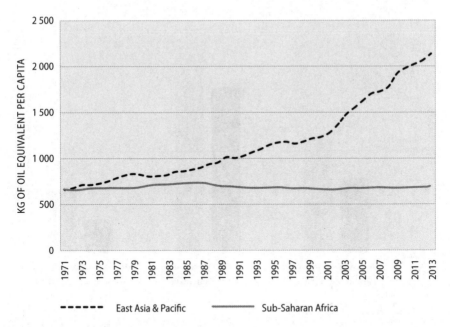

Figure 14.1: Comparative per capita energy consumption
Source: World Bank Databank, 2019.

capacity of electricity was 168 gigawatts in 2016,[5] compared with 334 gigawatts in India and 1 650 gigawatts in China. But South Africa accounts for
one-third of this capacity. To put this into perspective, Nigeria, which has
a population four times the size of South Africa's, has less than one-fifth
of South Africa's installed capacity. Per capita consumption of energy in
sub-Saharan Africa (excluding South Africa) is 180 kilowatts per capita,
compared to 13 000 kilowatts in the US and 6 500 kilowatts in Europe.[6]

As a result, fewer than half of Africans have regular access to electricity,
on and off the national grid.[7] This figure is skewed by the big gap between
electricity access in urban households (71%) versus rural households
(22%). And a large share is made up by private generators costing at least
three times as much to operate as power from national grids. Nigeria, for
example, is the world's largest purchaser of generators. Those who cannot
afford generators have to rely on biomass sources for cooking, heating and

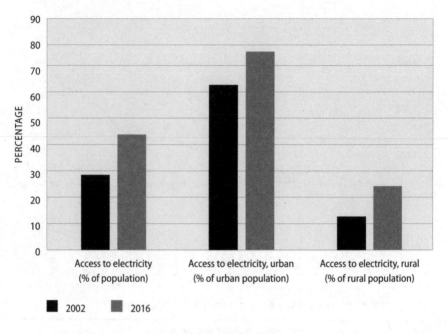

Figure 14.2: Electricity access in sub-Saharan Africa

Source: Sustainable Energy for All database.

lighting, with all the environmental and efficiency issues attached.

Though there is great discrepancy between states and rural and urban areas,[8] some 78% of Southeast Asians receive power from national grids. The overwhelming majority of this is from fossil fuels. In China, for example, this was the result of a nationwide electrification programme. Erdaoqiao, a settlement in south-west China, made headlines in 2015 for being the last village to receive power under this programme, which has seen electricity reach 900 million people since 1949, and much of it in the last 30 years.[9] (By comparison, Africa increased its electricity power capacity by less than 1 000 megawatts per annum on average between 2000 and 2018.)

The Chinese power sector, the world's largest since 2011, services 1.3 billion consumers with more than 1 700 gigawatts of installed capacity,

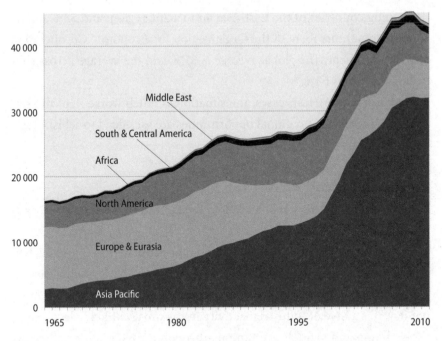

Figure 14.3: Annual coal consumption, measured in equivalents of annual terawatt hours

Source: BP Statistical Review of World Energy.

the equivalent of eight Germanys. The 13th Five-Year Plan, published in 2016, targets 2 000 gigawatts of capacity installed by 2020, a 20% increase. As noted in Chapter 9, much of this is reliant on new coal-fired sources, meaning China produces no less than a quarter of the world's emissions: it is not only the world's factory, but also the world's smokestack.

The challenge of diversification is felt even in Japan. The Fukushima nuclear accident in March 2011 was caused by a tsunami, which flooded the emergency generators, leading to a nuclear meltdown and the release of radioactive material. Following Fukushima,[10] a new energy plan was adopted by the Japanese government, aimed at reducing the reliance on nuclear power, then around 25% of power supplied. Fossil fuels compose over 80% of energy consumption in Japan, compared to 74% across the developing countries of the East Asia and Pacific region, and 58% among (high-income) members of the Organisation for Economic Co-operation and Development. The global average is 65%, and the average across sub-Saharan Africa is 64%.[11]

And, in some African cases, the situation is much worse than the statistics indicate, where national opportunities are sacrificed to selfishness.

Powering Africa

'Give us electricity,' says cobbler Peter Owyia, 'and I will double my daily production.'

Peter's calculation was common among the estimated 50 000 shoe, belt and bag makers in Ariaria market in the city of Aba in south-eastern Nigeria's Abia State. With each cobbler producing an average of 50 shoes per day, it is a hive of industrial activity in the most unlikely place. Abia's shoes, boots and sandals are famous throughout Nigeria and, increasingly, as the French labels on some products hint, now in parts of West Africa.

Underfoot is a sludge of mud, plastic and goodness knows what else. The road outside is a slippery track, temporarily worsened by a current project to install a parallel concrete drain. Just inside the entrance is a man focused on fixing a large pile of paraffin cookers. To the left are food vendors. To the right is a team of women manually weaving the leather straps for sandals, the hands a blur of twists, turns and flicks.

Industry is everywhere; the industriousness impressive.

Yet, there is one thing mostly missing amid the sights, smells and sounds of the market: the hypnotic *grrrrrr* of small generators. The margin and money are so tight that the shoes are manually cut out and sewn on foot-powered treadle sewing machines.

The cost of electricity supplied by Nigeria's grid is less than half that from generators. But the problem is there is no grid supply. A failure of the consumer to pay has undermined the production of power, the investment in the equipment and systems required and, in a vicious cycle, the supply of reliable power for which consumers are willing to pay. On paper, Nigeria should produce 7 100 megawatts based on installed generation capacity, but, in practice, it only generates 4 600 megawatts. This is still a far cry from the 200 000 megawatts of electricity Nigeria theoretically needs to meet the demand of its population.[12]

It does not have to be like this.

A stone's throw away from Ariaria market is the Apia power generation plant, a privately funded US$500-million, 141-megawatt facility. It is brand spanking new – and, so far, unused.

The Apia power plant has its origins in a group of local entrepreneurs, led by Bart Nnaji, a US university professor and, later, minister of power in Nigeria, who wanted to create a replicable model for sustainable power development in the country. Having obtained the concession for Aba from the federal government in 2005, the consortium built a state-of-the-art plant, rehabilitated the entire local distribution network, put up nearly 150 kilometres of overhead lines within the Aba metropolis, completed or refurbished 12 substations, and constructed a 27-kilometre gas pipeline from Imo River to supply the three General Electric turbines.

Then, with just 60 days work left on the project, the local Enugu Electricity Distribution Company was handed over to another party by the Bureau of Public Enterprises (BPE) without excising Aba from the sale. As Nnaji notes, 'The BPE, in effect, double-sold Aba metropolis. This is in spite of the very fact that the agreement we had clearly states that whenever there is privatisation, our company has first right to purchase the facility in Aba.'[13]

Aba now sits with a world-class electricity infrastructure that cannot be turned on, to the cost of both the investors and local industry, and which is bound to turn off other investors. In this way, Nigeria's greatest high-energy development asset is also its greatest problem: Nigerians themselves.

Yet, Nigeria's population will more than double to 415 million in the next generation. The five states of the south-east will increase to 45 million people over this time. To create the jobs their people crave, they will need an enabling environment for business and the infrastructure to power industry and get goods to market, starting with electricity.

A large sign above one of Ariaria market's alleyways reads: 'This is Big Line, Where God Makes People Big'. Even so, government has a critical role to play in setting a competitiveness vision, and acting on its promises by delivering the policies and hardware that enable business to compete. And that starts, in Abia's case, with turning on the electricity.

But it is government, not God, in partnership with others that is going to be responsible for progress in electricity, as across other infrastructure sectors, including transport, where Africa lags substantially.

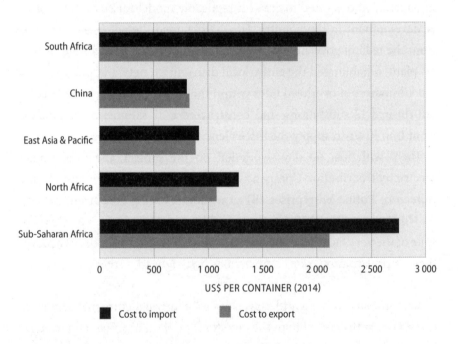

Figure 14.4: Cost of moving containers (US$ per container)

Source: World Bank Doing Business Index, 2014.

East Asia's success at improving communications and links with the global economy is as technologically impressive as it is enticing in offering glitzy, big-ticket solutions to infrastructure constraints.

Construction of Japan's Shinkansen, or 'bullet train', began in 1959. Five years later, the world's first line, Tōkaidō Shinkansen, was opened to the public. This pioneer of high-speed rail operates at a maximum speed of 300 kilometres per hour across nine lines, transporting nearly half a million passengers daily.

South Korea followed with its KTX high-speed rail, which became operational in April 2004, based on French technology. More than 85 000 passengers use the service daily. Taiwan High Speed Rail (THSR) was opened three years later at a cost of US$18 billion. Utilising Shinkansen technology, the THSR is one of the largest privately funded transport schemes worldwide, carrying 65 million passengers punctually each year.

Now China has become the regional leader in high-speed rail, putting over 25 000 kilometres of track into operation since 2008, more than the total for the rest of the world, logging over 1.7 billion passenger trips annually, changing patterns of urban development in the process through shortened travel times, improving labour flexibility and increasing tourism.

However tempting high-speed trains might be as a means to leapfrog development, and a symbol of a progressive-minded government, transport is not enough by itself to catalyse growth and jobs. What matters most is how transport, high speed or slow, is integrated with other infrastructure and wider policy, as Kenya illustrates.

Prioritising Africa's infrastructure, matching software

Hassan Ali Joho was first elected governor of Mombasa in 2013. By 2019, aged just 43, he was halfway through his second and final term.[14]

His city, which constitutes the smallest of Kenya's 47 counties by land mass, is the second wealthiest after Nairobi. It contains, he says proudly, the second-highest level of skills among its 1.5 million inhabitants, also just behind the capital. In addition, it is the point of access to 200 million Kenyans, Ugandans, Rwandese and Congolese in the hinterland.

He might have added, it is also the beneficiary of the largest infrastructure project undertaken in Kenya since independence – the 485-kilometre Standard Gauge Railway (SGR), shortening the journey time to Nairobi to just five hours. The Madaraka Express passenger service is clean, tidy, runs on time and there are apparently enough security and other checks (nine in total to board the train) for it to be considered secure.

The SGR is, too, a masterpiece of engineering, built by the Chinese contractor 18 months ahead of schedule in just three years, sweeping across 98 bridges and through nine passenger stations, each one built according to a wacky theme: Mombasa's terminus representing ripples in the ocean, Miasenyi the stripes of a zebra, Emali the closed fist of unity, and so on.

In theory, the upgrading of the railway seemed a good idea. The narrow (Cape) gauge colonial-era Rift Valley Railway (RVR), known as the Lunatic Express, had deteriorated as a result of a complete absence of post-independence funding and thus maintenance, and an ill-conceived privatisation process. Annual rail freight from Mombasa port had fallen from 4.8 million to 1.5 million tonnes as RVR's shareholders fought with the elements, the failing century-old inheritance and each other.

Constraints at the port of Mombasa had also not helped, driving up the transport component to around one-third of the cost of goods, compared to 4% in the most efficient trade corridors. Bring these down by reducing congestion on the road, the thinking went, and the economy could take off, leveraging Mombasa's position as the gateway to markets in East and Central Africa.

In practice, however, there have been problems with this new infrastructure.

Foremost has been the shattering short-term effect of the SGR on business in Mombasa itself. A blanket ban on trucks has taken away nearly all the transport business from the Container Freight Services depots, which were set up in Mombasa in 2005 to reduce port congestion by allowing containers to move to holding facilities outside the port. Here they were cleared by customs prior to onforwarding up the road to Nairobi. Taking strain and absent alternatives, business in Mombasa is angry, preferring to view the SGR through the prism of corruption, a deliberate slight by Nairobi against those on the coast – a divide that has political echoes.

This relates to a second challenge with SGR, which is to use the railway option to drive competitiveness rather than simply divert traffic from one system to another. Kenya must provide greater efficiencies for its burgeoning population, which is expected to increase from 50 million to 80 million by 2045, when the majority will be living in urban areas, with nearly 10%, at current rates of growth, in sprawling slums.

Yet, until now, government has been unable to link logistics with fresh employment initiatives.

Joho believes that Mombasa can cement its place as the second most important port in sub-Saharan Africa after Durban in South Africa, with a rich vein of opportunities in the oil and gas sector, tourism and the blue economy.

'To play to our strengths, as a gateway,' says the governor, 'we must reflect back on the origins of the port of Mombasa: for export and value addition. Today, it is mostly about imports.' To transform it once more into a source of economic growth and jobs, 'we need national policy alignment, to ensure that the export processing zones work, that the industrial development zones are integrated. This demands free trade regimes, and a taxation regime that is attractive,' he adds.

The absence of industry to soak up these numbers of unemployed can be seen in the import versus export figures. While some 1 600 containers arrive in Mombasa each day (of which 400 are in transit for the region outside Kenya), exports account for just 100.

Growth also requires better roads and traffic management.

Mombasa's road and traffic system is infamously bad, trucks and cars weaving through potholed and dusty roads to avoid swarms of tuk-tuks, boda-bodas (motorbikes) and suicidal matatu taxis. Two years after the completion of the SGR, Mombasa's main arterial roads were still being overhauled with the construction of the 10-kilometre Mombasa-Jomvu link, which was awarded to Third China Engineering Company. Why this US$65-million African Development Bank-funded project was a lesser priority than the SGR is hard to fathom.

Veteran opposition leader Raila Odinga, who served as prime minister between 2008 and 2013, is concerned about the cost of the project. 'Once we decided to go it alone on the Nairobi to Mombasa stretch, without the Ugandans, we conducted a feasibility study to the consultants' design,' he notes, 'and awarded the contract at $2.7 billion just before we left [the government]. The contract was then cancelled by the new government, readvertised, and then awarded to the same contractors for US$3.5 billion, which has ended up being US$4.2 billion.' He notes that Ethiopia built a similar length, if higher-specification, railway at much less cost, as has Tanzania. 'This has led to higher rates on the line to repay the loans,' he notes.

US$4.2 billion is a lot of money for a railway that does not possess a viable revenue model. It was a big bet on a single project, when raising the debt levels, as this did, could have funded many others, from Mombasa's roads to upgrading the existing line at a fraction of the cost.

In 1903, Britain's colonial administrator, Sir Charles Norton Edgecumbe Eliot, boldly stated of the railway that 'it is not uncommon for a country to create a railway, but it is uncommon for a railway to create a country'.

Whether the SGR becomes known as a reckless financial exercise or bold stroke of leadership genius, which unlocked infrastructure bottle-necks and spurred not only Kenyan but regional growth, will depend on the extent to which the railway is matched by policy to attract business. As Odinga puts it, 'as we have learnt from East Asia, to attract investors, you need to put in place attractive conditions, more attractive than in their home countries'. Likewise, while Ethiopia has been better able to get improved value for money in its infrastructure and has built it with the development of industry in mind, it also shows that these aspects are not enough. The macro-economic conditions are critical, too, in encouraging inward investment and export competitiveness.

Infrastructure: Not an end in itself

Hawassa. Some 270 kilometres south of Addis Ababa, the picturesque Rift Valley city has relied on agriculture as a source of income and employment. The regional Sidama coffee is one of Ethiopia's best-known brands and provides the name of the local football side.[15]

That was until the establishment of the Hawassa Industrial Park (HIP), inaugurated by the then Prime Minister Hailemariam Desalegn in June 2017. Flanked by Lake Hawassa, HIP is the largest government industrial park, built at a cost of US$250 million in just nine months by the contractor, the Chinese Civil Engineering Construction Corporation. The first phase covered 140 hectares with 52 factory sheds, and by the start of 2019 it housed 20 textile and apparel firms from 11 countries, employing 23 000 local workers and 700 expats.

Though it was not the first, other government industrial parks are modelled on Hawassa, which itself incorporated lessons from the first park at Bole Lemi in Addis.

The parks have been Ethiopia's response to the challenge of unemployment and the need for economic diversification. A team was assigned and led by Arkebe Oqubay, once the mayor of Addis, later the chairperson of the Ethiopian Industrial Parks Corporation. A study was made of the successes and failures of industrial parks around the world, looking at Nigeria, Mauritius, Taiwan, Vietnam, Singapore, South Korea and, of course, China. Nigeria, the government concluded, failed because of a lack of leadership, and because it was unsupported by the state beyond giving the developers land. Mauritius, which was a success, emphasised the value of location, logistics, clear policy and organisational structure.

The reasons for firms setting up in Ethiopia are clear: a package of incentives (including duty-free imports of capital equipment and tax exemptions of up to seven years) combined with cheap electricity at US0.04 kilowatts per hour, cheap rentals, duty-free access to the US market through the African Growth and Opportunity Act (especially important for the apparel sector), one-stop services in each facility, including customs and permits, and plentiful labour at cheap rates.

Ethiopia also offers some value-chain advantages to manufacturers. Huajian, for example, uses only Ethiopian leather on its shoe uppers. Located in the Horn of Africa, Ethiopia is Africa's largest livestock producer. And as much as 2.6 million hectares are suitable for cotton production.[16]

But it is labour that is the notable advantage. The average salary at Huajian is 900 birr, or US$30; while workers start at just 750 birr in Hawassa. The top end is 3 000 birr. Taking advantage of this requires freeing up the movement of labour along with continued education to remain competitive.

Sue Dong Linpei has been a manager of the Eastern Industrial Park for three years. 'We are here because of the size of the local market when we were originally focused on import substitution, and we stay because of comparative political stability, stable electricity and water, security, and the cost of labour. We learnt in China of the importance of industriousness and efficiency, and, less positively, of the need for environmental management.'

Some may be horrified at the low wages in the route on which Ethiopia has embarked to meet the annual inflow of 500 000 new job seekers, including 100 000 university graduates, into the market. At the same time, Addis had few other options. There is no one silver bullet. Together with tourism, agriculture and agro-industry, the government has bet that manufacturing will provide the bedrock of a new economy.

The government in Addis realised early on that an industrial park is not just about providing infrastructure. It is about the full package, which includes the regulatory and policy environment, the provision of one-stop facilities, clarity and efficiency on customs, labour law and visas, and relations with local government. It is about setting up a system, not just a shed.

Even this is not enough, as is evident from Ethiopia's inability to move out of low-value, small-margin manufacturing and create jobs on the scale that Vietnam has done. Logistics times and costs, while they have improved, continue to impose a premium, and make it difficult to raise labour rates without becoming uncompetitive. The integration of the parks with the US$3.2-billion Chinese-built SGR, linking the port of Djibouti with Addis, and the refurbishment of the port of Berbera in Somaliland and the highway between it and Ethiopia, are potential game-changers, but they are a long way from working.

And there is a need for consultation with business. Government has to view business as its customer, just as business appreciates the needs and demands of consumers. To do so, there is the need to ask business, not to assume the answer. 'Build and they will come' is not enough, given that Ethiopia is a long way from richer markets. Other things have to happen, such as macro- and micro-economic reforms necessary to attract business, including liberalising the exchange rate, opening up the banking sector, controlling public expenditure and inflation, and improving domestic revenue collection.

Industrial parks eventually also have to be weaned from government's support. This leads to greater efficiency and competitiveness, as in Asia. The Ethiopian government has been torn, however, between trying to fill the parks, cutting them loose as fiscal obligation and improving their competitiveness.

As one longstanding Japanese adviser to the Ethiopian government observes, government has to accept that business is there to make a profit, and that industrial parks, like infrastructure, are the means to that end, not an end in itself. [17]

There are examples of how to do big infrastructure right in Africa, to integrate it with logistics and match it with the needs and profit motive of business.

Integrating for success

Winston Churchill said of Marrakesh that it was 'simply the nicest place on earth to spend an afternoon'. The British leader had spent a little longer than that in Morocco, painting a winter holiday away in the North African country during his political 'wilderness years' in the 1930s, frustrated by the Baldwin government's refusal to give him a cabinet position. It was his first of six trips to Morocco in 23 years. In Tangier, Churchill stayed in the Hotel Continental, whose guests include the likes of Edgar Degas and the author Paul Bowles; and in Marrakesh at the La Mamounia, a tranquil and enchanting hotel oasis, rich in tiles, tapestries and history.[18]

Eighty years later, and 11 million annual foreign tourists seemingly agree that Morocco is a nice place to spend an afternoon or three. But there is much more to it than gentle cooling breezes over the medina and lounging in sun-baked gingerbread houses.

Morocco's high-speed train, Al-Boraq, running between Casablanca and Tangier, is the first of its kind on the African continent, inaugurated in November 2018 by King Mohammed VI. Named after the legendary winged Islamic courier, it is an impressive piece of hardware, reaching over 300 kilometres per hour and cutting the passenger time to Casablanca to just two hours. It has boosted downtown Tangier, part of a scheme to upgrade cities and infrastructure started by Mohammed VI on his inauguration 20 years ago on 30 July 1999. Like the Ethiopian and Kenyan SGRs, it is controversial, however, since not every Moroccan thinks the US$2-billion high-speed rail offers value for money.[19]

Al-Boraq is one high-profile element, however, of a longer-term, less dramatic reform strategy, at the heart of which were changes in the political environment. Reforms started by King Hassan II were accelerated after his death in 1999 by King Mohammed VI, known to many Moroccans even before taking power as the 'Prince of the Poor'. In 2003 the government adopted a proactive and aggressive economic growth strategy, aimed at gaining a greater slice of trade and investment through fresh privatisations, the signing of free trade agreements, and what was conceived of as the Emergence Plan.

This economic reform agenda identified seven sectors for export potential – aeronautics, agriprocessing, offshoring, fishing and other sea products, automobiles and parts, textiles, and speciality electronics – and was designed to complement other schemes, such as the Plan Azur objective to increase tourists, and the Green Morocco initiative promoting vertical integration and improved yields in agriculture.

While agriculture (and agribusiness) has historically been the largest contributor to the Moroccan economy, it is also the Achilles heel that has been behind dramatic downswings in economic growth and underdevelopment, given its dependency on rainfall and lack of mechanisation. Cereal yields, one proxy for agricultural productivity, have improved by an average of 2% per year since 1990, with production jumping from 11.6 million tonnes in 2015, to just 3.5 million in 2016, and back to nearly 10 million in 2017, with GDP growth rising and falling in tandem.

In a continent where complex development plans seldom survive contact with political and resource reality, Morocco is an impressive exception. Forty kilometres north of Tangier is the new Tangier Med port, the second phase of which was opened in June 2019, now capable of handling nine million containers annually, three times more than Egypt's Port Said, the next largest in Africa. The port operations have been concessioned between several operators on 30-year leases, split roughly between containers, car transporters and ferries, together totalling 14 000 ship movements in 2018.

Top ten best-connected countries and/or territories	2018 Score	Rank
China	187.8	1
Singapore	133.9	2
Korea, Rep.	118.8	3
Hong Kong SAR, China	113.5	4
Malaysia	109.9	5
Netherlands	98.0	6
Germany	97.1	7
United States	96.7	8
United Kingdom	95.6	9
Belgium	91.1	10
Top ten African connected countries		
Morocco	71.5	16
Egypt	70.3	17
South Africa	40.1	43
Djibouti	37.0	51
Togo	35.9	52
Mauritius	34.5	54
Cameroon	25.5	62
Congo, Rep.	25.5	63
Angola	25.1	64
Kenya	21.2	68

Table 14.1: UNCTAD's Liner Shipping Connectivity Index

Source: UNCTAD, Liner Shipping Connectivity Index, 2019.

This has pushed Morocco up the connectivity rankings. For example, the United Nations Conference on Trade and Development's (UNCTAD's) Liner Shipping Connectivity Index (Table 14.1) illustrates how well countries are connected and integrated into global shipping networks through a series of indices. It can be considered an indicator of the accessibility to global trade.[20]

Between Tangier and the port is the Renault-Nissan car plant, one of 900 companies in various special economic zones, which fills six 200-car trains per day to Tangier Med destined for export. The Renault plant, which employs 11 500 workers, and is the company's third largest world-wide, produced 402 000 cars in 2018, of which nearly 360 000 were sold abroad, mostly in Europe.

The port and associated logistics infrastructure cost US$3.5 billion, sourced from government equity and multilateral and private loans. It is a model public-private partnership on a continent that usually pays lip service to the term, brought about because government insisted on 'offsets' in the form of local job opportunities in return for their support.

On the quayside at Tangier Med 1 were giant wind turbine blades. This hints at another big Moroccan infrastructure bet.

Africa has options

Asia teaches – and Africa reminds us – that having no electricity is the worst polluter of all, whatever the source. The use of charcoal, for one, for cooking and coal for domestic heating produces considerably more carbon dioxide than electricity production per unit. This explains why, for example, urban air pollution in China did not increase as quickly as the energy consumption and vehicle population, and in some indicators was reduced during the 1990s,[21] even though Beijing was listed among the world's top ten most polluted cities because of coal combustion and a rapid increase in vehicles. This was a result of the reduction in traditional coal burning. Still, air pollution and related health costs are an important issue to consider regarding the impacts of high-speed urban development.

Asia also teaches that expanding energy capacity and usage is not easy, and is fraught with political tensions and trade-offs. In Asia, for example, it has made more sense to focus on grid expansion to highly populated urban centres rather than rural areas. As a result, out of the total population of

640 million people living in Association of Southeast Asian Nations (ASEAN) member states, 65 million did not have access to electricity in 2015 and 250 million relied on biomass for cooking, most of them living in remote rural areas.[22]

East Asian countries are increasingly turning to renewable, off-grid solutions to bridge this rural-urban gap. Myanmar, which has one of the lowest electricity penetration rates among ASEAN member states at just 26%, has embarked on a rural electrification programme using solar energy to supply electricity. The government aims to generate 30 megawatts each from off-grid sources to power some 500 000 households in the first five years of the programme, which started in 2017. Cambodia aims to connect 70% of households to the national grid by 2030 and has similarly adopted a masterplan to facilitate rural electrification, promoting the development of mini-grids that utilise solar home systems, small hydropower and solar photovoltaic systems in rural areas.[23]

Technological advances in renewable options, like solar, are useful for increasing access, such as for rural consumers in sparsely populated areas through localised provision and mini-grids, and might even power industrial-size projects that create jobs or for densely populated urban situations.

Of the alternatives to coal, dams for hydro upset delicate environmental balances, nuclear remains controversial, wind power kills birds and is unsightly, and solar is a costly option, if decreasingly so, and one better suited to sun-kissed countries. But difficult choices will have to be made. Indecision is not an option. While coal has made sense for much of Asia, Africa's realities are different, and so are the times.

At the outset, there is an imperative to make full use of all resources. Currently, according to the World Bank, just 40% of Africa's output reaches its potential customer market due to problems of distribution and transmission.[24] In Nigeria, 28% of electricity is 'lost' between the generator and the customer,[25] not to mention seven power stations that stand idle, and many more (in Nigeria and elsewhere) that produce under capacity. Africa also harnesses just 7% of its hydro potential, compared to 65% globally.[26]

Achieving universal electricity access in sub-Saharan Africa by 2025 will, according to the African Development Bank, take between US$60 billion and US$90 billion of annual investment.[27] How will and should Africa fund this?

Financing development

China has led in infrastructure development, as noted in Chapter 9, through a largely unsustainable cocktail of high debt and low-input costs. This cannot be Africa's way, even if China is offering to finance it, and precisely because, in part, Chinese institutions are offering to do so. The opacity of African governments' financing deals with Chinese banks is particularly concerning, especially with African government external debt owed to China at around 20% and growing.

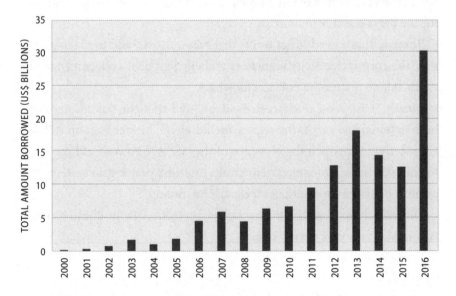

Figure 14.5: Chinese loans to Africa, 2000–16

Source: Johns Hopkins School of Advanced International Studies China-Africa Research Initiative, 2019.

Other financing models will have to be considered. The examples of East Asian countries show several innovative measures of mobilising domestic capital to fund infrastructure: Singapore instituted a system of mandatory savings through its Central Provident Fund, which were used to fund such large-scale projects as the major housing developments that continue today. South Korea used state-owned banks to direct subsidised credit at low rates to *chaebols*, the large conglomerates that dominated the country's export industries. Because they were owned by the state, these banks could take on a higher level of risk than private banks, and could channel lending towards sectors identified as strategic. These financing models depend, critically, on a disciplined state.

Foreign capital provides options for Africa's infrastructure, but will require governments to reduce the frictional costs – the regulatory, financial and administrative barriers, and political and security considerations – that drive up financing costs and deter investment. This confirms, yet again, the crucial role of government in creating the conditions necessary for the private sector to flourish.

There is also a need to set tariffs that recoup costs, and to make people pay. The role of electricity regulators and efficient debt-collecting systems is crucial, no matter the political blowback.

Finally, East Asia is characterised by well-thought-out masterplans, both national and across the region, including the Master Plan on ASEAN Connectivity, in which the objective of the ASEAN Power Grid project is to enhance transborder electricity trade, interlink power grid systems and create a platform for multilateral electricity trading.

Difficult choices, such is the overall lesson from Asia, lie ahead if Africa is going to reduce its energy deficit.

Conclusion: The future is brighter

Just 30 minutes' flying from Marrakesh over the High Atlas Mountains is the sweltering city of Ouarzazate. Known as Little Hollywood on account of its role in the global film industry (it was the location for the *Game of Thrones*, *Gladiator* and James Bond in *The Living Daylights*, among other hits), it has become the centrepiece of Morocco's drive for renewable energy. The Concentrated Solar Power (CSP) tower and the 3 000 hectares of solar panels can be seen blinking from a long way out on the flight approach, hardly surprising since the Inconel-plated tower of the 150-megawatt Noor 1 facility heats up to no less than 560 degrees Celsius. Noor 1 alone has half a million solar mirrors installed.

When completed, Noor's four stages will produce 580 megawatts of power from a combination of (mostly) CSP and (some 70 megawatts) from photovoltaic cells. It is expensive (at US$2.2 billion) and faces long-term technological challenges, including the storage of heat for peak usage, but costs are coming down fast to the point that, at US$0.08 per kilowatt hour, the plant currently makes money.

Like the high-speed train and Tangier Med 1 and 2, Noor is a calculated gamble. Again, it is funded by a combination of government and concessional loans. But Morocco had little option given its dependency on imported coal for most of its energy. It aims to shift the energy mix to mostly renewables by 2030, from a combination of hydro, wind power and solar.

The lesson of Morocco's contemporary success at delivering big infrastructure assets and then using them efficiently is down to a combination of leadership, vision, delivery – the need, simply, for both software and hardware. Just providing infrastructure is not enough. You need skills and systems, too, and a supportive policy environment.

The share of government financing has come from two sources: an increase in borrowing (and thus the fiscal deficit) to over 3% of GDP, and a threefold real increase in the tax collection rate in the last 20 years. As the spending catalyst for growth kicked in, so too did revenue expand.

The positive cycle does not end there. The Renault plant has a government-funded training facility alongside, which has produced more than 10 000 graduates since the factory opened in 2012. With more growth has come greater demand for talent.

Likewise, the Aerospace Hub clustered around Casablanca employs 16 700 in 140 companies, now a US$1.7-billion industry for Morocco, making everything from wings to wiring harnesses for the likes of Boeing, Airbus and Bombardier. Workers are trained at a government-funded facility, Institut des Métiers de l'Aéronautique (IMA), inside the free trade zone, which, like Renault, has produced 7 000 graduates since 2011.

Firms are no doubt attracted by Morocco's labour rates, which, at US$350 per worker per month, are a fraction of European costs, with virtually identical geography and thus logistics. But as the IMA's Hamid Benbrahim El Andaloussi explains, the 'best incentives are those for long-term activity, not those which governments might provide. In aerospace,' he notes, 'the critical drivers are innovation, cost and talent. We are not able to compete in the first area, but we can do so in the latter two respects. We say Morocco is the place to be if you want to be competitive in Europe.'

There is more to this than plans and technology, however. Mohcine Jazouli, Morocco's minister for African co-operation, highlights a final but, as he observes, 'most critical' prior aspect of Morocco's twenty-first-century development story. 'We once had a contested national identity. Were we Berbers, Arabs, Mediterranean, Muslims or North Africans? Today we are clear: we are Moroccans.' This reflects, he says, a leadership with an inclusive national narrative and a developmental agenda to match.[28]

There are ongoing challenges in improving health care, education and the justice system. But in identifying these, and acting on them, Morocco is increasingly the face that modern Africa needs.

Chapter 15

Open Up to Keep Control

India grows at night while the government sleeps … But we should also grow during the day. We cannot have a story of private success and public failure.

— Gurcharan Das, 2012

The People's Committee Head Office of Ho Chi Minh City would not be out of place in Paris, which presumably was the whole idea when it was built by the French in 1908 as the Hotel de Ville de Saigon. Outside, its elegant yellow and white facade offers an insight into the country's colonial past; inside its marble foyer a rich red and gold carpet leads up a sweeping staircase to the meeting chamber, with its painted tapestries, grand chandeliers and painted blue-sky ceiling.

It is a most incongruous site for a discussion on total factor productivity (TFP).

'We envision Vietnam to become a country of industry and modernity by 2025,' stated Le Thanh Liem, the vice chairperson of the city in 2016, his seniority denoted by a gold party lapel badge.[1]

'To achieve this,' he says, 'we use our internal strengths and mobilise external reserves through investment. We aim to try and make investors feel welcome here. Capital is key, as is the development of human resources, and, increasingly, total factor productivity' – the improvements in outputs not accounted for by labour and capital improvements, including technology and governance. It is not often you hear a functionary talking about such terms. 'Although the city is growing,' he observes, 'at 9.6% per annum, our year-on-year increase in TFP has grown from 20% in 2014 to 32% in 2015.'

Letting go of state-led development

The debates on whether globalisation is good or evil have become irrelevant and the consensus reached that the most successful countries were those that opened up their borders to the world. The ideological claptrap of 'America first' is equally inapt for a country where trade makes up one-third of GDP. Many Asian countries recognise that the economic growth necessary to achieve their development goal is contingent on a healthy, dynamic private sector. This requires the state to get out of the way.

The extent of Vietnam's liberalisation can be seen in the declining number and importance of state-owned enterprises (SOEs). Many have successfully made the leap from state to a commercial enterprise.

Started by a Soviet-trained engineer in 1976, Vinamilk is based north of Ho Chi Minh City at My Phuoc. There, its US$120-million, state of the art hyper-automated factory is capable of producing 400 million litres annually. Vietnam's annual milk consumption has risen from just 10 litres per person in 2010 to 17 litres five years later, mostly the result of improved wealth. This is still some way behind Chinese (26 litres), Thai (35 litres) and Malaysian (58 litres) consumption, hence plans to double the Tetra Pak-built factory's capacity. Vinamilk attracted a number of foreign investors to its initial public offering (IPO) in 2003. The same is true of Vinatex, the textiles firm and former SOE, which moved to become a 'joint stock company' through its US$57-million, September 2014 IPO listing.

To achieve this, the state has had to get *out* of business, not the reverse. The attraction of foreign businesses has required competitive tax breaks, good logistics and openness to the outside world, as evident in a plethora of free trade agreements, remarkable given the country's pro-Soviet and anti-American history. As Liem put it, 'Increasing competitiveness demands meeting the challenge of international integration.'

While wages are low in Vietnam, in backing up Liem's point, competitiveness is not a cage fight on cheaper labour costs, a 'race to the bottom'. Generally, the richer the market, the better the manufacturing business. The notion that Vietnam's growth success is just about incentives or cheap wages is a cop-out for critics. It is about a whole lot more, not least the commitment of government to openness, however bumpy that path.

Incentivising investment

Foreign direct investment (FDI) is increasingly required by those African countries looking to develop much-needed infrastructure or diversify their economies and create jobs. This requires an investor-friendly stance from government, and, crucially, the removal of 'frictional costs' – those costs added by corruption, cumbersome bureaucratic processes and lack of necessary infrastructure, which add a premium to the returns an investor would hope to make from investing in an emerging market.

Economists call these 'transaction costs'. The Nobel laureate Douglass North stated that institutions, or the set of rules governing a society, are a key determinant of these costs, which fall into three broad categories: search and information costs, as a result of market and policy opacity; bargaining costs, which relate to the lack of a fixed price, corruption and permit fraud; and, finally, policing and enforcement costs, which are a result of the quality of the legal and law enforcement system, and the overall level of crime and corruption.[2]

Addressing these frictions and making it easier for investors to enter the country has been central to the success of countries like Vietnam, Thailand and Singapore. Zambia shows the heavy cost of the alternative.

The cost of antagonism

In May 2019, the Zambian government applied to place Konkola Copper Mines (KCM), the country's largest private employer, into provisional liquidation. This seemed to be a sign that an increasingly desperate government, starved of resources to pay the salaries of a burgeoning civil service and of cash to meet the international debt it had rung up in record time, was thinking of nationalising the mines. After all, Zambia had been here before – and with devastating consequences last time around.

KCM was, at the time, Zambia's largest pay as you earn (PAYE) tax provider with more than 13 000 workers at its mines at Nchanga and Konkola. It had invested more than US$3 billion into these facilities since its acquisition of a majority share after Anglo American's withdrawal from the project in 2002, including sinking a deep shaft, commissioning a new smelter and opening three new concentrators.

Whereas KCM's lack of productivity had made it one of the biggest contributors to the daily US$1-million loss of the mines before Zambia Consolidated Copper Mines' privatisation in 2000, since then it usually has contributed about one-fifth of Zambia's 800 000-tonne annual copper production.

The most benign explanation for this action was of an honest if clumsy attempt to try to recoup money owed to the state. Vedanta, which owns four-fifths of KCM, with a record of environmental problems and faltering production, was the softest target for such a move among the big miners. The liquidation application came shortly after Vedanta reported an annual loss of US$165 million, blamed on import taxes on concentrate from the Congo and the weakening of the kwacha.

But government's liquidation action had less to do with the mine, and its profitability, than Zambia's precarious debt situation.

In 2005, Zambia's debt had largely been forgiven. By the start of 2019, however, the country was once more up to its eyeballs in debt, and the government had no plan to stop spending. External debt had increased to

US$10.1 billion, of which about US$3 billion was in eurobonds, US$1.8 billion multilateral and US$2.9 billion from China (mainly Exim Bank). On top of this, Zambia had announced a further US$1-billion loan from the Chinese, while there were other ongoing contracts committed but not disbursed.

As external debt payments invariably ramp up to be larger than inflows, Zambia's foreign exchange reserves have declined, and with it external debt costs have increased. There seemed to be no way out from these debt challenges without an International Monetary Fund programme or another credit line, or both, and a radical economic turnaround.

Zambia has one seemingly intractable problem: politics.

As the opposition leader Hakainde Hichilema, popularly known as HH, has put it, 'Zambians see the government as a fraud and recognise it as such.

'It has a negative impact on the rule of law,' he notes. 'Why would you trust a government that came to power in questionable circumstances, and is willing to change or ignore the rules to suit itself? All this erodes investor trust and confidence, and increases risk and thus the costs of capital. In sum,' Hichilema concludes, 'if you get the politics wrong, the economics will follow.'[3]

The problem with the approach to government taken by Zambia's ruling party is that eventually, to paraphrase Margaret Thatcher, they would run out of someone else's money. Thus, a recovery strategy would have to be less about from where Lusaka was going to source its next loan or create a tax bonanza than how they could grow the overall economic pie, diversify away from mining, improve productivity, ease logistical constraints, and reduce government red tape and overheads.

In this sense, 'opening up' refers not only to the process of integrating into the global economy. In successful cases in East Asia, it has also meant opening up the economy to the private sector, and commercialising some state functions in the interest of competitiveness.

This is illustrated by the case of Singapore.

A commercial and meritocratic imperative

S. Dhanabalan has enjoyed a stellar career as a Singaporean law-maker, minister and public servant. After his retirement from government, he has served, among other positions, as chairperson of Singapore Airlines, DBS Holdings and, for 17 years until August 2013, Temasek Holdings.[4]

Temasek is the investment arm of the Singapore government. With a portfolio of US$160 billion, Temasek owns stakes in many of Singapore's largest and iconic companies, such as Singtel, DBS, Singapore Airlines, Port of Singapore Authority International, SMRT Corporation, Singapore Power and Neptune Orient Lines. Since it branched out into the region in 2002, by 2018 three-quarters of underlying assets were in Asia, with 25% concentrated in China.

Temasek was born out of the decision to divest the Singaporean Economic Development Board (EDB) from various businesses in the late 1960s since the 'government decided that, in addition to its role in investment promotion, there was too much under its one roof', says Dhanabalan.

Unbundling followed, and, as a result, Jurong Industrial Estate assumed EDB's land portfolio, DBS Bank took over EDB's financing role, while the Ministry of Finance took over EDB's equity stakes. Later, Temasek was created in June 1974 with a share capital of just US$250 million to assume the equity in the various businesses, including the airline (which had been created out of the split in Malaysian-Singapore Airlines). Government-owned entities, such as telecoms, ports and power, were later corporatised and passed over to Temasek.

Its annualised total shareholder return since inception has been 15%. Some 45 years later, Temasek is valued as a US$230-billion company.[5]

Critically, from the outset, Temasek's governance model relied on an independent board, which comprised mainly public servants who were made responsible for supervising the management. Similarly, the various companies under its control were run mostly by professionals with independent boards. Strict commercialisation sets it apart from most other state-owned enterprises.

'The purpose', Dhanabalan says, 'was not jobs for the boys, but to make the investments pay.'

Unusually for SOEs, Singapore's make money. 'It's an investment house,' he stresses, 'not an investment promotion agency.'

The reasons for lack of profitability in many SOEs, Dhanabalan says, are 'never because people don't know what to do. We get many, including many from Africa, coming to ask us how it is that Singapore's state-owned enterprises make money. Technically the answer is textbook. You can find this out anywhere. But the answer to why Singapore and not others has managed it is in the governance framework. It makes decisions on commercial principles and commercial needs.'

For example, he explains further, in the 1970s, 'Singapore Airlines had decided to make a US$1-billion order for new aircraft, the largest ever at the time.' Even though the government was, through Temasek, the major shareholder, they did not go to it for permission. In every other country politicians want to have their say. 'In Singapore's case, it is different. If the company does not make money, then the administration would be sacked, but not for any other reason.'

Under Lee Kuan Yew, the state's actions were guided by commercial principles, not least since it had to make its investments (even those in public housing) pay for themselves in order to ensure sustainability.

Temasek sees its success as being able to take a long-term view, with no redemption date or preferred method. And its investments have been secured by the independence of the SOEs in which it so heavily invested. 'Even in those companies where Temasek is a 100% shareholder,' one of its senior executives notes, 'Temasek does not sit on the board.' With its foreign investments it is also politically 'agnostic', less worried 'about who is running the country than whether you can get your money out'. The discipline comes, they say, 'from the top, from LKY, who at the start said: "If you fail [referring to Singapore Airlines], I will not be here to bail you out."[6]

But Singapore's extraordinary development success is not just about institutions or, for that matter, planning alone. It is about growth, jobs, governance, business and people.

Singapore ranks at the top end of the key Doing Business indicators, from the ease of starting a company to best labour force and intellectual property rights protection. Hence, the 7 000-plus multinational companies now present on the island.

In essence, politicians have allowed the planners and professionals to get on with it.

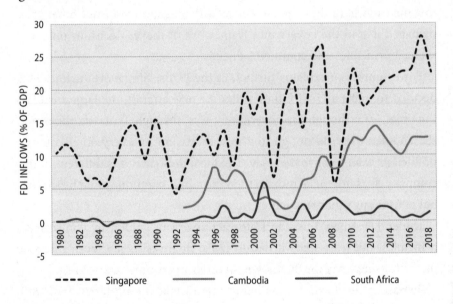

Figure 15.1: Comparative FDI inflows

Source: World Bank Databank, 2019.

Cambodia has similarly used a well-positioned and empowered body like Singapore's EDB in the form of the Council for the Development of Cambodia (CDC) to attract investment. Underlying this was the honest recognition that the private sector is a friend of development, not an enemy.

The CDC was promoted to the highest decision-making level of government for private sector investment. Its operational arms, the Cambodian Investment Board and the Cambodian Special Economic Zone Board, review investment applications and grant incentives to investment projects that meet the requirements laid out in the country's investment laws. This law streamlined the foreign investment regime and provided generous and competitive incentives for direct private sector investment. For example, companies can enjoy corporate tax holidays of up to nine years with a tax rate of only 20 per cent thereafter. Capital goods can also be imported duty-free, and there are no restrictions on capital repatriation.

A latecomer, ravaged by civil war until 1991, Cambodia jumped at the chance to learn from other countries' experiences. Early success was the result of choosing a niche in hi-tech investments. Having studied FDI inflows to Malaysia and Thailand, the Cambodian Investment Board concluded that the hi-tech investment process was too cumbersome and regulation-heavy. To benefit from their neighbours' shortcomings, Cambodia then set up a one-stop shop for investors in hi-tech.

As one example of how this might be translated to Africa, take the example of South Africa. Despite immense strengths in its mineral and natural resource endowments, a sophisticated financial and business services sector, its proximity to fast-growing African markets, high-quality universities, and a modern, productive agricultural sector, South Africa's share of FDI on the African continent and worldwide has been sliding as a result of incoherent policies that are antagonistic to foreign capital. If South Africa can make it easier for business to invest its money, business will come.

Across East Asia, including in socialist countries such as Vietnam, SOEs are routinely allowed to fail, or are sold, in pursuit of greater competitiveness and less reliance on the state's resources. In most cases in Africa, SOEs have proven spectacularly unsuccessful, fraught with jobs for pals, opaque contracting, inflated salaries and poor management. So, where they are successful, as in the case of Ethiopian Airlines, they stand out, and their lessons are worth learning, even though this does not excuse overall the imperative for relentless reforms in the search for strategic opportunity and cost-competitiveness.

Ethiopian Airlines: How SOEs can do it

Users of Ethiopian Airlines (ET) have a common complaint: great airline, lousy airport. Despite this, ET has grown to become the largest African airline in terms of passengers, and the world's fourth-largest by the number of countries served. This century the airline has expanded passenger numbers from one million to nearly 11 million in 2018, and its aircraft from 26 to 117. And the airport is catching up, with a new extension opened during 2019, along with the institutionalisation of a visa-on-arrival system.

The airline stands out in Africa where carriers will lose US$300 million, or US$3.50 per passenger during 2019, even though some governments, including Ghana, Uganda, Tanzania, Zambia and Chad, continue to be drawn to the idea of financing national airlines. South African Airways has only survived on gargantuan and escalating taxpayer bailouts, while in July 2019 Kenya's parliament voted to fully nationalise the debt-burdened Kenya Airways.[7] A combination of fuzzy nationalism and rent-seeking opportunities continue to plague the sector, in part explaining why longstanding plans to liberalise the continental air traffic market have effectively been stillborn.

ET is perhaps the best example of how good governance can promote a vibrant service company, and of the advantage of technocrats being allowed to get on with their jobs, free from political interference.[8]

Its CEO, Tewolde Gebremariam, speaks with disarming frankness about the airline's plans. Having joined ET aged 18 in 1984, he returned to Ethiopia from New York in 2004, where he had headed up ET's operations. Vision 2010 followed, 'which repositioned the airline', he says. The goal was to increase turnover from US$400 million in 2005 to US$1 billion within five years.

By 2010, the airline's turnover was US$1.3 billion. Cargo and passenger numbers also exceeded projections. Vision 2025 was then put in place. By that date, ET aimed to have 120 aircraft flying to 90 destinations internationally and 20 within Ethiopia, with revenue of US$10 billion. Yet, by 2019, ET was flying to 127 destinations, now turning over US$2 billion.

ET has been a notable success story during a period when the aviation business has been seen, in the words of Warren Buffett, as a 'great way to make a small fortune from a large one'. Its success, however, is not in spite of the absence of deep pockets, but because of scarcity. There are plenty of competitors capable of outspending ET. Turkish Airlines has an increasingly active African network, while Emirates already handles more than five million African passengers annually. In fact, the share of African carriers of the continental market has fallen from 80% to 20%, though overall numbers rose to 88 million by 2019.

Tewolde highlights several factors critical to the airline's success.

The first is the strong foundation laid by its management contract with Trans World Airlines (TWA) in 1945. These managerial traits continued beyond TWA's role, and despite the various governments, from the emperor through to the communist Derg, and into the twenty-first century. Even though ET remains wholly government-owned, 'there is no government interference'. In this Tewolde sees the 'government-owned, commercially-run' model as having big advantages for a such a strategic asset, just as China has been able to achieve, enabling the means to 'run the airline for the long term, not just for one-quarter', driven by the views of outside analysts.

This horizon is demanded by the nature of capital programmes. 'The new technology of aircraft,' explains Tewolde, 'like the 787 and A350, demanded a longer-term horizon.'

In all of this, there is a serious commitment to cost management. 'Cost is critical for the airline business,' he reminds us, 'since it is very difficult to make profits.' As a result, 'we are very prudent, and very frugal'. The CEO drives a modest 15-year-old Honda. Likewise, ET's headquarters, just a stone's throw from the main terminal at Addis Ababa's Bole Airport, is true to the government's mantra about keeping overheads low. 'You cannot,' he warns, 'be as lavish as South African Airways, and expect to survive.'

In all this, Tewolde says, 'governments need to make flying easy, affordable and safe for the public if countries want to trade'. Yet, he notes, 'most governments do not have an understanding of the value of aviation but rather see it as a cash cow to pay for other things – they see it as a Minister of Transport for the Rich, so they tax it too high, and constrain growth and service.'

ET not only stands out among SOEs in Africa, but among the 25 state corporations in Ethiopia itself, most of which have done poorly, especially the Ethiopian Sugar Corporation, along with those concerned with telecoms, railways, agriculture and chemicals. Overarching problems of corporate management in these bodies have been compounded by preferential political access. METEC, an engineering corporation run essentially by the military, and EFFORT (the Tigrayan firm with its fingers in all manner of pies), offer, for example, a quite different story from ET, one that threatens to undermine the economy while prompting increasing levels of corruption.

ET's list of possible reforms is a microcosm of those of Ethiopia itself: shed non-core businesses, including catering, ground handling and hotels. For the Ethiopian state, the reform ledger includes measures to encourage foreign businesses to take stakes in previously closed sectors, such as telecoms, while focusing on its 'core business' of ensuring macro-economic stability (including exchange rate and inflation management), the rule of law and security, and removing overall the frictions of doing business.

Removing frictions

If they are to emulate East Asia, African countries will have to address the frictions and institutional backlogs preventing capital markets from functioning effectively and investors from looking at sectors other than natural resources. A comparison of African countries based on the frictional costs they add to investors' returns reveals some interesting results.

The first is in the number of things that are directly within government's control to change, if only they had the will. This includes a long list, ranging from the cost of money (increased by policy uncertainty or an ill-suited exchange rate regime), credit controls and the ease of profit repatriation, openness to trade and membership of free trade areas and tax treaties, to the ease of travel (visas and direct flights), the state of logistic networks, labour market conditions (freedom of movement and work permits), to good old corruption and tax collection.

The second revelation is that these frictions have a direct cost to society: they reduce the number of jobs available, and impose a ceiling on growth and development. As the example of Nigeria shows clearly in Chapter 14, electricity is needed for growth, investors are needed for electricity, but government needs to come to the party and improve conditions for investors before they will be willing to trust in the country.

A third and final observation from this comparison between Africa and Asia is that corruption is omnipresent, whether as a 'lubricant for business', as some have called it, or an intrinsic part of human nature. But in Asia, it seems, corruption takes place at the point of delivery, with rents being captured *after* completion of a job – relating back to Asia's commitment to popular welfare perhaps. In Africa, more often than not, corruption is present at the point of transacting, hampering delivery, and at a direct cost to job creation and the distribution of wealth.

Finally, then, in the quest for sectors that might create jobs for Africa's burgeoning populations, Kilifi County in Kenya hints at one of the answers: tourism. It is, coincidentally, also a result of greater openness and receptiveness towards foreigners.

The coconut plot

Patrick stood at the base of the palm tree, a pile of freshly harvested coconuts at his feet. The plot was at the end of Bofa Road, running on the northern bank of the Kilifi River in Kenya. Coconuts are a hard way to earn one's keep, retailing at 30 shillings (US$0.30) in the shops. Two hundred metres away in the blazing sun and seeping humidity was Paul Ngari's operation, a coral quarry.

Battered Italian stone-cutting machinery ran along wonky rails, a giant blade cutting the ancient coral base into strips, from which 14 inch by 7 inch by 7 inch rectangular building blocks were prised by teams of women. The better grades at the top of the coral sold for 36 shillings, those towards the bottom of the ten layers around 25 shillings. And there was delivery on top of that, reminded Paul, who has two other similar quarries among some 35 operational in the vicinity.

His workers, most caked in a fine white coral powder, were paid 350 shillings a day.

It may be a tough and sweaty way to make a living, but an even tougher place to find a job. Most of the county of Kilifi's 1.5 million people survive on subsistence farming, like Patrick, and income from tourism.

Tourism is a major 'export' for Kenya, offering first-class safaris closer to European and Asian markets than South Africa, and an unparalleled 'beach and bush' experience. The second-largest source of foreign exchange revenue after agriculture, Kenya's international tourism accounted for US$1.5 billion of income from two million visitors in 2018.

While many of the top-end safari camps are thriving, others are struggling, and the sector has not reached anything near its potential, despite a recent recovery. This is the story, too, of Africa, which received US$44 billion in income from 64 million visitors in 2016, a fraction of the global US$1.6-trillion and 1.3-billion tourist market.

In Kenya's case this is down, in part, to terrorist events and the resultant advisories, which slam travel. The Westgate attack and subsequent 80-hour siege by al-Shabaab on 21 September 2013, in which militants stormed Nairobi's top shopping mall, resulted in 67 deaths, and started a downward tourism trend. International arrivals were, for example, 877 602 in 2016, down from 1.18 million in 2015 and 1.35 million the year before, 1.5 million in 2013 and 1.7 million in 2012.

This downturn has had a big impact on a job-scarce market place.

Under 10 million at independence, Kenya's population topped 50 million in 2019, and is projected to hit 150 million by 2100.

Kilifi has just 400 beds, or half that number of rooms suitable for international tourists. There is no conference facility that will absorb more than 50 attendees. The nearest airport is 60 kilometres away, down a bumpy and dangerous main road.

What Kilifi needs is a Club Med, or something like it, and a few of them. That will bring better infrastructure, and lower operating costs and larger margins. It will also improve competition and service. Such a facility will inevitably raise standards and encourage local procurement and specialised training on a grand scale, both of which would have massive spin-offs. And it might, in its own self-interest, promote the systematic cleaning up of the environment, especially the plastic flotsam and jetsam that blight Kenya's beautiful beaches.

The government says that Kilifi is at the centre of its tourism plans. The governor for the area, Amason Kingi, stresses the 'virgin potential' of the area compared to the 'chock-a-block beaches' on the south coast beyond Mombasa.

Kilifi's spectacular natural beauty, its warm water and white beaches are crying out for further, sensitive development.

But the government, say operators, will have to play its part, in putting in place a better road network, opening up the airlinks, and reducing taxes on hotel investors. Government will also have to make travel easier, perhaps by creating visa-free access for all countries with a higher GDP per capita than Kenya.

The band of young men in front of the coconut plot told their own story about joblessness and poverty. As did the women ferrying stacks of firewood on their heads down the Bofa Road and the skinny cattle criss-crossing the traffic and the goats feeding in the spilt mounds of rubbish. As the foreman at the coral quarry shrugged when asked if one could make a living on 350 shillings a day, 'Maybe, maybe not, but what else is there?'

Why these areas have not yet been opened up properly to the global market reflects a failure of policy and, at its heart, the uncompetitiveness of the political system. Politicians continue to find it too easy to make decisions in the interests of a tiny elite, caring more about their houses than hotels, and the size of their personal cars, not the health and safety of public transport. And they have gotten away with it, until now, with con-stituencies divided by tribe and geography, more concerned about whose turn it is to eat than issues of political performance and service delivery.

In the circumstances, absent an enlightened leadership, an enraged citi-zenry becomes the most likely conduit of change.

Conclusion: An open nation is greater than the sum of its parts

Liberalisation and openness, as successful Asian examples have shown over and over again, are a necessary step and countries that have been more open have generally fared better. This is the lesson not only from Asia's successful export-driven growth model, which has spurred competi-tiveness to the benefit of domestic consumers, but also from countries that have liberalised in terms of fundamental rights, democracy and freedoms, for they have fared better in comparison to those that have not.

Japan, for example, has long been unable to increase labour force par-ticipation and workplace inclusion (especially in managerial positions) for women, and this may well have contributed to slow growth – as having one half of your labour force underutilised will surely do. Vietnam, meanwhile, with its limits to media freedom has no doubt suffered from less account-ability, while Thailand's slide into autocracy has hurt its precious tourism industry by creating instability.

Financial liberalisation, as argued in Chapters 13 and 14, is a necessary but insufficient condition for growth absent the underlying basics, such as education, productivity increases and infrastructure. There can be very limited leapfrogging without improving skills and productivity levels, or growth will be unsustainable. But civic freedoms, in terms of human rights and inclusion, are the surest (although not necessarily the quickest) road to a stable society.

Openness relates also to a willingness to learn, and to permit and even encourage external influences. This was the fundamental lesson from Japan throughout the Meiji Restoration, which provided the catalyst for the entire region to develop and prosper. Singapore relied heavily on external advisers, and deliberately sought to attract multinational companies, given that they brought in not only skills, capital and technology, but logistics and ready markets. While the diaspora was encouraged to return home, or at least send a portion of their hard-earned capital home, as notable in Taiwan and through Vietnam's Viet Kieu (Overseas Vietnamese, about two million of whom live in the US), this was not where openness began and stopped. Far from it. A decade before the US withdrawal from Vietnam, Ho Chi Minh said of the Americans, 'We will spread a red carpet for you to leave Vietnam. And when the war is over, you are welcome to come back because you have technology and we will need your help.'[9] Magnanimity, or pragmatism, or just plain smart?

Africa has the largest population of young people in the world. While other regions continue to age, Africa will in the coming decades become the world's energy centre – the human battery, if you like. In order to take advantage of worldwide shifts in production and economic activity, it will have to take deliberate steps to enable its youth to enter the global economy.

CONCLUSION

What if Lee Kuan Yew was African?

We had our backs to the wall. We had no money, no skills and no resources. But we had a group of leaders with a common purpose and a common vision.

— S.R. Nathan, president of Singapore, 2014

The task of the leaders must be to provide or create for them a strong framework within which they can learn, work hard, be productive and be rewarded accordingly. And this is not easy to achieve.

— Lee Kuan Yew, *The Singapore Story*

Singapore's leaders certainly didn't have a roadmap. It is only with the benefit of hindsight (and the help of a growing literature on the subject) that we are able to discern their strategy. To an extent, Lee Kuan Yew and his colleagues managed by a healthy combination of curiosity and pragmatism. When asked the secret of his success, Prime Minister Lee admitted that there was no miracle, but that, rather, 'we did a few things right and well, and continued to do them right and well, widening and deepening them all the time'.[1]

Still, there are many good reasons for Africa to learn from East Asia. The regions, we note, share similar colonial histories. More importantly, Asia shows the possibility of focused development within a short time frame, which reached those at the bottom of the socio-economic pile, thereby alleviating poverty through inclusive growth. This required a fundamental and not just rhetorical commitment to growth involving strategic structural reforms, which, at times, were counter to the professed ideological tenets of the ruling party, such as in Vietnam and China. It is the willingness to make tough reform choices, which have been locally owned, that separates much of Africa from East Asia.

It also illustrates the power of regional exemplars and proximity. Japan moved first, inspiring the region, and debunking the myth of Asian inferiority. In so doing, the success of one country contributed to the success of the whole region. Across East Asia, economic crises were used to good effect, creating the political space to implement necessary, if otherwise unpopular, reforms. Asia's success was enabled by population density and geographic proximity (to both internal and external markets), which assisted the flow of goods and movement of investment across the region. It is essentially the phenomenon economists describe as the multiplier effect.

As was shown in the Introduction, Africa's challenge is that its share of global income has not increased as fast as (or faster than) its share of population. East Asia has been doubly advantaged with a dramatically rising income share and falling population share. Parenthetically, the income share of sub-Saharan Africa has fallen. The bottom line is that a major advantage for Asia over the last several decades is that they have had proximity, which Africa has lacked. Instead, African countries tended to cut themselves off from world trade while managing the disadvantages of distance (physical and informational) and division (trade restrictions, tariffs and overvalued exchange rates).[2] At the same time, Africa has had little success in extending regional markets, not least because of weak infrastructure, suspicion and a lack of trade complementarity.

But Asia's progress was not preordained. When Lee started as the leader of independent Singapore in 1965, the island was a fragile, poor backwater. Born amid crisis arising from the separation of the Malaysian Federation and Konfrontasi with Indonesia, the city-state was riven with racial, ethnic and religious fault lines. Its infrastructure was geared to colonial purpose, including the dockyards. Two-thirds of its then 1.6 million people lived in overcrowded slums, most without waterborne sewerage, and many without employment, on a tiny island-state of just 580 square kilometres.

Fifty years later, Singapore's GDP per capita stood at more than US$50 000 – over 100 times more than at independence and 25% greater than that of the UK, the former colonial power. Over the same period, per capita incomes in sub-Saharan Africa had increased by just US$200 to average US$1 000 in constant terms.

In the 1960s, as former Prime Minister Raila Odinga reminds us in the Foreword to this volume, Singapore looked to Africa for lessons on growing its economy, while Africa has been slow to learn the lessons since.[3]

The catalytic role of Lee, among other regional leaders, raises the question: how might development be pursued in Africa by a leadership steeped in the experience of Asia? Put differently, what would an African Lee Kuan Yew do?

Principles for action

While recognising historical differences, both between East Asia and Africa and between African countries themselves, what lessons might Africans usefully take from Singapore? A dozen stand out:

1. Unity of purpose: One of the prominent features of Lee's time in office was the vision he had for Singapore and his ability to allow others, notably the private sector, to help bring it to reality. He understood that the role of government was in creating the conditions that enable growth – as opposed to being the main driver for growth – and took development decisions towards that end by investing in education, housing, infrastructure and policies that made it easier to do business in Singapore. Growth was a 'national project' behind which people could rally.

2. Make the difficult trade-offs: Lee knew that you cannot do

everything at once, and that focus was required to succeed at anything. As noted in Chapter 3, from the slums of the 1960s, by 2015, 83% of Singapore's population lived in publicly supplied Housing Development Board apartments, 90% own their own homes, the rivers are clean, the island is 15% larger as a result of land reclamation, and despite the population increase, green cover has increased to 47% of the territory. Singapore's mandatory Central Provident Fund savings scheme, promoted by Lee, enabled the construction of housing and home ownership on a grand scale, and also seemingly offers a way around the chronically low savings rate across Africa. Success has depended, not on a few big or iconic infrastructure projects or even the provision of necessary funding, housing and land, but fundamentally on setting clear targets and making the difficult decisions that would allow them to become a reality.

3. Change the pattern of the colonial economy: Lee quickly realised that with Singapore's 'limited options' to survive, the country had to 'make extraordinary efforts' and in the process 'render obsolete our role as the entrepôt and middleman for the trade of the region. We had to be different,' he concluded, 'in order to address high unemployment and social tension.' This change saw Singapore, first, move into low-cost manufacturing, then convert the British military facilities, which unexpectedly closed in 1971, to civilian use, and all the while attract multinational companies to the island. Its strategy required continuous improvement and reinvention: from manufacturing through services and a digital transition, to its contemporary green economic phase. This did not mean ignoring the country's colonial past but rather a dogged pragmatism in using the resources available at the

time to move Singapore to a future that was not defined by the structures put in place by its former colonial masters.

4. Build institutions: While the state under Lee was undoubtedly at the helm of this transformation, additional lessons include the guiding of all actions by commercial principles, balance of power through devolution, and shared responsibility among fellow founding fathers. Contrary to the notion of one person running things from the centre, the reality of Lee's rule was quite different. His government, and those of his successors, involved top-quality peers, not just one 'big man'. Singapore has been reliant on institutions in the pursuit of development, a mindset and practice cultivated by Lee but which far outlived his tenure.

5. Integrate, don't isolate: Singapore's transformation has been underpinned by a drive to globalise rather than nationalise. Whereas African countries routinely make it difficult to move goods in and out, Singapore has capitalised on its strategic geographic crossroads by matching policies and the focus of institutions. There is a zero tariff on imported goods, low tax rates (personal and corporate tax rates are capped at 20% and 18% respectively), a range of free trade agreements, and vigorous trade and export promotion. Lee used his international engagements, including a sabbatical at Harvard in 1968, to understand better the ebbs and flows of world politics and economics and, importantly, to win investors over. The Singaporeans set up the Economic Development Board in 1961 specifically to provide a one-stop shop for investors and promote investment through its overseas offices. But Lee backed this up with personal commitment. Every time he visited the US he would arrange to meet 20–50 executives, to enable those CEOs who 'had not

time to visit Singapore … to see and assess the man in charge before they set up a factory there'. He was able to gauge how these investor minds worked. 'They looked', Lee wrote, 'for political, economic and financial stability and sound labour relations to make sure that there would be no disruption in production that supplied their customers and subsidiaries around the world.'[4]

6. Attract talent: Singapore made sure that the best and brightest were in government, that they were paid properly, and that they were given full support by leadership to do their job. As Lee observed, 'Equal opportunities for all and meritocracy, with the best man or woman for the job, especially in leaders in government, were basic principles that have helped us progress.' Moreover, 'legitimacy through performance' was central to gaining and maintaining the confidence that the island's citizens had in its impressive leaders. In proving the adage that 'any country with a skills problem has an immigration problem', the importation of talent has also been a key aspect to Singapore's success. From little over one million people at independence, Singapore's population stands at 5.6 million, including around 1.5 million expatriates, permanent residents and migrant workers. The injection of immigrants is part of a strategy to maintain GDP targets, and syncs with the need for continuous innovation and the search for a competitive advantage.

7. Invest in infrastructure that makes growth possible: Singapore's focus on being a welcoming environment for international investment meant creating the logistical and infrastructural framework to support that investment. An endeavour is clearly seen in the Port of Singapore. As noted earlier, more than 34 million containers are offloaded at

the port yearly, the world's second busiest behind Shanghai. The customs clearance time is officially under ten minutes, though, in practice, this is as quick as a mouse click for 99.9% of imports. Singapore's efficiency has been achieved through technology and the implementation of seemingly straightforward procedures, such as profiling customers and goods, and imposing strict penalties for transgressors. By comparison, cargo dwell times (the time cargo spends in the port) average about 20 days in African ports. The reason for such tardiness and the failure of solutions, ranging from privatisation to expanded port facilities, says the World Bank, 'is that the long dwell times are in the interest of certain public and private actors in the system'.[5]

8. Catalyse, don't capture: African governments like to cite Singapore as an example in the maintenance of their own parastatals and 'partystatals' (companies owned and/or run by ruling parties), both routinely notorious for crowding out private sector competition to the advantage of narrow financial and patronage interests. Again, such lessons are wide off the mark. An example of how to do this differently is in Temasek Holdings, the government-owned US$230-billion Singapore investment company. Despite its statist origins, Temasek's strategy and role are based on commercial and capitalist rather than political rationales. This avoids the intellectual suffocation and bureaucratic inertia of nationalised entities and creates a powerful investment vehicle for Singapore.

9. Manage labour relations: Labour relations in Singapore have been driven by the maxim that 'it is better to have a low-paying job than no job at all', balanced by a set of laws that spelt out minimum employment conditions, placing limits

on retrenchment benefits and overtime benefits. This created a co-operative environment between government, the unions and business. Lee realised early on that union practices were 'forcing employers to become capital-intensive, investing in expensive machines to get the work done with the minimum of workers [creating] a small group of privileged unionised workers getting high pay and a growing band of underpaid and underemployed workers'. He thus made it illegal for a union to take strike or industrial action without a secret ballot, continuously stressing the importance of wider employment over narrow privilege, and was able to decrease strikes from 153 in 1961–2 to zero in 1969.

10. Work with comparative advantages: Lee must have known Singapore's limits, which were imposed by its population and land size, and natural resource base. He therefore opted for development through sectors that could take advantage of the country's strengths, particularly its geographical position. This is how the development of Singapore into a regional air flight hub came about. This search for comparative advantage demands, as Chapter 9 among others shows, not aiming too high, and seeking gradual progress up the value chain of industrial progress.

11. Don't be a cheap date; use aid well, but don't rely on it: Despite the fad to bash aid as the explanation for all of Africa's problems, Asian countries have used the aid they received to some benefit. During the 1960s, aid per capita received by both regions was similar. Whereas some Asian countries enjoyed especially large aid flows (South Korea and Taiwan), and this has continued until recently (Vietnam), aid has not been relied upon as the single source of income. Asian countries have put aid to good use, with improved governance,

sound policies, effective planning and clearer, firmer local ownership of projects. Lee was, however, adamant that his government should nurture a 'spirit of self-reliance', avoiding an 'aid-dependent mentality. If we were to succeed,' he stated, 'we had to depend on ourselves.' Or as he put it to Singaporean workers: 'The world does not owe us a living. We cannot live by the begging bowl.' This move from victimhood, and the perception of Africa as a mere recipient of policies generated elsewhere, aligns with a reality of increasing African agency in the international system.[6]

12. Do some things differently: A final lesson, although not straight out of Lee's playbook, is that modern challenges call for an altogether different type of growth from that of Singapore and, for that matter, much of East Asia. Today, we are aware of the cost of infrastructure- and consumption-driven growth on the environment, as we see the effects of more than a century of unchecked fossil fuel use on our air quality, changing climate and the plastic debris in our oceans and rivers. There are other pressing issues, not least inequality, decent work and human rights, that were barely recognised in Lee's day. This applies also to the nature of manufacturing operations. When Japan was recovering from the devastation of the war and catching up with America and Europe, it was still possible to protect a domestic manufacturing industry by high tariff barriers. This condition does not exist anymore for relative latecomers. Moreover, car manufacturing is increasingly capital-intensive and less labour-intensive. There are significantly greater rewards for Africa, at least in the short term, for investment in comparatively job-intensive sectors, including agribusiness and tech services. To gain this sort of investment, the same conditions, however, apply to Africa

as Asia: long-term sustainability must take precedence over short-term gains.

The global context has shifted dramatically since most Asian countries started their reform journeys. Climate change and digital technology have closed off some avenues of growth. At the same time, they have opened up others, easing connectivity, reducing the barriers to global financial and market integration, and freeing the flow of ideas and skills. Perhaps most importantly, Africa has an advantage that East Asia did not possess in the power of this development example, where its 'rules' of development still apply.

Take the right lessons and deliberate steps

Asia's example does not tell us exactly *what* each African country should do, but it does give some clues on *how* to do it. Creating market space – domestically, regionally and internationally – and becoming a friend of business and facilitator of the flow of capital, skills and technology is imperative, as is the need to build a sense of a national project. Playing identity politics or inventing ideological cul-de-sacs and trotting out shibboleths about donors or the dire effects of structural adjustment might be politically convenient, but shifts the responsibility away from the local setting and the actors that matter. It also encourages corruption and clientelism. A positive alternative, Asia shows, is a political economy of change that gets stuck into the future and not in the past. It has to be driven by pragmatism and a leadership obsessed with execution.

East Asia's process of diversification, which drove job creation, pivoted the economy away from the elites to the citizenry – what we have termed a commitment to popular welfare. The institutionalisation of this approach was enabled through the establishment of a meritocracy, through education in the longer term and skills enhancement in the short term, the adoption of a full package of reforms from infrastructure to bureaucratic red tape, and by citizens taking a greater responsibility for their own destiny and holding leaders to account. This included a willingness to learn from anyone, including foreigners, and the instilling of a culture of continuous improvement.

The selection of low-hanging fruit helps to create momentum; while there were consistent building blocks across Asia, including the development of agriculture and light manufacturing, both were immediately pro-poor. The agriculture revolution was focused principally on improving yields, and that reflected a critical combination of improved market access, finance, technology and techniques. Economic inclusion mattered more than land restitution. Donors were important in oiling the wheels of Asian success but only because their programmes and the projects they spawned were locally instigated and thus owned.

Investing heavily in infrastructure has enabled countries to move quickly up the value chain and efficiently access markets. Yet, East Asia's focus has been on using infrastructure well, whatever its physical extent. This means matching hardware with human and institutional software, focusing on reducing delays and costs, and squeezing as much out of it as possible. Devising a financing model, public or private or public-private, remains a challenge across much of Africa, in part because of government autarky, regulatory discretion and policy unpredictability. Rather than trying to extend governance and costly infrastructure over wide expanses with often fraught politics, in some cases a focus on municipal governance may be cheaper and reap greater rewards.[7]

Africa today has a comparably greater store of technological innovation than much of East Asia possessed at take-off in the 1960s. What Asia did much better than Africa, however, was in providing the market space for entrepreneurs to employ their ideas and inventions.

East Asia also teaches that there is no single silver-bullet solution, and no easy answers. Asia is not one thing, and neither is Africa.

Often the wrong lessons – of a belief in the value of a benign dictator, for example – are taken by those seeking single-issue answers. Singapore's path shows that it is as wrong to extol the virtues of colonialism as it is to promote the benefits of authoritarianism. Lee's style of governance was also consultative in nature, the prime minister being careful to build public support, making it quite different, despite the caricatures to the contrary, from dictatorial systems. Legitimacy through delivery – or 'performance legitimacy' – was central to the political philosophy of Asia's first leadership generation.[8]

Overall, while better choices made in the interest of a majority matter, policy has to be continuously reinforced by strong leadership and strong institutions. Development depends on the ability to pull together. In this, East Asia teaches us that the sum of reforms is greater than its individual parts.

'Jambo Express' (Greg Mills/Robin Auld)

Out of the darkness and into the light
Amathemba … not out of sight
Looking for direction
To get where we wanna beeee ….

All aboard
Vuta Pamoja
All aboard
On the Jambo Express
How long it takes we just can't say
We gonna make a plan any way
All aboard
On the Jambo Express

No one would have said
Asia could make it pay
The power of the Confucian
The plastics revolution
Made in Japan
Taiwan in a can
Tigers and their cubs they grew
What to do … if you are Lee Kuan Yew

Prisoners of our past
Won't make it last
Karl, Joe and Ho,
No place to go
Turning on the track
Never looking back
Leaders on their toes
Hell no, we don't need superheroes

Notes

All the website references in the notes below were working links when accessed during the
researching and writing of this book.

INTRODUCTION

The Asian Aspiration

1 The 620-million person, ten-country ASEAN (Association of South East Asian
   Nations) grouping, comprising, as of 2019: Brunei, Cambodia, Indonesia, Laos,
   Malaysia, Myanmar, Philippines, Singapore, Thailand, Vietnam, for example, largely
   the focus of the case studies in this volume, has seen the average Human Development
   Indicator improve from 0.543 to 0.719 between 1990 and 2018, reflecting
   improvements in both the expectancy and quality of life, according to the Human
   Development Index Trends, 1990–2017.

2 On the importance of 'having a good crisis', see Jared Diamond, *Upheaval: Turning
   Points for Nations in Crisis*. New York: Allen Lane, 2019.

3 Unless otherwise indicated, the statistical basis used throughout this volume reflects
   that of the World Bank's data groupings for East Asia and the Pacific (EAP) and
   Sub-Saharan Africa (SSA). The EAP group comprises: American Samoa, Australia,
   Brunei Darussalam, Cambodia, China, Fiji, French Polynesia, Guam, Hong Kong
   SAR China, Indonesia, Japan, Kiribati, North Korea (Democratic People's Republic),
   South Korea (Republic), Lao PDR, Macao SAR China, Malaysia, Marshall Islands,
   Micronesia Federated States, Mongolia, Myanmar, Nauru, New Caledonia, New
   Zealand, Northern Mariana Islands, Palau, Papua New Guinea, Philippines, Samoa,
   Singapore, Solomon Islands, Thailand, Timor-Leste, Tonga, Tuvalu, Vanuatu, Vietnam.
   SSA is made up of: Angola, Benin, Botswana, Burkina Faso, Burundi, Cabo Verde,
   Cameroon, Central African Republic, Chad, Comoros, Côte d'Ivoire, Democratic
   Republic of Congo, Equatorial Guinea, Eritrea, Eswatini, Ethiopia, Gabon, Gambia,
   Ghana, Guinea, Guinea-Bissau, Kenya, Lesotho, Liberia, Madagascar, Malawi, Mali,
   Mauritania, Mauritius, Mozambique, Namibia, Niger, Nigeria, Republic of Congo,
   Rwanda, São Tome and Principe, Senegal, Seychelles, Sierra Leone, Somalia, South

Africa, South Sudan, Sudan, Tanzania, Togo, Uganda, Zambia, Zimbabwe.

4 African Development Bank, 'Jobs for Youth in Africa', 2016, https://www.afdb.org/fileadmin/uploads/afdb/Images/high_5s/Job_youth_Africa_Job_youth_Africa.pdf.

5 World Bank, 'Literacy Rate, Youth Total (% of People Ages 15–24)', 2019, https://data.worldbank.org/indicator/SE.ADT.1524.LT.ZS?locations=ZG-8S-Z4-ZJ.

6 BBC, 'World Bank: Extreme Poverty to Fall Below 10%', 5 October 2015, http://www.bbc.com/news/world-34440567.

7 'Towards the End of Poverty', The Economist, 1 June 2013, http://www.economist.com/news/leaders/21578665-nearly-1-billion-people-have-been-taken-out-extreme-poverty-20-years-world-should-aim.

8 See https://www.imf.org/en/Publications/WEO/Issues/2016/12/31/Legacies-Clouds-Uncertainties; reported at https://www.foxnews.com/world/china-surpasses-u-s-to-become-largest-world-economy.

9 See https://www.gapminder.org/answers/where-do-people-live/.

10 See https://www.atlanticcouncil.org/images/files/global-trends-2030-nic-lo.pdf.

11 According to a survey undertaken by The Brenthurst Foundation during June and July 2019, polling some 300 individuals living and working in Africa.

12 According to respondents in 36 African countries. See Afrobarometer, Round 6, Dispatch No. 122, 24 October 2016, http://afrobarometer.org/sites/default/files/summary_results/ab_R6_afrobarometer_global_release_highlights.pdf.

13 Gideon Rachman, Easternization: War and Peace in the Asian Century. London: Vintage, 2016.

14 See http://rabble.ca/toolkit/on-this-day/us-secret-bombing-cambodia.

15 Parag Khanna, The Future is Asian. London: Weidenfeld & Nicolson, 2019.

16 This is based on three trips to Cambodia in 2009, 2010 and 2014.

17 See https://data.worldbank.org/indicator/NY.GDP.PCAP.KD?locations=KH.

18 Joe Studwell, How Asia Works: Success and Failure in the World's Most Dynamic Region. London: Profile, 2014.

19 See, for example, Human Rights Watch, 'The Secret Underbelly of the Cambodian Garment Industry', 24 October 2016, https://www.hrw.org/news/2016/10/24/secret-underbelly-cambodian-garment-industry.

20 According to the Kuznets curve, inequality rises as countries develop, before reaching a maximum and declining as growth increases further.

21 World Bank, 'The East Asian Miracle', 1993, http://documents.worldbank.org/curated/en/975081468244550798/pdf/multi-page.pdf.

22 See https://data.worldbank.org/indicator/NY.GNS.ICTR.ZS.

23 Botswana, Cabo Verde, Cameroon, Djibouti, Kenya, Malawi, Mauritius, Morocco, Namibia, Senegal, South Africa, Swaziland, Tanzania and Zambia.

24 See https://www.forbes.com/sites/leezamangaldas/2017/10/25/india-and-china-both-struggle-with-deadly-pollution-but-only-one-is-fighting-it/#4a66f370707a.

25 See http://www.globalwaterforum.org/2012/06/09/water-pollution-in-asia-the-urgent-need-for-prevention-and-monitoring/.

26 See, for example, Richard Partington, 'Is It Time to End Our Fixation with GDP and Growth?', The Guardian, 17 June 2019, https://www.theguardian.com/news/2019/jun/17/is-time-to-end-our-fixation-with-gdp-and-growth.

PART ONE: CASE STUDIES FROM ASIA

Chapter 1: Japan: The Power of Example and Innovation

1 David Pilling, *Bending Adversity: Japan and the Art of Survival*. London: Penguin Books, 2014.
2 See Michael Porter, *The Comparative Advantage of Nations*. New York: Free Press, 1990.
3 According to Saburo Okita, quoted in Pilling, *Bending Adversity*.
4 According to Marius B. Jansen, *Sakamoto Ryoma and the Meiji Restoration*. Princeton: Princeton University Press, 1961, p.335.
5 This chapter is based on a research trip to Japan in July 2019. Unless otherwise indicated, the interviews cited here were conducted during this time.
6 A shuttle is the container that holds the yarn, and was previously manually changed by machine operators, slowing down production.
7 Cited in Henry Kissinger, *On China*. London: Penguin, 2011, p.79.
8 Masa Sugano, deputy Africa representative at the Japan External Trade Organisation, interview, 31 May 2019.
9 Pilling, *Bending Adversity*, p.32.
10 In constant 2005 dollars. See https://fas.org/sgp/crs/natsec/RL33331.pdf.
11 Abe Aamidor, *Shooting Star: The Rise and Fall of the British Motorcycle Industry*. Canada: ECW Press, 2009.
12 See https://focus2move.com/world-car-group-ranking/. Top in 2018 was Volkswagen, followed by Toyota, Renault-Nissan, General Motors, Hyundai-Kia, Ford, Honda, FCA, PSA and then Suzuki.
13 With sales of 1.6 million in 2018, behind Honda (19.5 million), Yamaha (5.4 million), Hero (7.6 million), Bajaj (3.4 million) and TVS (3.3 million). See https://www.mbaskool.com/fun-corner/top-brand-lists/17638-top-10-bike-companies-in-world.html.
14 Chalmers Johnson, *MITI and the Japanese Miracle*. California: Stanford University Press, 1982. See also http://www.e-ir.info/2008/06/15/the-developmental-state-and-economic-development/ for a summary of these arguments.
15 While worldwide sector sales are over 60 million units annually, growth is driven by the largest market in 2018, India, with 21.5 million units, having more than doubled in the last decade. China is in second place at 15.5 million units, followed by Indonesia (6.4 million), Vietnam (3.4 million), Pakistan (1.9 million), Thailand (1.8 million), the Philippines (1.6 million) and Brazil (960 000). See https://motorcyclesdata.com/2019/05/20/world-motorcycles-market/.
16 Toyota has done likewise. In 1990 it produced 4.2 million cars in Japan, and 680 000 elsewhere. The crossover point at which more cars were produced abroad than at home occurred in 2005. By 2019, 5.7 million were manufactured elsewhere, and 3.1 million in Japan. Southeast Asia made up 2.5 million of this total.
17 Interview, Pretoria, 4 June 2019.
18 Pilling, *Bending Adversity*, p.xxvii.
19 We are grateful to Ambassador Norio Maruyama for these points. Discussion,

Johannesburg, 6 September 2019.

20 According to officials from Honda's External Relations Division, interviewed on 23 July 2019.

Chapter 2: Taiwan: The Subcontractor

1 See https://www.reuters.com/article/us-usa-trade-china-apple/designed-in-california-made-in-china-how-the-iphone-skews-u-s-trade-deficit-idUSKBN1GX1GZ.

2 According to a presentation at the Hsinchu Science Park Bureau on 18 July 2019.

3 At 1996 prices.

4 Information provided by Chung-Hua Institution for Economic Research, 19 July 2019.

5 Ibid.

6 See http://hdr.undp.org/en/content/income-gini-coefficient.

7 See, for example, The Committee of the Conference of the Taiwan Experience, UNISA (ed.), *The Taiwan Experience: Implications for South Africa*. Johannesburg: Consulate-General of the Republic of China, December 1995; Yu Tzong-shian, *The Story of Taiwan*. Republic of China: Government Information Office, undated; Joseph S. Lee (ed.), *The Emergence of the South China Growth Triangle*. Taipei: Chung-Hua Institution for Economic Research, 1996.

8 Figures based on a visit to the Taiwan Land Reform Museum on 22 July 2019.

9 See, for example, 'In Praise of Paranoia', *The Economist: A Survey of Taiwan*, 7 November 1998; Koo Chen-Fu, 'The "Economic Miracle": A Commentary', *Free China Review* 48(12), December 1998: 37–9.

10 Provided by TAITRA, Taipei, 19 July 2019.

11 See https://ws.ndc.gov.tw/Download.ashx?u=LzAwMS9hZG1pbmlzdHJhdG9yLzEwL3JlbGZpbGUvNTYwNy83MzQvMDAxNDc5MC5wZGY%3D&n=RWNvbm9taWWMgRGV2ZWxvcG1lbnQsIFIuTy5DLiAoVGFpd2FuKS5wZGY%3D&icon.pdf.

12 See http://reports.weforum.org/global-competitiveness-report-2018/country-economy-profiles/#economy=TWN.

13 See https://www.worldbank.org/content/dam/doingBusiness/country/t/taiwan-china/TWN.pdf.

14 See http://focustaiwan.tw/news/aeco/201609130024.aspx.

15 See, for example, https://www.reuters.com/article/us-taiwan-china-campaign-insight/pro-china-groups-step-up-offensive-to-win-over-taiwan-idUSKCN1TR01H.

16 Based on a visit to ITRI on 18 July 2019.

17 Intellectual property to initial public offering.

18 See https://www.forbes.com/global/1998/0601/0105042a.html#2f7e72ad67f4.

19 Ibid.

20 This is based on a visit to the Kavalan Distillery on 20 July 2019. See also https://www.forbes.com/sites/forbesasia/2017/01/16/distilled-succession-albert-lee-guides-familys-food-and-beverage-group-with-a-premium-whisky/.

21 The CIER was established by the government in 1979 in reaction to the severing of US diplomatic recognition, and self-labels as 'Taiwan's most prestigious think tank'.

22 Information provided by Chung-Hua Institution for Economic Research, 19 July 2019.

23 See http://focustaiwan.tw/news/aipl/201805140029.aspx.
24 Seehttps://www.forbes.com/sites/ralphjennings/2018/03/19/taiwans-wages-are-as-low-as-mexicos-blame-china/#23d055c64888.

Chapter 3: Singapore: Have a Good Crisis

1 See, for example, http://www.worldairportawards.com/awards/world_airport_rating.html.
2 See http://data.worldbank.org/indicator/NY.GDP.PCAP.CD?page=6.
3 In an interview with Liu Thai Ker on 31 August 2012, published in *Urban Solutions* 2, 2013.
4 See Huang Lijie and Joyce Fang, *Front Page Stories of Singapore since 1845*. Singapore: Straits Times Press, 2015.
5 Jules Verne, *Celebrated Travels and Travellers*. Oxford: Oxford University, 1881, p.1002.
6 Iain Manley, *Tales of Old Singapore*. Hong Kong: Earnshaw Books, 2010.
7 Commonly held to include Lee Kuan Yew, lawyer David Marshall, unionist Devan Nair, lawyer Eddie Barker, economist Goh Keng Swee, Lim Kim San, Ong Pang Boon, Othman Wok, S. Rajaratnam and Toh Chin Chye.
8 Cited in The New Paper Team, *Founding Fathers*. Singapore: Straits Times Press, 2015, p.123.
9 I.M. Pei, who inter alia had designed the pyramid at the Louvre, and Kenzo Tange were roped in to improve the cityscape of Singapore in the 1970s. Lee had met Tange when receiving an honorary degree at the University of Hong Kong in 1970, and the following year invited him to the Istana. Tange redesigned the United Overseas Bank building, while Pei designed the Raffles City complex and rebuilt the Overseas Chinese Banking Corporation.
10 Discussion, HDB, Singapore, 5 December 2013.
11 See http://eresources.nlb.gov.sg/history/events/c4c0b6bf-d674-4851-a3d4-fcc0b9d785d2.
12 See Stephen Dobbs, *The Singapore River: A Social History, 1819–2002*. Singapore: Singapore University Press, 2003.
13 See 'UNDP and the Making of Singapore's Public Service: Lessons from Albert Winsemius', http://issuu.com/undppublicserv/docs/booklet_undp-sg50-winsemius_digital.
14 Thanks to Ambassador Barry Desker for this insight.
15 Cited in Manley, *Tales of Old Singapore*, p.132.
16 See Lee Kuan Yew, *From Third World to First*. Singapore: Marshall Cavendish, 2008.
17 Email correspondence, 27 June 2019. See also Chua Beng Huat, *Liberalism Disavowed: Communitarianism and State Capitalism in Singapore*. Singapore: NUS Press, 2018.
18 Interview, Singapore, 23 May 2018.
19 Comments by Ambassador Barry Desker by email, 19 August 2019.

Chapter 4: South Korea: Incentivising Competitiveness

1 See https://www.bbc.com/news/world-asia-41228181.

2 This is based on a research trip to South Korea by Greg Mills in September–October 2018. Thanks are expressed to the Korea-Africa Foundation for its role in organising an itinerary. Unless otherwise indicated, the interviews cited were conducted during this time.

3 Cited in Joe Studwell, *How Asia Works: Success and Failure in the World's Most Dynamic Region*. London: Profile, 2014, p.109.

4 See Louis Kraar, 'The New Power in Asia', *Fortune*, 31 October 1994.

5 See Sung-hee Jwa, *The Rise and Fall of Korea's Economic Development: Lessons for Developing and Developed Economics*. Cham, Switzerland: Palgrave Macmillan, 2017.

6 Jong-dae Park, *Re-inventing Africa's Development: Linking Africa to the Korean Development Model*. Cham, Switzerland: Palgrave Macmillan, 2019.

7 Cited in Max Hastings, *The Korean War*. London: Pan, 1987, p.336.

8 Jong-dae Park, *Re-inventing Africa's Development*.

9 See http://english.chosun.com/site/data/html_dir/2010/07/07/2010070701203.html.

10 See Hwang Kyung Moon, *A History of Korea*. London: Macmillan, 2010.

11 See https://ewn.co.za/2018/10/05/south-korea-jails-former-president-lee-for-15-years-on-corruption-charges.

12 In 1963, 1967, 1971, 1972, 1978.

13 For details of these processes and movements, see Seo Joong-seok, *Contemporary History of South Korea – 60 Years*. Seoul: Korea Democracy Foundation, 2007.

14 See http://english.yonhapnews.co.kr/national/2015/08/07/84/0301000000AEN201508 07006800315F.html.

15 These and other growth statistics are generated from the World Bank's World Development Indicators. See http://databank.worldbank.org/data/reports. aspx?source=world-development-indicators. Chapter 5: The Philippines: Beware Elites

Chapter 5: The Philippines: Beware Elites

1 This is based on two research trips by Greg Mills to the Philippines, in February 2017 and September 2018. Unless otherwise cited, the interviews were conducted during this time. Thanks are expressed to the South African Embassy in Manila and especially to Ambassador Martin Slabber and his staff for their kind assistance in this regard. Thanks are also due to Archie Muzenda and Nicola Doyle for their assistance with this section.

2 Joe Studwell, *How Asia Works: Success and Failure in the World's Most Dynamic Region*. London: Profile, 2014, p.88.

3 Peter Church, *A Short History of South-East Asia*. Singapore: Wiley, 2017, p.148.

4 Joe Studwell, *Asian Godfathers: Money and Power in Hong Kong and Southeast Asia*. London: Profile, 2007, p.25.

5 Studwell, *Asian Godfathers*, p.26.

6 A.B. Villanueva, 'Post-Marcos: The State of Philippine Politics and Democracy during the Aquino Regime, 1986–92', *Contemporary Southeast Asia* 14(2), September 1992, pp.174–87.

7 This was, in 2015, eclipsed only by India, the leading recipient country, which

received US$72 billion, and China, US$64 billion. See https://news.abs-cbn.com/business/01/12/16/which-countries-receive-the-highest-remittances.

8 See http://www.magellan-solutions.com/blog/whats-the-number-analysis-of-the-latest-statistics-of-the-bpo-industry/.

9 See https://www.sunstar.com.ph/article/142793 and http://m.hktdc.com/business-news/article/Research-Articles/The-Philippines-Special-Economic-Zones/rp/en/1/1X000000/1X0AAKZD.htm.

10 With thanks to his office for providing this information.

11 See https://www.rappler.com/nation/77094-aquino-legacy-good-governance.

12 See http://www.newmandala.org/philippine-chief-justice-serenos-undemocratic-ouster/.

13 See https://www.unescap.org/sites/default/files/03Chapter1.pdf.

14 Studwell, *How Asia Works*.

15 See https://www.theguardian.com/global-development/2019/jul/08/waste-recycling-smell-pollution-philippines-plastic-city.

16 See https://www.scmp.com/news/asia/southeast-asia/article/3025486/philippines-has-plastic-pollution-crisis-and-poverty-makes.

17 Interview, Professor Maria Atienza, University of Manila, September 2018.

18 Correspondence with his office, 12 October 2018. See also https://joeam.com/2018/03/14/a-letter-to-president-aquino-and-his-response/.

19 See www.sws.org.ph/swsmain/artcldisppage/?artcsyscode=ART-20180710155308.

20 See http://cnnphilippines.com/transportation/2018/02/23/JICA-P3.5-billion-traffic.html.

21 See http://www.nytimes.com/2014/08/04/business/international/strained-infrastructure-in-philippines-erodes-the-nations-growth-prospects.html?_r=0.

22 See https://www.transparency.org/country/PHL.

23 See https://freedomhouse.org/report/freedom-world/2018/philippines.

24 See https://news.abs-cbn.com/news/02/22/18/ph-score-in-world-corruption-index-falls-to-lowest-in-5-years.

25 See, for example, https://www.washingtonpost.com/news/theworldpost/wp/2018/03/20/duterte/?noredirect=on&utm_term=.36c51dc0a782.

26 See https://tribunecontentagency.com/article/understanding-dutertes-mind-boggling-rise-to-power/.

27 Interview, SGV, Manila, September 2018.

Chapter 6: Malaysia: Managing Diversity

1 This chapter is based, in part, on a visit by the authors to Malaysia in May 2019. Unless otherwise cited, the interviews were conducted during this time.

2 Victoria Glendinning, *Raffles and the Golden Opportunity*. London: Profile, 2012, p.15.

3 This is based on a trip to Penang by Greg Mills in August 2014.

4 Ooi Keat Gin, 'Disparate Identities: Penang from a Historical Perspective, 1780–1941'. *Kajian Malaysia* 33(2), 2015, pp.27–52.

5 See http://www.mida.gov.my/home/incentives-in-manufacturing-sector/posts/.

6 See https://www.asiaone.com/health/penang-tops-list-medical-tourism.
7 These statistics were acquired from the Ministry of Economic Affairs, Kuala Lumpur, 29 April 2019.
8 See https://data.worldbank.org/indicator/ST.INT.ARVL?locations=MY.
9 See https://www.thestar.com.my/business/business-news/2019/01/03/airasia-targets-100-million-passengers-in-2019/.
10 See http://povertydata.worldbank.org/poverty/country/MYS.
11 ASEAN average excluding Singapore and Brunei.
12 See http://www.mida.gov.my/home/competitiveness-ranking/posts/.
13 Tom Wright and Bradley Hope, *Billion Dollar Whale: The Man Who Fooled Wall Street, Hollywood, and the World*. New York: Hachette Books, 2018.
14 See https://www.theguardian.com/world/2019/apr/02/the-trial-of-najib-razak-former-pm-to-face-court-of-over-global-1mdb-scandal.
15 International Monetary Fund, Global Financial Stability Report.
16 Kenichi Takayasu and Yosie Yokoe, 'Non-performing Loan Issue Crucial to Asia's Economic Resurgence', *JRI Research Journal* 44, 1991.
17 Joe Studwell, *Asian Godfathers: Money and Power in Hong Kong and Southeast Asia*. London: Profile, 2007, p.277.
18 Studwell, *Asian Godfathers*, p.26.
19 Mahathir bin Mohamad, *The Malay Dilemma*. Singapore: Asia Pacific Press, 1970, p.44.
20 See https://umexpert.um.edu.my/file/publication/00006071_124301.pdf.
21 Interview with Greg Mills, Petronas Towers, Kuala Lumpur, April 2007.
22 See World Bank, 'Malaysia Economic Monitor June 2019: Re-energizing the Public Service', 30 June 2019, https://www.worldbank.org/en/country/malaysia/publication/malaysia-economic-monitor-june-2019-re-energizing-the-public-service.
23 Discussion, Tan Sri Rastam Mohd Isa, Kuala Lumpur, 29 April 2019.
24 See http://www.mpc.gov.my/productivity-performance/.
25 Interview, Singapore, September 2014.
26 Studwell, *Asian Godfathers*, p.xxi.
27 Studwell, *Asian Godfathers*, p.xix.

Chapter 7: Indonesia: The Cost of Corruption, the Benefits of Growth

1 This is based, in part, on two trips to Indonesia: to Jakarta, Semarang, Yogykarta and Japara in August 2014; and Bandung and Jakarta in January 2016.
2 See Joe Studwell, *How Asia Works: Success and Failure in the World's Most Dynamic Region*. London: Profile, 2014, p.152. See also Elizabeth Pisani, *Indonesia Etc.: Exploring the Improbable Nation*. New York: W.W. Norton, 2014.
3 See http://www.doingbusiness.org/rankings.
4 See https://www.pri.org/stories/2016-12-30/indonesia-s-rapidly-disappearing-forests-four-charts.
5 See https://data.worldbank.org/indicator/ST.INT.ARVL?locations=ID; https://data.worldbank.org/indicator/ST.INT.RCPT.CD?locations=ID.
6 Pisani, *Indonesia* Etc., p.1.

7 See http://thediplomat.com/2015/03/indonesias-migrant-workers-dreams-and-tears/.
8 Raoul Oberman, Richard Dobbs, Arief Budiman, Fraser Thompson and Morten Rossé, 'The Archipelago Economy: Unleashing Indonesia's Potential', *McKinsey & Company*, September 2012, http://www.mckinsey.com/insights/asia-pacific/the_archipelago_economy.
9 See https://www.statista.com/statistics/304829/number-of-facebook-users-in-indonesia/.
10 See https://www.transparency.org/research/gcr/gcr_political_corruption/0/.
11 See, for example, Peter Lewis, *Growing Apart: Oil, Politics and Economic Change in Indonesia and Nigeria*. Ann Arbor: University of Michigan Press, 2007. See also Ahmad Helmy Fuady, 'Aid and Policy Preferences in Oil-rich Countries: Comparing Indonesia and Nigeria', *Third World Quarterly* 36(7), 2015: 1349–64; 'A Tale of Two Giants: Why Indonesia has Beaten Nigeria Hands Down', *The Economist*, 13 January 2000, https://www.economist.com/special-report/2000/01/13/a-tale-of-two-giants.
12 See https://www.bbc.com/news/world-africa-11399866.
13 See http://hdr.undp.org/en/content/income-gini-coefficient.
14 See https://economics.mit.edu/files/2130.
15 See http://hdr.undp.org/sites/all/themes/hdr_theme/country-notes/IDN.pdf.
16 See https://unesdoc.unesco.org/ark:/48223/pf0000002930.
17 See http://data.uis.unesco.org/Index.aspx?queryid=166.
18 See https://knoema.com/atlas/Nigeria/topics/Education/Literacy/Adult-literacy-rate.
19 See https://www.indonesia-investments.com/finance/macroeconomic-indicators/poverty/item301.
20 See A. Garba, 'Alleviating Poverty in Northern Nigeria', Paper presented at the annual convention of the Zumunta Association, Minneapolis, 28–29 July 2006.
21 See https://databank.worldbank.org/data/download/poverty/33EF03BB-9722-4AE2-ABC7-AA2972D68AFE/Global_POVEQ_NGA.pdf.
22 Discussion, Japara, August 2014.
23 See https://www.bcg.com/publications/2013/center-consumer-customer-insight-consumer-products-indonesias-rising-middle-class-affluent-consumers.aspx.
24 See http://www.indonesiabriefing.com/news/manufacturing-setup-indonesia.
25 Lewis, *Growing Apart*, pp.278–9.
26 Lewis, *Growing Apart*, p.285.
27 See https://www.bbc.com/news/world-africa-11399866.
28 Amartya Sen, *Beyond the Crisis: Development Strategies in Asia*. Singapore: Institute of Southeast Asian Studies, 1999, pp.15–37.
29 We are grateful to Jonathan Pincus for this point. Telephonic interview, 1 July 2019.
30 See https://www.transparency.org/cpi2018.
31 Peter Church, *A Short History of South-East Asia*. Singapore: Wiley, 2017, p.69.

Chapter 8: Thailand: Closed Politics, Open Tourism

1 See https://mashable.com/2014/12/26/tsunami-10-year-anniversary/.
2 See https://www.worldbank.org/en/country/thailand/overview.
3 Ibid.

4 See https://www.doingbusiness.org/content/dam/doingBusiness/country/t/thailand/ THA.pdf.
5 Based on an interview with Dr Kiatipong Ariyapruchya at the World Bank in Bangkok, 8 August 2019.
6 The Columbia-educated economist later went on to establish the TDRI in 1984. See https://tdri.or.th/wp-content/uploads/2014/09/Prof.Sanoh_1-final.pdf.
7 Email exchange with Makoto Sasagawa of Toyota's IIES, Tokyo, 8 August 2019.
8 Based on an email exchange with Abhisit Vejjajiva, 9 August 2019.
9 This is based on an interview in Bangkok, 8 August 2019. See also his article charting Thailand's economic transformation and future growth model at https://tdri.or.th/2015/04/tdri-quarterly-review-march-2015/.
10 See https://amcn.com.au/editorial/triumph-thailand-factory/.
11 Email correspondence, 7 August 2019.
12 See https://motorcyclesdata.com/2019/07/20/thailand-motorcycles/.
13 Kaname Akamatsu, 'A Historical Pattern of Economic Growth in Developing Countries', *Journal of Developing Economies* 1(1), 1962, pp.3–25.
14 See 'Relocating Labour-Intensive Industries from Thailand to Neighbouring Countries', http://www.aseancenter.org.tw/upload/files/outlook009-06.pdf.
15 See https://www.eeco.or.th/en/content/targeted-industries.
16 Based on an interview in Bangkok on 8 August 2019.
17 See, for example, http://www.entrepreneurialleaders.com/downloads/sb_eleaders/ EntrepreneurialExpertGordonRedding.pdf.
18 See https://www.newmandala.org/counting-thailands-coups/.
19 See https://www.bbc.com/news/world-asia-44507590.
20 See https://freedomhouse.org/report/freedom-world/2019/thailand.
21 This interview was conducted via email, 4 August 2019.
22 See https://www.bangkokpost.com/learning/advanced/1272197/thai-business-shuns-regime-invests-overseas.
23 See https://www.bloomberg.com/news/articles/2018-10-10/travelers-spend-more-money-in-thailand-than-anywhere-else-in-asia.
24 See https://newsroom.mastercard.com/wp-content/uploads/2016/09/FINAL-Global-Destination-Cities-Index-Report.pdf.
25 The index is regarded as an indicator for the purchasing power of an economy. The average price for a Big Mac burger in Switzerland was US$6.62 in January 2019, the most expensive; Russia was the cheapest at US$1.65.
26 See https://www.economist.com/finance-and-economics/2018/01/20/our-big-mac-index-shows-fundamentals-now-matter-more-in-currency-markets.
27 See https://www.numbeo.com/cost-of-living/rankings.jsp.
28 See https://www.worlddata.info/cost-of-living.php.
29 See https://businessblog.trivago.com/trivago-hotel-price-index/.
30 See https://media.hopper.com/articles/asias-top-ten-backpacking-destinations.
31 See https://www.rvo.nl/sites/default/files/2017/06/factsheet-toerisme-in-thailand.pdf.
32 See https://www.expatistan.com/cost-of-living/comparison/beijing/ bangkok?currency=USD; https://www.expatistan.com/cost-of-living/comparison/ tokyo/bangkok.

33 See https://www.bloomberg.com/news/articles/2018-10-10/travelers-spend-more-money-in-thailand-than-anywhere-else-in-asia.
34 See https://www.scbeic.com/en/detail/file/product/2953/ekn1rppsq7/EIC_Insight_ENG_Tourism_2016.pdf.
35 See https://data.worldbank.org/indicator/ST.INT.ARVL?locations=TH.
36 See https://www.imf.org/en/News/Articles/2018/06/07/NA060818-Thailands-Economic-Outlook-in-Six-Charts.
37 See https://www.scbeic.com/en/detail/file/product/2953/ekn1rppsq7/EIC_Insight_ENG_Tourism_2016.pdf.
38 See https://www.policyforum.net/challenging-times-for-thai-tourism/.
39 See https://www.scbeic.com/en/detail/file/product/2953/ekn1rppsq7/EIC_Insight_ENG_Tourism_2016.pdf.
40 See https://www.scbeic.com/en/detail/file/product/2953/ekn1rppsq7/EIC_Insight_ENG_Tourism_2016.pdf.
41 This chapter is based in part on a research trip to Thailand by Greg Mills and Emily van der Merwe in August 2019.
42 See https://www.panynj.gov/airports/pdf-traffic/ATR2017.pdf .
43 See https://12go.asia/en/post/8038/expansion-of-don-mueang-airport-to-be-completed-by-2024.
44 See https://www.independent.co.uk/travel/news-and-advice/best-airports-2019-world-changi-singapore-skytrax-awards-tokyo-seoul-a8843431.html.
45 See https://www.internationalairportreview.com/article/32311/top-20-largest-airports-world-passenger-number/.
46 See https://tastythailand.com/how-long-does-it-take-to-get-through-suvarnabhumi-airport-bangkok-immigration/.
47 See http://www.nationmultimedia.com/national/30356743.
48 See https://www.bangkokpost.com/business/1701300/thai-tourism-still-wounded.
49 See https://www.bangkokpost.com/thailand/general/1674364/maya-bay-to-remain-closed-till-mid-2021.
50 See https://www.bangkokpost.com/business/1523562/on-phuket-hotel-guests-check-out-of-plastic-waste.
51 Based on an interview at TAT's offices in Bangkok on 9 August 2019.
52 See https://www.scbeic.com/en/detail/file/product/2953/ekn1rppsq7/EIC_Insight_ENG_Tourism_2016.pdf.
53 See https://www.grandviewresearch.com/press-release/global-medical-tourism-market.
54 See https://www.theguardian.com/world/2018/dec/31/almost-200-die-in-three-days-on-thailands-roads-as-holiday-carnage-returns.

Chapter 9: China: Cats, Mice and Cement

1 Interview, Shanghai, September 2018.
2 See http://www.worldbank.org/en/country/china/overview#3.
3 See www.worldportsource.com.
4 Ibid.

5 See https://www.forbes.com/sites/niallmccarthy/2018/07/06/china-produces-more-cement-than-the-rest-of-the-world-combined-infographic/.

6 Based on an interview with Justin Lin in Beijing on 30 July 2019.

7 See https://www.telegraph.co.uk/travel/destinations/asia/china/articles/Qufu-China-a-tour-of-Confuciuss-home-town/.

8 Cited in Devesh Kapur, John Prior Lewis and Richard Charles Webb, *The World Bank: History*. Washington, D.C.: Brookings, 2008, p.145.

9 See Bin Zhao, 'Consumerism, Confucianism, Communism: Making Sense of China Today', www.shehui.pku.edu.cn/upload/editor/file/20181102/20181102103058_2959.pdf.

10 See https://newleftreview.org/issues/I222/articles/bin-zhao-consumerism-confucianism-communism-making-sense-of-china-today.

11 See https://www.straitstimes.com/asia/east-asia/xi-gives-trump-a-chinese-history-lesson.

12 Based on an interview on 30 July 2019 in Shanghai.

13 Jonathan Fenby, *Tiger Head, Snake Tails: How It Got There, and Where It is Heading*. London: Simon & Schuster, 2012, p.3.

14 Loren Brandt and Thomas G. Rawski (eds), *China's Great Economic Transformation*. Cambridge: Cambridge University Press, 2008.

15 Cai Fang, Guo Zhenwei and Wang Meiyan, 'New Urbanisation as a Driver of China's Growth'. In Ligang Song, Ross Garnaut, Cai Fang and Lauren Johnston (eds), *China's New Sources of Economic Growth*, Volume 1. Canberra: Australian National University Press, 2016, pp.43–64.

16 The ratio of the working-age population to dependants, or those under 15 and above 65.

17 See https://www.ceicdata.com/en/indicator/china/gross-savings-rate.

18 Based on an interview on 2 August 2019 in Shanghai.

19 See www.bbc.com/news/business/China_urban_rural_inequality.

20 Patrick Skene Catling, '"Wicked Old Paris of the Orient": A Portrait of 1930s Shanghai', *The Spectator*, 4 June 2019, https://www.spectator.co.uk/2016/06/wicked-old-paris-of-the-orient-a-portrait-of-1930s-shanghai/.

21 See http://travel.cnn.com/shanghai/life/historic-shanghai-flowers-shanghai-669685/.

22 Taras Grescoe, *Shanghai Grand: Forbidden Love and International Intrigue on the Eve of the Second World War*. London: Pan Macmillan, 2016.

23 Based on an interview on 30 July 2019 in Beijing.

24 Justin Yifu Lin and Célestin Monga, *Beating the Odds: Jump-starting Developing Countries*. Princeton: Princeton University Press, 2017, p.3.

25 Discussion, Embassy of the People's Republic of China, Johannesburg, 17 January 2019.

26 Yuen Yuen Ang, 'Autocracy with Chinese Characteristics', *Foreign Affairs*, May/June 2018, p.46.

27 See http://www.bbc.com/news/world-asia-china-43453769.

28 See https://www.eastasiaforum.org/2016/05/17/chinas-soe-sector-is-bigger-than-some-would-have-us-think/.

29 See Ligang Song, 'The Past, Present and Future of SOE Reform in China', *East Asia Forum*, 25 October 2018, https://www.eastasiaforum.org/2018/10/25/the-past-present-

and-future-of-soe-reform-in-china/.

30 See https://thediplomat.com/2018/03/can-china-keep-controlling-its-soes/.

31 See https://bruegel.org/2018/09/inequality-in-china/.

32 See https://www.lowyinstitute.org/publications/clear-waters-and-green-mountains-will-xi-jinping-take-lead-climate-change.

33 See https://ourworldindata.org/fossil-fuels.

34 See https://www.forbes.com/sites/judeclemente/2019/01/23/coal-is-not-dead-china-proves-it/#4540606365fa.

35 Based on an interview in Shanghai on 1 August 2019.

36 Sky Television report, 28 June 2019.

37 See, for example, https://www.chathamhouse.org/publications/twt/how-one-party-state-may-shape-our-future.

Chapter 10: Vietnam: Making Better Development Choices

1 The visit to the Giap house and the events and individuals cited here were, unless otherwise indicated, part of the findings of a research trip to Hanoi and Ho Chi Minh City in May 2019. Other research trips on which this chapter is based were conducted during November 2018 and August 2019.

2 Related during a roundtable event organised by the Vietnam Academy of Social Sciences and the Institute of African and Middle East Studies, 2 May 2019.

3 World Bank, *Vietnam 2035: Towards Prosperity, Creativity, Equity, and Democracy.* Washington, D.C.: World Bank, 2016.

4 See https://gro-intelligence.com/insights/vietnamese-coffee-production.

5 Unless otherwise stated, all data was sourced from the World Bank Development Indicators. See https://databank.worldbank.org/data.

6 See https://data.worldbank.org/indicator/NY.GDP.PCAP.CD?locations=VN; https://www.worldbank.org/en/news/press-release/2016/02/23/new-report-lays-out-path-for-vietnam-to-reach-upper-middle-income-status-in-20-years.

7 Email correspondence, 6 June 2019.

8 Email correspondence, 21 May 2019.

9 See https://www.undp.org/content/dam/vietnam/docs/Publications/4585_oda2000.pdf.

10 See 'Labour-related Difficulties Lie Ahead for Vietnamese Textile Companies', *Viet Nam News*, 3 August 2019.

11 See https://www.scmp.com/news/china/diplomacy-defence/article/2152150/dont-give-our-land-away-clash-interests-vietnams-anti.

12 See, for example, the analysis on Vingroup, https://www.ft.com/content/84323c32-9799-11e9-9573-ee5cbb98ed36.

13 See https://www.mckinsey.com/~/media/McKinsey/Featured%20Insights/Asia%20Pacific/Sustaining%20growth%20in%20Vietnam/MGI_Sustaining_growth_in_Vietnam_Full_Report.ashx.

14 World Bank, 'Taking Stock: Recent Economic Developments of Vietnam. Special Focus: Vietnam's Tourism Developments', 2019, http://documents.worldbank.org/

curated/en/439611561653730211/Taking-Stock-Recent-Economic-Developments-of-Vietnam-Special-Focus-Vietnams-Tourism-Developments-Stepping-Back-from-the-Tipping-Point-Vietnams-Tourism-Trends-Challenges-and-Policy-Priorities.

15 Yoshino Takeyama, 'Reform of State Owned Enterprises: A Big Challenge to the Vietnamese Economy', 2018, https://www.iima.or.jp/en/docs/newsletter/2018/NL2018No_12_e.pdf.

16 'Spotlight on Viet Nam: The Leading Emerging Market', *PwC Vietnam*, https://www.pwc.com/vn/spotlight-on-vietnam.

17 See https://www.k12academics.com/Education%20Worldwide/Education%20in%20Vietnam/teaching-quality-issues.

18 See https://www.indexmundi.com/facts/vietnam/school-enrollment.

19 See http://www.doingbusiness.org/en/data/exploreeconomies/vietnam#DB_gc.

20 See https://e.vnexpress.net/projects/sidewalk-economics-what-the-future-holds-for-vietnam-s-ubiquitous-street-vendors-3565620/index.html.

21 See https://e.vnexpress.net/news/news/saigon-s-captain-sidewalk-steps-down-after-cleanup-campaign-fails-3695873.html.

22 See https://www.transparency.org/country/VNM.

23 See https://freedomhouse.org/report/freedom-world/2018/vietnam.

24 See Peter Church, *A Short History of South-East Asia*. Singapore: Wiley, 2017.

25 See https://www.amnesty.org/download/Documents/ASA4181622018ENGLISH.PDF.

26 See https://data.worldbank.org/indicator/ST.INT.ARVL?locations=VN.

27 World Bank, 'Taking Stock'.

28 World Bank, 'Taking Stock'.

29 Finn Tarp, 'Viet Nam, the Dragon that Rose from the Ashes', UNU-WIDER Working Paper, 2018/126.

30 See https://climateknowledgeportal.worldbank.org/country/vietnam.

31 UNU-WIDER, 'The Cost of Climate Change in Vietnam', *Recom*, 2013, http://www1.wider.unu.edu/recomenvironment/article/cost-climate-change-vietnam.

PART TWO: FIVE KEY LESSONS FOR SUCCESS FROM ASIA

Chapter 11: The Premium of Leadership and Institutions

1 See, for example, Meredith Woo-Cumings, *The Developmental State*. Ithaca, NY: Cornell University Press, 1999; Stephen Haggard, *Pathways from the Periphery: The Politics of Growth in the Newly Industrializing Countries*. Ithaca, NY: Cornell University Press, 1990.

2 See Greg Mills, Olusegun Obasanjo, Jeffrey Herbst and Tendai Biti, *Democracy Works: Rewiring Politics to Africa's Advantage*. Johannesburg: Pan Macmillan, 2019.

3 Daron Acemoglu and James Robinson, *Why Nations Fail: The Origins of Power, Prosperity and Poverty*. London: Profile, 2012.

4 Milton Osborne, *Southeast Asia: An Introductory History*. Sydney: Allen & Unwin, 2013.

5 We are grateful to Christopher Clapham for this point.

6 Osborne, *Southeast Asia*, p.45. To an extent with the exception of Vietnam, where there was always much greater state control from the centre.

7 Osborne, *Southeast Asia*, p.43.

8 Osborne, *Southeast Asia*, p.111.

9 Osborne, *Southeast Asia*, p.107.

10 See http://www.intracen.org/exporters/statistics-export-country-product/.

11 Mancur Olson, *Power and Prosperity: Outgrowing Communist and Capitalist Dictatorships*. New York: Basic Books, 2000.

12 Discussion, Johannesburg, 28 September 2019.

13 Daron Acemoglu, Simon Johnson and James Robinson, 'The Colonial Origins of Comparative Development: An Empirical Investigation', *The American Economic Review* 91(5), 2001, pp.1369–401.

14 Francis Fukuyama, *Political Order and Political Decay: From the Industrial Revolution to the Globalization of Democracy*. London: Profile, 2015.

15 Fukuyama, *Political Order*, p.302.

16 Jared Diamond, *Guns, Germs and Steel: The Fates of Human Societies*. New York: W.W. Norton, 1997.

17 David Lamb, *The Africans*. New York: Random House, 1987, p.17.

18 See https://www.worldometers.info/world-population/south-eastern-asia-population/; http://worldpopulationreview.com/continents/eastern-asia-population/.

19 See https://www.worldatlas.com/articles/african-countries-by-population-density. html.

20 Jeffrey Herbst, *States and Power in Africa: Comparative Lessons in Authority and Control*. Princeton: Princeton University Press, 2001.

21 Tilly argued that European states were forced, because of their competition and military rivalry with each other, to raise taxes (thus extending and improving governance over their territories) and apply technologies (including military technologies). The same intense conditions of territorial contestation, technological invention and application did not apply to China – and, for that matter, contemporary Africa. See Charles Tilly, 'Westphalia and China', Keynote address given at a conference on 'Westphalia and Beyond', Enschede, Netherlands, July 1998.

22 With thanks to Johnny Clegg for highlighting this. See also http://www.nomadsed.de/fileadmin/user_upload/redakteure/Dateien_Publikationen/Mitteilungen_des_SFB/owh6sigrist.pdf.

23 Joe Studwell, *Asian Godfathers: Money and Power in Hong Kong and Southeast Asia*. London: Profile, 2007, p.xix.

24 Studwell, *Asian Godfathers*, p.xvii.

25 Comments made at the review meeting of this manuscript, 22–24 September 2019.

26 Discussion, Hargeisa, 2 September 2019.

27 Herbst, *States and Power in Africa*, p.15.

28 Comments made at the review meeting of this manuscript, 22–24 September 2019.

29 Two recent examples stand out from South Africa. By July 2019, South African Airways had experienced more than 70 board members (where there were 11 members on average at any given time), seven board chairs and 14 CEOs since 2002. The electricity parastatal, Eskom, has had no fewer than 84 board members (where 14 was the average

membership), 11 CEOs and 8 board chairs over the same 17-year period. There are other, even more extreme examples. Mobutu Sese Seko, the former Zairean president, survived three decades through a combination of brutal repression (including public hangings of opponents), huge inflows of foreign aid (estimated at US$9 billion with the US the third-largest donor after Belgium and France), nationalisation of foreign interests (including the rich copper and cobalt mines), and the development of a personality cult through his choice of clothing, along with personalised name changes. There were more subtle means of maintaining power. A key part of his strategy was to institutionalise political discontinuity among his potential rivals, and delivering patronage, in part by staging more than 50 full cabinet changes in three decades.

30 On the lessons from Asia, see Mills Soko, 'What SA Can Learn from Japan, Singapore and China', *Fin24*, 12 August 2019, https://www.fin24.com/Opinion/mills-soko-what-sa-can-learn-from-japan-singapore-and-china-20190812.

31 See https://pursuit.unimelb.edu.au/articles/in-praise-of-technocracy-why-australia-must-imitate-singapore.

Chapter 12: Don't be a Prisoner of the Past

1 Unless otherwise indicated, this chapter is based on several research trips to Singapore, including August–September 2014, January 2016 and February 2018. The interviews with S.R. Nathan were conducted in December 2013 and September 2014, and with Goh Chok Tong in February 2018.

2 Lee Kuan Yew, *From Third World to First*. Singapore: Marshall Cavendish, 2008, p.67.

3 Interview, Singapore Management University, December 2013.

4 World Bank national accounts data and OECD national accounts data files. See https://data.worldbank.org/indicator/NY.GDP.PCAP.CD?end=1964&locations=IN-GH-KR&start=1960.

5 See https://english.vietnamnet.vn/fms/business/194379/vietnam-s--2-400-income-per-capita-disappoints-economists.html.

6 See https://saigoneer.com/saigon-news/11578-saigon-s-per-capita-income-to-reach-$9,800-by-2010-official.

7 Unless otherwise cited, these interviews were conducted by Greg Mills during several visits to Vietnam, including to Saigon in March 2016, and, most recently, Hanoi in November 2018.

8 See https://www.census.gov/foreign-trade/balance/c5520.html#1995.

9 See https://www.export.gov/article?id=Vietnam-Market-Overview.

10 See https://business.inquirer.net/240699/vietnam-us-sign-12-billion-trade-deals.

11 Anthea Jeffery, *The People's War: New Light on the Struggle for South Africa*. Johannesburg: Johnathan Ball, 2009, p.4.

12 Govan Mbeki, *Sunset at Midday*. Braamfontein: Nolwazi Educational Publishers, 1996, p.xxxiii.

13 Mbeki, *Sunset at Midday*, p.43.

14 Quoted in Herbert N. Foerstel, *From Watergate to Monicagate: Ten Controversies in Modern Journalism and Media*. Connecticut: Greenwood Press, 2001, p.110.

15 Martin Legassick, 'Myth and Reality in the Struggle against Apartheid', *Journal of South African Studies* 24(2), 1998, pp.443–58.

16 Mbeki, *Sunset at Midday*.

17 Howard Barrel, 'The Turn to the Masses: The African National Congress Strategic Review of 1978–79', *Journal of Southern African Studies* 18(1), 1992, pp.64–92.

18 David Lamb, *Vietnam Now: A Reporter Returns*. New York: PublicAffairs, 2003, p.63.

19 Lamb, *Vietnam Now*.

20 Based on an interview in Tokyo on 24 July 2019.

21 Shigetaka Komori, *Innovating Out of Crisis*. Berkeley: Stone Bridge Press, 2013.

22 Erik Brynjolfsson, Andrew McAfee and Michael Spence, 'New World Order: Labor, Capital, and Ideas in the Power Law Economy', *Foreign Affairs* 93(4), 2014, pp.44–53.

23 See https://www.forbes.com/sites/ericsavitz/2011/03/31/
acer-ceo-lanci-quits-board-split-over-growth-strategy/#6a67a98f159f.

24 See https://variety.com/2019/gaming/news/
video-games-300-billion-industry-2025-report-1203202672/.

25 See https://www.nytimes.com/2016/09/21/opinion/jefferson-and-vietnam.html.

26 Cited in Lamb, *Vietnam Now*, p.181.

Chapter 13: Get the Basics Right for Growth

1 Joe Studwell, *How Asia Works: Success and Failure in the World's Most Dynamic Region*. London: Profile, 2013, p.3.

2 World Bank, *The East Asian Miracle: Economic Growth and Public Policy*. Washington, D.C.: Oxford University Press. 1993.

3 We are grateful to Professor Kenichi Ohno for this apt expression.

4 Interview, Tokyo, 23 July 2019.

5 Masafumi Nagao, 'Education and Development: The Japanese Experience', *Journal of International Cooperation in Education* 15(18), 2005, p.7.

6 See https://stats.oecd.org/#.

7 TIMSS 1995, 2003, 2007, 2011, 2015. See http://timssandpirls.bc.edu/timss2015/
international-results/wp-content/uploads/filebase/full%20pdfs/T15-International-
Results-in-Science-Grade-8.pdf.

8 See http://timssandpirls.bc.edu/timss2015/international-results/wp-content/uploads/
filebase/full%20pdfs/T15-International-Results-in-Mathematics.pdf.

9 Nagao, 'Education and Development'.

10 Interview, Singapore, 23 May 2018.

11 See http://acetforafrica.org/acet/wp-content/uploads/publications/2016/10/Second-
Asian-Development-Forum-remarks.pdf.

12 See, for example, http://geography.about.com/od/economic-geography/a/Rostow-S-
Stages-Of-Growth-Development-Model.htm.

13 See 'Agriculture in Sub-Saharan Africa: Prospects and Challenges for the Next Decade'. In *OECD-FAO Agricultural Outlook 2016–2025*. Paris: OECD Publishing, https://doi.
org/10.1787/agr_outlook-2016-5-en.

14 See https://www.bbc.com/news/magazine-25811724.

15 Discussion, Dave Barry, Mombasa, October 2019.
16 Information provided by Carol Chen of the International Cooperation Section of the Council of Agriculture in Taipei.
17 Based on a presentation by Professor Hsu on 22 July 2019 in Taipei, Taiwan.
18 Based on an interview with Yu Zhu, a professor of geography and demographics at Fujian Normal University on 2 August 2019 in Shanghai.
19 See https://www.theguardian.com/cities/2017/mar/20/china-100-cities-populations-bigger-liverpool.
20 Based on an interesting methodology that utilises Facebook data to track migratory patterns. See https://www.urbangateway.org/news/lagos-leads-global-urban-migration-according-facebook.
21 Based on a survey by The Brenthurst Foundation, which polled more than 500 Lagos residents during July and August 2017. See Nchimunya Hamukoma, Nicola Doyle, Sarah Calburn and Dickie Davis, 'Lagos: An Urban Everest', Discussion Paper 3/2019, http://www.thebrenthurstfoundation.org/workspace/files/brenthurst-paper-2019-03.pdf.

Chapter 14: Build and Integrate

1 See http://siteresources.worldbank.org/INTAFRICA/Resources/aicd_factsheet_energy.pdf.
2 See 'Powering Africa', *McKinsey & Company*, February 2015, https://www.mckinsey.com/industries/electric-power-and-natural-gas/our-insights/powering-africa.
3 See https://robertrotberg.wordpress.com/2019/07/06/africas-need-for-power/.
4 See https://qz.com/africa/1271252/world-bank-recommendations-on-electricity-in-sub-saharan-africa/; http://documents.worldbank.org/curated/en/292931523967410313/pdf/125329-REPLACEMENT-PUBLIC.pdf.
5 See https://www.afdb.org/en/the-high-5/light-up-and-power-africa---a-new-deal-on-energy-for-africa.
6 Ibid.
7 See https://data.worldbank.org/indicator/EG.ELC.ACCS.ZS?locations=ZG.
8 The range between ASEAN member states varies vastly. On one end of the spectrum are countries like Singapore and Brunei, which have achieved 100% electrification, and on the other end are countries like Myanmar with an electrification ratio of just 26%. See https://theaseanpost.com/article/electrifying-rural-asean.
9 See https://www.powermag.com/powering-the-dragon-how-chinas-power-sector-is-evolving/.
10 For analysis on the implications, see https://www.intechopen.com/online-first/nuclear-energy-policy-after-the-fukushima-nuclear-accident-an-analysis-of-polarized-debate-in-japan.
11 See https://ourworldindata.org/fossil-fuels.
12 Based on a rule of thumb that 1 000 megawatts are needed for every one million people.
13 Discussion, Enugu, October 2017.
14 This section is a result of two research trips by Greg Mills to Mombasa in March and October 2019.

15 Unless otherwise cited, this section is based on research trips to Ethiopia in January/ February 2019, and to Morocco in January 2019.

16 Lena Partzch and Laura Kemper, 'Cotton Certification in Ethiopia: Can an Increasing Demand for Certified Textiles Create a "Fashion Revolution"?', *ScienceDirect*, 2018, https://www.sciencedirect.com/science/article/pii/S0016718518303543.

17 Discussion, National Graduate Institute for Policy Studies, Tokyo, July 2019.

18 This is based on several trips to Morocco, most recently by Greg Mills and Olusegun Obasanjo in July 2019. The interviews cited here were conducted during that time.

19 See https://www.bbc.com/news/live/world-africa-47639452/page/5.

20 See https://data.worldbank.org/indicator/IS.SHP.GCNW.XQ.

21 See, for example, Jiming Hao and Litao Wang, 'Improving Urban Air Quality in China: Beijing Case Study', *Journal of the Air and Waste Management Association* 55(9), 2005, pp.1298–305.

22 See https://www.iea.org/southeastasia/.

23 See https://theaseanpost.com/article/electrifying-rural-asean.

24 See documents.worldbank.org/curated/en/292931523967410313/pdf/125329-REPLACEMENT-PUBLIC.pdf.

25 See https://medium.com/@Edmund_Olotu/the-electricity-situation-in-nigeria-3f53c8ae0267.

26 See https://www.projectfinance.law/publications/2008/November/hydropower-in-africa.

27 See https://www.afdb.org/en/the-high-5/light-up-and-power-africa---a-new-deal-on-energy-for-africa.

28 Discussion, Johannesburg, 6 September 2019.

Chapter 15: Open Up to Keep Control

1 Interview, Ho Chi Minh City, March 2016.

2 Douglass North, *Transaction Costs, Institutions, and Economic Performance*. San Francisco: ICS Press, 1992; Douglass North, 'Transaction Costs through Time', Economic History, University Library of Munich, 1994.

3 Email correspondence with Greg Mills, 5 July 2019.

4 S. Dhanabalan was interviewed in Singapore by Greg Mills in January 2016.

5 See https://www.temasek.com.sg/en/news-and-views/news-room/news/2018/temasek-review-2018--record-net-portfolio-value-of-s-308-billion.html; 'Temasek Grim on Returns Outlook as Trade Wars Bite', *Business Day*, 10 July 2019, https://www.pressreader.com/south-africa/business-day/20190710/281887299873322.

6 These insights were gained during a visit to Temasek in May 2018.

7 'Blue-Sky Thinking', *The Economist*, 31 August 2019.

8 This is based on several interviews in Addis during 2016, 2018, 2019 and January 2020. See also Greg Mills, 'Ethiopian Airlines: An Example to SAA?', *Daily Maverick*, 17 June 2016, http://www.dailymaverick.co.za/article/2016-06-17-ethiopian-airlines-an-example-to-saa/#.WEASbHecbNA.

9 See https://www.latimes.com/archives/la-xpm-2000-nov-19-mn-54241-story.html.

CONCLUSION

What if Lee Kuan Yew was African?

1 Visit by Olusegun Obasanjo with the African Leadership Forum to Singapore, 8–10 November 1993.
2 See, for example, World Bank, *World Development Report 2009: Reshaping Economic Geography*, 2009, https://openknowledge.worldbank.org/handle/10986/5991.
3 Discussion with Greg Mills, Nairobi, 1 February 2016.
4 Lee Kuan Yew, *From Third World to First*. Singapore: Marshall Cavendish, 2008, p.220.
5 See Gaël Raballand, Salim Refas, Monica Beuran and Gözde Isik, 'Why Does Cargo Spend Weeks in Sub-Saharan African Ports? Lessons from Six Countries', 2012, https://unctad.org/meetings/en/Contribution/dtltlbts-AhEM2018d3_WorldBank_en.pdf.
6 We are grateful to Christopher Clapham for this point.
7 See, for example, Ken Menkhaus, 'If Mayors Ruled Somalia: Beyond the State-building Impasse', *The Nordic Africa Institute*, Policy Note 2, https://www.gpplatform.ch/sites/default/files/If%20mayors%20ruled%20Somalia.pdf.
8 Email correspondence with Professor Barry Desker, 27 June 2019; and teleconference, 1 July 2019.

Index

Page numbers in italics indicate figures and tables.